DUMBARTON OAKS
MEDIEVAL LIBRARY

Jan M. Ziolkowski, General Editor

RICHER OF SAINT-RÉMI

HISTORIES

VOLUME II

DOML 11

Histories

RICHER OF SAINT-RÉMI

VOLUME II
BOOKS 3–4

Edited and Translated by

JUSTIN LAKE

DUMBARTON OAKS
MEDIEVAL LIBRARY

HARVARD UNIVERSITY PRESS
CAMBRIDGE, MASSACHUSETTS
LONDON, ENGLAND
2011

Library of Congress Cataloging-in-Publication Data
Richer, of Saint-Rémy, 10th cent.
    [Historiae. English & Latin]
    Histories / Richer of Saint Rémi ; edited and translated by Justin Lake.
        p. cm. — (Dumbarton Oaks medieval library; 11)
    Latin with facing English translation.
    Includes bibliographical references and index.
    ISBN 978-0-674-06003-6 (v. I : alk. paper) — ISBN 978-0-674-06159-0
(v. II : alk. paper) 1. France — History — To 987 — Early works to 1800. 2.
France — History — Capetians, 987–1328 — Early works to 1800.   I. Lake,
Justin.   II. Title.
    DC70.A3R513 2011
    944'.01 — dc22   2011008840

Contents

BOOK THREE

I

Peractis autem exequiis, Gerberga regina legatos dirigit fratribus suis, Ottoni regi ac Brunoni, ex presule duci, necnon et Hugoni Galliarum duci, petens per eos Lotharium filium suum in regnum patri defuncto succedere. Adveniunt itaque ab Ottone rege omnes ex Belgica duce Brunone principes, sed et ex Germania aliqui. Adest etiam Hugo Galliarum dux. Conveniunt quoque Burgundiae et Aquitaniae simulque et Gothiae principes. Episcopi etiam e diversis regionum urbibus conveniunt. Atque hi omnes in urbem Remorum apud Gerbergam reginam pari voto collecti sunt. Omnium fit consensus; omnibus animo inest Lotharium patri defuncto succedere.

2

Universorum itaque consensu a domno Artoldo Remorum metropolitano, favente Brunone eius avunculo principibusque diversarum gentium laudantibus, Lotharius duodennis rex creatur in basilica sancti Remigii, ubi pater suus

I

After the funeral Queen Gerberga dispatched messengers to her brothers, King Otto and Archbishop Bruno (who
had been made a duke),[1] and to Duke Hugh of the Gauls,
seeking their assistance so that her son Lothar could succeed to the throne in place of his late father. At Otto's behest, all the leading men of Belgica came to her, with Bruno
at their head, as well as some from Germany. Duke Hugh of
the Gauls was also present. In addition, the leading men
of Burgundy, Aquitaine, and Gothia came, along with the
bishops of various cities in these lands. All of these men assembled before Queen Gerberga in the city of Reims with
the same purpose. There was unanimous agreement among
them; all were of the mind that Lothar should succeed his
deceased father.[2]

2

And so with universal consent, with the support of his
uncle Bruno, and with the approbation of the leading men
of various peoples, the twelve-year-old Lothar was consecrated king by Archbishop Artald of Reims in the basilica of
Saint-Rémi, where his father had been buried and lay at rest

tumulatus cum aliis regibus sepultis quiescebat. Creatusque rex, a matre Gerberga simulque et principibus Laudunum, ubi ex antiquo regia esse sedes dinoscitur, magna rerum ambitione inclitus deducitur. Dux continue ei individuus assidet. Et ad multam regis benivolentiam animum intendens, postquam principes in sua discessere, privatis cum rege colloquiis coutebatur. Et ut suae fidelitatis virtutem penitus demonstraret, regem eiusque matrem suas urbes et oppida in tota Neustria visere petit obtinetque.

3

Deducitur ergo a duce rex cum matre regina per Neustriam ac ab eo decentissime excipitur Parisii, Aurelianis, Carnoti, Turonis, Bleso, aliisque quam plurimis Neustriae urbibus oppidisque. Inde quoque cum exercitu in Aquitaniam feruntur. Et premissis legatis, cum Wilelmus princeps occurrere nollet, Pictavim adoriuntur, principem ibi esse rati. Cum ergo exercitus vehementissime urbem attereret et diutissime pugnam urbanis inferret, a quibusdam regiis castrum sanctae Radegundis urbi contiguum clandestina irreptione captum atque succensum est. Comperto vero principem non adesse, tandem post duorum mensium dies, victus indigentia exercitu fatigato, ab obsidione disceditur.

amid the tombs of other kings.[3] Afterward his mother Gerberga and the leading men escorted him with great pomp and circumstance to Laon, which is known to have been the seat of kings of old.[4] The duke remained by his side constantly, and in an effort to ingratiate himself with the king, he took part in private conversations with him after the leading men had left for home. And in order to demonstrate more fully the strength of his loyalty, he successfully petitioned the king and his mother to visit his cities and strongholds in Neustria.

3

And so the duke escorted the king and the queen mother 955 throughout Neustria, giving them a fitting welcome at Paris, Orléans, Chartres, Tours, Blois, and a great many other cities and strongholds of Neustria. Thereafter they advanced into Aquitaine with an army. They sent out envoys in advance, and when Duke William refused to come meet them, they attacked Poitiers, because they believed that the duke was there. The army had been mounting a violent assault upon the city and doing battle with the townsmen for quite a while, when some of the king's men made a surprise attack on the fortified abbey of Saint-Radegund, which adjoined the city, capturing and burning it. When they discovered that the duke was not there, however, then, finally, after two months, with the army in a state of exhaustion from the lack of provisions, they raised the siege.[5]

4

Wilelmus vero Arverniae fines perlustrans, quae est Aquitaniae pars, ab oppidis milites educebat, ad pugnam exercitum colligens, collectoque in regem fertur. Quo rex comperto, duce favente exercitum in hostem reducit signisque infestis congreditur. Acerrime dimicatum est, nonnullis utrimque fusis. Sed regio equitatu prevalente, Aquitanos fuga exagitat. Regiae vero acies promtissime insecuntur. In qua fuga nonnulli Aquitanorum interfecti, plurimi autem capti fuerunt. Wilelmus vero devia secutus, cum duobus vix per abrupta profugit.

5

Rex ergo prospero belli successu insignis, acies iterum Pictavis inferri iubet. Arbitrabatur etenim urbem tunc facillime capi posse, cum exercitus recentis belli animositate adhuc ferveat, et urbani multo detineantur metu ob princi-

4

In the meantime William was making a circuit through the Auvergne (which is part of Aquitaine), taking his fighting men out of his strongholds and mustering an army for battle. After he had assembled his forces, he advanced against the king. When Lothar learned of this, he led his army back against his enemy with the duke's support. The armies met, and battle was joined. There was fierce fighting and many men were killed on both sides, but the king's knights got the upper hand and put the men of Aquitaine to flight. The royal army pursued them without hesitation. In the course of their retreat a number of the Aquitainians were killed and many more were captured. Duke William, however, by following remote paths, managed with difficulty to escape through the rugged countryside with two of his companions.[6]

5

The king, therefore, having distinguished himself through the successful outcome of the battle, ordered his troops to mount a second assault on Poitiers. For he believed that he would have little difficulty taking the city now, because the army was still fired with courage from the recent battle, and the townsmen were immobilized with great fear due to the

pis sui fugam eiusque militum infelicem eventum. Dux itaque regis magnanimitatem multo favore excipiens, exercitum, licet fatigatum, et tamen sua benignitate captum, urbi
reducit. Urbani vero belli casu exanimes vitam deposcunt et
pro urbis illesione supplicant. Cum autem exercitus urbem
vi vellet irrumpere et spolia asportare, dux, habita apud eos
dissuasione, intactam rege iubente reliquit. Rex autem ab
urbanis obsides quot vult capit. Sicque duce interveniente,
urbs ab exercitu liberata est, et sub pace sequestra obsidio
solvitur. Prosperaque rerum fortuna rex cum duce et exercitu Laudunum repetit. Dux vero Parisii receptus, in egritudinem decidit, qua nimium affectus, vitae finem accepit.
Sepultusque est in basilica sancti Dionisii martiris.

6

Interea Ottone rege Bulizlao Sarmatarum regi bellum in-
ferente, Ragenerus quidam, quem Otto rex ob custodiam in
Belgica dimiserat, multa quae illicita erant presumebat. Inter quae aedes regias et predia regalia Gerbergae reginae
quae in Belgica erant tirannica temeritate pervadit. Regina
vero apud suos de repetendis prediis et aedibus regiis priva-
tim consultare non distulit.

flight of their lord and the defeat of his soldiers. The duke welcomed the king's boldness of spirit and led the troops, who, in spite of their exhaustion, were won over by his benevolence, back to Poitiers. Terrified at the turn the war had taken, the townsmen begged for their lives and entreated him to spare the city. Although the soldiers wanted to force their way in to plunder, the duke advised them against it, and at the king's command the city was left unharmed. Lothar, however, took as many hostages as he wanted from the townsmen. And in this way, through the intervention of the duke, the city was delivered from the army and the siege was raised under terms of truce. Amid this good fortune the king set off for Laon with the duke and his army. Upon his arrival in Paris, however, the duke fell ill, and when the sickness overcame him, he died.[7] He was buried in the basilica of Saint-Denis.

956

6

In the meantime, while King Otto was waging war against King Boleslav[8] of the Sarmatians,[9] a man named Reginar,[10] whom Otto had sent to safeguard Belgica, began to undertake many unlawful actions. Among other things, with tyrannical audacity he seized control of royal palaces and estates in Belgica that belonged to the queen. For her part, the queen lost no time in taking counsel with her men privately to see how she could recover her estates and palaces.

955

956

7

Inter quos cum pater meus huius rei dispositioni videretur idoneus, ab eo id summopere ordinandum petebatur. Quod etiam ipse disponendum suscipiens, 'Sinite,' inquit, 'per dies aliquot me istud explorare. Et si quidem nostris viribus id par fuerit, procul dubio per hoc temporis intervallum contemplabimur. Ad alia interim vos ipsos conferte. Illud tantum a vobis expediatur, ut si a deo nobis rei gerendae oportunitas conferatur, apud vos nulla mora attemptandi opus habeatur.' Sic quoque a sese soluti sunt.

8

Pater meus itaque ad oppidum predicti Rageneri quod dicitur Mons Castrati Loci, ubi etiam uxor eius cum duobus filiis parvis morabatur, quosdam suorum quos ipse in militaribus instruxerat dirigit, qui loci habitudinem militumque numerum, rerum etiam fortunam ac famulorum exitum vigilumque diligentiam cautissime considerent. Procedunt itaque duo tantum in habitu paupertino ac usque ad oppidi portam deveniunt. Exstruebantur tunc muri per loca potio-

7

Among the queen's men my father was deemed ideally suited to oversee this operation, and he was asked to devote all of his efforts to devising a plan. As he took the matter in hand he told them: "Give me a few days to look into this. I have no doubt that within this span of time we will be able to determine whether or not our forces are equal to the task. In the meantime, devote your efforts to other matters. There is only one thing that you must be prepared to do. If God gives us the opportunity to carry out this deed, then there must be no hesitation on your part to make the attempt." And with that they parted from one another.

8

My father dispatched some of his men, whom he himself had trained in the arts of war, to one of Reginar's strongholds called Mons, where Reginar's wife and also his two young sons were staying. His men were instructed to take careful note of the layout of the site, the size of the garrison, and the material conditions there, as well as the departures of the servants and the vigilance of the guards. Two men alone were sent, dressed in the garb of paupers, and they arrived at the gates of the stronghold. At the time improvements were being made to the walls in various places, and

ribus aedificiis. Unde et lapidum caementique portitores saepe per portam egrediebantur regrediebanturque presente eo[1] qui operi presidebat. Adsunt exploratores et ad comportandum lapides offerunt sese. Deputantur operi, daturque eis clitellaria sporta. Comportant itaque caementum ac lapides, ac nummos singulos singuli in dies accipiunt. Ante dominam etiam cum latomis et caementariis bis cibati sunt, curiose omnia contemplantes. Dominae etiam cubiculum eiusque natorum diverticulum, sed et famulorum egressum et regressum actionumque tempestatem, ubi etiam oppidum insidiis magis pateat multa consideratione pernotant. Et diebus IIII consumtis, dies imminebat[2] dominica. Sicque accepta laboris mercede, ab opere soluti sunt. Redeunt igitur omnibus exploratis ac patri meo talia referunt.

9

Ille in multa spe omnia ponens, regina conscia cum duabus cohortibus oppidum adit ac ducentibus iis quos premiserat, per locum competentem nocturnus ingreditur. Portas et exitus omnes pervadit ac custodes, ne quis effugiat, deputat. Ipse ad cubiculum dominae ferventissimus tendit. Eumque ingressus, matrem cum duobus natis comprehendit. Alii

workers carrying stones and mortar were constantly passing in and out of the gates in front of the overseer. The scouts came up to him and offered to help carry stones. They were subsequently put to work, and each of them was given a basket. They helped to carry rocks and mortar, and every day they each received a single coin. On two occasions they also dined with the stone-masons and bricklayers in the presence of the mistress, and they observed everything attentively. They took careful note of her bedroom and the children's side-chamber, the comings and goings of the servants, the hours of their activities, and the places where the stronghold was most vulnerable to a surprise attack. When four days had passed, Sunday was approaching, and after receiving their wages they were discharged from their labors. Having investigated everything thoroughly, they returned and told my father what they had learned.

9

Wagering everything on his great hopes for success, he took two cohorts and set off for the stronghold with the queen's knowledge. Guided by the scouts whom he had sent out earlier, he entered during the night at a suitable location. He took control of all the gates and points of egress and assigned guards to make sure that no one escaped. He himself made for the lady's chambers with furious haste. Upon entering, he took her and her two children captive, while others busied themselves with carrying off her finery.

vero ornamentis asportandis insistebant. Comprehendit et
milites oppidumque succendit. Quo combusto, cum domina
et natis militibusque comprehensis ad reginam Gerbergam
reversus est.

10

Quod Ragenerus comperiens, tanta necessitate ductus,
Brunonem fratrem reginae postulat ut mature colloquium
quo iubeat regina constituatur, ubi ipse uxorem et natos re-
cipiat, et regina aedes et predia resumat. Quod etiam statuto tempore factum est. Nam habitis utrimque rationibus,
regina a tiranno predia recepit, et ipse uxorem et natos militesque reduxit.

11

His ita gestis, Rotbertus Trecarum princeps, Heriberti
tiranni filius, Hugonis vero abdicati frater, Lothario regi
iniuriam hac arte molitus est. Castrum regium quod Divion
dicitur, secus Oscaram torrentem conditum, multa cupidi-

He then took the garrison prisoner and set fire to the stronghold. When it had been reduced to ashes, he returned to Queen Gerberga with the lady and her children, as well as the soldiers whom he had captured.[11]

10

When Reginar learned of this, he was driven by the desperation of his circumstances to beseech Bruno, the queen's brother, to arrange a meeting as soon as possible wherever the queen wanted, so that he could get his wife and children back and she could recover her houses and estates. At a fixed time the meeting was held. After negotiations between the two parties, the queen received her estates back from the tyrant, and he took back his wife, his children, and his men.[12]

11

Afterward Count Robert of Troyes, the son of the tyrant Heribert and the brother of the deposed Hugh, plotted to do mischief against King Lothar in the following way. He longed to get his hands on the royal castle of Dijon, which was located on the Ouche River, because he thought that

959

tate sitiebat, eo quod per eum, si id habere posset, optimam Burgundiae partem ad suum ius transire posse arbitrabatur. Illum itaque qui castro preesse videbatur de transfugio ad sese per legatos alloquitur, plurima spondens et maiora sub iureiurando pollicens; apud regem quoque multam rerum inopiam asserens, apud sese vero sufficientes opes, oppida nonnulla aliaque desiderabilium insignia vehementissime protestans. Tunc iuvenis rerum cupidine captus, pro trans- fugio mercedem quaerit. At illi mercedis nomen edicunt. Ille vero ex promissis iusiurandum postulat capitque. Et tempore congruo tirannum cum multa militum manu intra oppidum excipit, ac sese ei commitens, fidem pro militia ac- commodat. Pervaso autem oppido, regii milites contume- liose pelluntur. Deputantur vero ibi milites tiranni.

12

Perlata sunt haec ad regem. Rex vero Brunoni avunculo le- gatos dirigit, copias ab eo postulans. Nec moratur Bruno et cum duobus milibus armatorum ex Belgica terram tiranni occupat urbemque Trecasinam obsidione circumdat. Rex vero cum matre erepto castro exercitum inducit. Cum ergo duplici exercitu tirannus urgeretur, cedit[3] et ab rege indul-

once it was his, the better part of Burgundy would fall under his sway. So he sent messengers to speak to the castellan about deserting over to his side, making all sorts of promises and pledging under oath to do even more. While claiming that the king was oppressed by poverty, he declared emphatically that he himself was blessed with great wealth, a number of strongholds, and other desirable marks of distinction. The young man fell victim to his greed and asked for a bribe in exchange for deserting. The messengers set a price for his reward, and he in turn demanded and received from them an oath on what they had promised. At an opportune time he let the tyrant and a large band of his troops into the stronghold, and committing himself to Robert, he swore an oath to become his vassal. The stronghold was seized, and the king's troops were driven out in humiliating fashion, whereupon the tyrant's men were installed in their place.[13]

12

When news of these events reached the king, he dispatched messengers to ask his uncle Bruno for troops. Bruno immediately marched into the tyrant's territory with two thousand armed men from Belgica and invested the city of Troyes.[14] Meanwhile, the king took his mother and led his army to the castle that had been snatched away from him. Because he was now under threat from two different armies, the tyrant surrendered and asked the king for pardon. He

960

gentiam petit; coactusque obsides et sacramenta dat, et insuper oppidi proditorem victus tradit. Qui mox prolata ab
rege sententia, ante oppidi portam coram patre decollatur.

13

Rex vero oppido potitus, cum matre Laudunum redit.
Huc ex diversis regionibus ad regem principes confluunt.
Adsunt quoque ducis defuncti filii duo, Hugo et Otto, qui
etiam regi fidelem militiam per iusiurandum coram omnibus spondent. Quorum benignitati rex non imparem libera-
litatem demonstrans, Hugonem pro patre ducem facit et
insuper terram Pictavorum eius principatui adicit, Ottonem
vero Burgundia donat.

14

In qua rerum distributione cum domnus ac reverendus
Artoldus metropolitanus admodum in die laborasset et pre
solis fervore toto corpore sudasset, cum vestem abiceret,
per poros calore apertos frigus autumnale irrepsit. Natoque

was compelled to give hostages and take oaths, and as a condition of his surrender he handed over the man who had betrayed the castle of Dijon. As soon as the king had pronounced judgment, the traitor was beheaded before the gates of the stronghold in the presence of his own father.[15]

13

Having regained control of the stronghold, Lothar returned to Laon with his mother. The leading men from different regions assembled there before the king. Also present were the two sons of the deceased duke, Hugh[16] and Otto,[17] who also pledged under oath before everyone there to do faithful service to the king. Demonstrating a generosity that was in no way inferior to the goodwill that they had shown him, the king made Hugh duke in place of his father and added Poitou to his duchy, while he bestowed Burgundy upon Otto.[18]

14

While this allotment of territory was taking place, the reverend archbishop Artald was hard at work during the day, and his whole body became drenched in sweat from the heat of the sun. As he undressed, the autumn cold crept into his

961

ex interno frigdore epatis morbo, nimiis doloribus confectus, pridie Kal. Octob. a suo presulatu anno XX diem vitae
clausit extremum.

15

Cuius peractis exsequiis, Hugo nuperrime dux Francorum ab rege factus, regem suppliciter adit petitque pontifi-
calem dignitatem ei restitui, eo quod ipse ante Artoldum ipsam adeptus fuerit; et non suo facinore sed Rodulfi regis
invidia Artoldum ei superductum memorat. Persistebat itaque ut redderetur. Et statim decreto regio sinodus episcoporum post dies XL habenda indicitur.

16

Colligitur ergo consummatis diebus in pago Meldensi secus fluvium Matronam, in vico qui vocatur . . . ex Remensi ac
Senonensi provinciis sinodus XIII episcoporum, preside

pores, which had become dilated from the heat, and as a result of an internal chill he contracted a disease of the liver. Racked with severe pains, he concluded the final day of his life on September 30, in the twentieth year of his episcopacy.[19]

15

After Artald's funeral, Hugh, who had just been made duke of the Franks by the king, went to him and humbly requested that the office of archbishop be restored to the other Hugh on the grounds that the latter had held this office prior to Artald. He pointed out that Hugh had not been replaced by Artald because of any misdeed on his part, but as a consequence of the hostility of King Radulf. The duke was persistent in requesting that Hugh be restored to office, and immediately thereafter it was announced by royal decree that a synod of bishops would be held forty days hence.[20]

962

16

When the forty days had elapsed, a synod of thirteen bishops from the provinces of Reims and Sens assembled in the county of Meaux by the Marne River in a village called

Senonense pontifice. Inter quos etiam fautores aliqui pro parte Hugonis videbantur, et maxime illi qui duci consuescebant, utpote Aurelianensis et Parisiacus, Silletensis quoque. Atque hi publice consultabant. Renitentibus autem Roricone Laudunensi et Gubuino Catalaunico episcopis, et vehementissime asserentibus quod a multitudine episcoporum excommunicatus, a minore eorum numero absolvi non posset, relinquitur ratio differenda usque ad interrogationem papae Romani.

17

Nec multopost et legatio dirigitur in Gallias a domno Iohanne papa, qui iam succedebat Octoviano, domni Agapiti successori, asserens predictum Hugonem abdicatum tam sinodo Romana quam Papiae nuperrime habita ab episcopis Italiae anathematizatum, nisi ab iis quae illicite repetebat quiesceret. Qua legatione omnibus intimata, quaerimoniae ratio pessumdata est. Hugo itaque a fratre suo Rotberto receptus, nimia anxietate intra dies paucissimos Meldi defunctus est.

<. . . ,>[21] with the archbishop of Sens[22] presiding. Among them were several supporters of Hugh's party—principally those who, like the bishops of Orléans, Paris, and Senlis, were on familiar terms with the duke—and these men deliberated publicly. But when bishops Rorico of Laon and Gibuin of Châlons opposed them and argued vehemently that a man who had been excommunicated by a great number of bishops could not be absolved by a smaller number of them, further discussions were postponed until such time as they could consult the pope.[23]

17

Not long after this a legation was dispatched to Gaul by Pope John, who had succeeded Octavian (himself the successor of Pope Agapitus),[24] declaring that at synods held at Rome, and most recently at Pavia, the Italian bishops had proclaimed the deposed Hugh excommunicate until such time as he should abandon his illegitimate claims.[25] When the pope's message had been made known to everyone, it put an end to any grounds for complaint. Hugh was subsequently taken in by his brother Robert and died at Meaux a few days later from mental anguish.[26]

18

Bruno itaque metropolitanus et dux cuidam ex collegio canonicorum Mettensium nomine Odelrico apud regem presulatum quaerebat. Quod cum obtinuisset, coram adesse facit. Qui vir memorabilis, cum esset divitiis et nobilitate litterarumque scientia adeo clarus, an rege largiente episcopatum suscipere audeat sciscitatur. Etenim tunc expetebatur a quodam illustri, cui a duce auxilium ferebatur. At ille, utpote vir magnanimus, si rex largiatur sese contra omnes et suscepturum et defensurum respondit. Quod etiam multam sibi ducis invidiam comparavit.

19

Ordinatur itaque in basilica sancti Remigii ab episcopis Remensis metropolis diocesaneis, Widone scilicet Suessonico, Roricone Laudunensi, Gibuino Catalaunico, Hadulfo Noviomensi atque Wicfrido Virdunensi. Factusque presul, mox tirannos qui suae aecclesiae res pervaserant ut ad satisfaciendum redeant iure aecclesiastico advocat. Atque inde per tres dierum quadragenas concessit esse consulendum.

18

Bruno, the duke and archbishop, now asked the king to bestow the archbishopric of Reims upon a member of the college of canons at Metz named Odelric. When the king granted his request, Bruno brought Odelric before him. This remarkable man, who was distinguished by wealth, noble birth, and knowledge of letters, was asked if he would have the courage to accept the office of bishop if the king were to bestow it upon him; for at that time a certain prominent person was seeking the office for himself with the support of the duke. In keeping with his boldness of spirit, Odelric replied that if the king were to grant him the see, then he would take it up and defend it against everyone, an answer that won him considerable hostility from the duke.[27]

19

And so Odelric was ordained in the basilica of Saint-Rémi by the suffragan bishops of the province of Reims, namely Wido of Soissons, Rorico of Laon, Gibuin of Châlons, Hadulf of Noyon, and Wicfrid of Verdun.[28] Shortly after assuming office, he called upon the tyrants who had usurped the possessions of his church to come and make satisfaction to him in accordance with ecclesiastical law. And from that time he allowed them thrice forty days to think the matter over.[29]

963

25

20

Evoluto vero tempore, Tetbaldum Turonicum cum aliis rerum aecclesiasticarum pervasoribus anathemate damnat. Post non multos autem dies, penitentia ducti, ad presulem satisfacturi redeunt atque res pervasas legaliter reddunt. Recipit itaque domnus presul ab Heriberto quidem Sparnacum vicum populosum ac opulentum, ab Tetbaldo vero castrum Codiciacum, eosque a vinculo anathematis absolvit. Et Tetbaldi quidem filio, qui sese sibi commiserat militaturum, castrum sub conditione servandae fidelitatis concedit.

21

Quo etiam tempore Arnulfus Morinorum princeps hac vita decessit. Cuius terram Lotharius rex ingressus, filio defuncti liberaliter reddit eumque cum militibus iure sacramentorum sibi annectit.

20

When this period of time had elapsed, he condemned Theobald of Tours and the other usurpers of church property with an anathema.[30] Not long after this, however, they were moved by repentance to come before him and make satisfaction, and in accordance with the law they returned the property that they had seized. The archbishop recovered Épernay, a wealthy and populous village, from Heribert, and the fortress of Coucy-le-Château from Theobald, after which he released them both from the bonds of anathema. He then granted the fortress to Theobald's son,[31] who had committed himself to becoming his vassal, on the condition that he keep his oath of fealty.[32]

964

965

21

At this time Count Arnulf of Flanders also departed from this life. King Lothar entered his lands and generously restored them to Arnulf's son,[33] binding him and his vassals to himself with an oath of fealty.[34]

22

Huic quoque regalis nobilitatis vir Adalbero, ex Mettensium similiter collegio, strenue ac feliciter successit. Qui quanto suis profuerit et quanta ab aemulis plus iusto passus sit, opere sequenti declarabitur. Hic in initio post sui promotionem structuris aecclesiae suae plurimum studuit. Fornices enim qui ab aecclesiae introitu per quartam pene totius basilicae partem eminenti structura distendebantur penitus diruit. Unde et ampliore receptaculo et digniore scemate tota aecclesia decorata est. Corpus quoque sancti Kalisti papae et martiris debito honore in ipso aecclesiae ingressu, loco scilicet editiore, collocavit. Ibique altare dedicans, oratorium fundendis deo precibus commodissimum aptavit. Altare precipuum crucibus aureis insigniens, cancellis utrimque radiantibus obvelavit.

23

Preter haec etiam altare gestatorium non viliori opere effinxit. Super quod sacerdote apud deum agente, aderant IIII evangelistarum expressae auro et argento imagines, sin-

22

He[35] was succeeded by Adalbero, likewise a man of royal blood, from the college of canons at Metz, who proved to be an energetic and effective successor. The rest of this work will show how greatly he benefited his own men and how many injustices he suffered at the hands of his rivals. In the period following his accession Adalbero devoted himself to the buildings of his church. He completely tore down the lofty superstructure of arches that extended from the entrance of the basilica over almost a quarter of its length; as a result the nave was expanded and the whole church was given a more impressive layout. He gave the body of the saint and martyr Pope Callistus a deserved place of honor in a more elevated location at the very entrance to the church. He also dedicated an altar there and constructed an oratory that was ideally suited for offering prayers to God. He adorned the main altar with gold crosses and covered it on both sides with gleaming chancels.

23

In addition to this he had a portable altar made of equally fine workmanship. As the priest performed the divine office upon the altar, images of the four evangelists fashioned from gold and silver could be seen, each standing in a different

gulae in singulis angulis stantes. Quarum uniuscuiusque alae extensae duo latera altaris ad medium obvelabant. Facies vero agno inmaculato conversas intendebant. In quo etiam ferculum Salomonis imitari videbatur. Fecit quoque candelabrum septifidum, in quo cum septem ab uno surgerent, illud significare videbatur, quod ab uno spiritu septem gratiarum dona dividantur. Nec minus et arcam opere eleganti decoravit, in qua virgam et manna, id est sanctorum reliquias, operuit. Coronas quoque non minima inpensa fabrefactas in aecclesiae decus suspendit. Quam fenestris diversas continentibus historias dilucidatam, campanis mugientibus acsi tonantem dedit.

24

Canonicos etiam, qui in propriis hospiciis degentes tantum sua curabant, iure communitatis vivere instruxit. Unde et claustrum monasterio addidit, in quo die morantes cohabitarent, necnon et dormitorium ubi noctu in silentio quiescerent, refectorium quoque ubi de communi considentes reficerentur. Legesque ascripsit, ut orationis tempore in ecclesia nihil nisi signo peterent, preter quod necessitatis afferret inpulsio; cibum una taciturni caperent; post prandium in gratiarum actione laudes deo decantarent; completorio

corner. The wings of each of them were spread out so as to cover both sides of the altar all the way to the middle, while their faces were turned toward the immaculate lamb. In this respect, too, it clearly imitated Solomon's litter.[36] In addition, Adalbero had a candelabrum made with seven branches issuing from one stem to signify that the seven gifts of Grace arise from one Spirit, and he had a chest decorated with elegant workmanship to house the rod and manna, that is, the relics of the saints.[37] To beautify the church he hung up crowns that had been made at considerable expense. He also illuminated it with windows depicting different stories and made it thunder, as it were, with the pealing of bells.

24

Adalbero also instructed the canons of the cathedral, who had been living in their own houses and attending only to their own affairs, to live according to a communal rule. For this reason he added a cloister to the church where they were to spend their time together during the day, a dormitory where they were to sleep silently at night, and a refectory where they were to sit together and take their meals communally. He also prescribed certain rules: during prayer time in the church they were not to ask for anything except by giving a sign, unless some sudden necessity dictated otherwise; they were to take their meals together in silence; after the midday meal they were to sing hymns to God in thanksgiving; after Compline was over they were not to

vero expleto, silentium usque laudes matutinas nullatenus violarent; iam horoscopo pulsante excitati, ad laudes persolvendas sese prevenire contenderent. Ante horam diei primam libertas egrediendi a claustro nemini concessa erat, preter hos qui curis eorum insistebant. Et ne quis per ignorantiam quicquam faciendum relinqueret, sancti Augustini instituta patrumque decreta cotidie eis recitanda indixit.

25

Monachorum quoque mores quanta dilectione et industria correxit atque a seculi habitu distinxit, sat dicere non est. Non solum enim religionis dignitate eos insignes apparere studuit, verum etiam bonis exterioribus augmentatos nullomodo minui prudens adegit. Quos cum multo coleret amore, precipua tamen beati Remigii Francorum patroni monachos caritate extollebat. Unde et eorum res stabiliri in posterum cupiens, Romam concessit. Et utpote vir nobilis et strenuus, et fama celibis vitae omnibus clarus, a beatae memoriae Iohanne papa cum multa reverentia exceptus est. A quo etiam post mutua colloquia iussus, in die natalitia do-

break their silence in any way until Lauds; and when they were awoken by the striking of the clock,[38] they were to compete with one another to arrive first for the office of Lauds. No one was given license to leave the cloister before the first hour of the day except those who were attending to their responsibilities. And so that no one would neglect anything out of ignorance, he prescribed that the rules laid down by Saint Augustine and the decrees of the fathers should be read aloud to them every day.

25

As for the monks, it is scarcely possible to say enough about the love and diligence with which he corrected their habits and kept them apart from the ways of the world. For not only did he take pains that they should be conspicuous for the worthiness of their devotion, but he was also careful to ensure that the external goods with which they had been endowed should not be diminished in any way. He cherished them all with great love, but he promoted the monks of Saint-Rémi, patron of the Franks, with particular affection. Thus he traveled to Rome out of a desire to see their property firmly secured for the future. As befitted a man of his nobility and energy, and one whose reputation for chastity was known to all, he was received with great respect by Pope John[39] of blessed memory, and after they had spoken together he was asked to celebrate mass on Christmas day in a

971

mini, XII procedentibus episcopis, missarum sollempnia celebravit. In tanta eius gratia habitus, ut ab eo rogaretur petere, si quid optaret.

26

Quod metropolitanus Adalbero de rebus sancti Remigii a papa Iohanne privilegium fieri petit[4]

Tunc vir memorabilis sic exorsus: 'Quoniam,' inquit, 'pater sanctissime, multa caritate filium complexus ad te amplius attraxisti, quod tibi onerosum sit petendum non arbitror. Novi enim quod diligens pater interdum filio gravari gaudeat. Sed illud petere me proposui, quod et tanto patri onerosum non fiat et petenti satis commodi comparet. Est mihi in Galliis monachorum coenobium, non longe ab urbe Remorum situm. Ubi etiam beati Remigii Francorum patroni corpus sanctissimum decentissime quiescit, cui etiam honor exhibetur debitus. Cuius res in posterum stabiliri firmiter quaerens, vestrae auctoritatis privilegio confirmari in-

procession with twelve bishops. He was held in such favor by the pope that he was asked to request anything that he wanted.

26

Archbishop Adalbero Requests a Privilege for the Property of Saint-Rémi from Pope John

Thereupon that remarkable man replied as follows: "Because you have embraced your son and drawn him close to you with great affection, most Holy Father, I do not think it is appropriate to make a request that would be burdensome to you. I know that a loving father is sometimes happy to be inconvenienced by his son, but it is my intention to ask for something that will impose no burden upon you, my great father, and yet will confer a substantial benefit upon the one making the request. I have a monastery in Gaul, not far from the city of Reims, where the most holy body of Saint Remigius, the patron of the Franks, lies in a most honorable state, receiving the reverence that is due to it. In my desire to see the monastery's property securely established for the future,

presentiarum deposco, terras videlicet cultas atque incultas, silvas et pascua, vineas ac pomeria,[5] torrentes et stagna. Castri quoque illorum immunitatem villarumque liberalem intra et extra potestatem, tandem etiam res omnes mobiles atque inmobiles vestri apostolatus dignitas solidet atque confirmet. Abbatiam quoque sancti Timothei martiris, quae nostri iuris esse videtur, sub vestri presentia horumque episcoporum testimonio eis concedo, ut inde pauperibus administretur, et memoria nostri servis dei in coenobio habeatur. Haec igitur superioribus addita in ius predicti sancti transeat atque illius propria vestra similiter auctoritate confirmetur.'

27

Ad haec domnus papa: 'Res,' inquit, 'domni ac patroni nostri Remigii nostri apostolatus sententia stabiliri tutasque in perpetuum fieri, quin etiam de tuo quicquid placet addi, libentissime concedo. Scripto etiam id roborari non solum

I hereby request that a privilege deriving from your authority be issued to confirm the monastery's holdings: that is, the lands both cultivated and uncultivated, the woods and pastures, the vineyards and orchards, the streams and ponds. May your apostolic dignity strengthen and confirm the immunity of their fortifications, the free exercise of their authority upon and outside of their estates, and all of their movable and immovable property. Moreover, in your presence and with these bishops here as witnesses, I hereby grant the abbey of Saint Timothy the martyr, which is within my jurisdiction, to the monks to be administered on behalf of the poor and to be held by the servants of God among the possessions of their monastery in memory of me. May these things be added to those mentioned above and pass to the authority of Saint Remigius, and may his property likewise be confirmed by your authority."

27

To this the pope replied, "I most willingly grant that the possessions of our lord patron Remigius should be firmly established by virtue of the authority of our apostolic dignity, and that these possessions, and whatever else it pleases you to add of your own property, should be secured in perpetuity. And I further ordain that it shall be confirmed in writing

mea, set et horum qui adsunt episcoporum auctoritate constituo.' Moxque scriptum iri iussit coramque scriptum legi precepit.

28

Cuius textus huiusmodi est: 'Iohannes servus servorum dei . . .'

29

Quod in auribus omnium qui aderant perlectum, sigilli sui nota insignivit atque episcopis roborandum porrexit. Quibus gestis, metropolitanus domni papae atque episcoporum licentia digressus, Galliis sese recepit, directoque itinere sancti predicti sepulchrum devotus petiit eique in collegio monachorum privilegium scriptum legavit. Monachi datum excipientes, archivo servandum mandant gratiasque pro tanta liberalitate decenter impertiunt.

not only by my authority, but by the authority of all the bishops who are present here." He then ordered the document to be drawn up and gave instructions that it be read out in public.[40]

28

The text of the document read as follows: "John, servant of the servants of God <...>"[41]

29

When the document had been read out before all who were present, the pope affixed his seal to it and gave it to the bishops for them to confirm. Afterward, when the archbishop had been given leave to depart by the pope and the bishops, he returned to Gaul, where in his devotion he proceeded directly to the tomb of Saint Remigius and bequeathed the papal privilege to the saint in the presence of the assembled monks. Accepting this gift from him, the monks entrusted it to their archives for safekeeping and offered fitting thanks to him for his generosity.

30

Quod Adalbero privilegium in sinodo ab episcopis confirmari facit[6]

His ita habitis, post sex mensium tempus ad montem sanctae Mariae, qui locus est Remorum diocesaneus, ab eodem metropolitano sinodus episcoporum habita est. Quibus considentibus, post quaedam sinodo utilia atque sanctae aecclesiae commoda, metropolitanus coram sic concionatus ait: 'Quoniam, patres reverendi, gratia sancti spiritus hic collecti sumus et quae de statu sanctae aecclesiae visa sunt utilia ordinavimus, restat adhuc res mihi adeo placens et nonnullis nostrae aecclesiae filiis nunc et in posterum profutura. Quam etiam vestrae dignitati indicandam arbitror atque roborandam. Ante septem mensium dies, ut vobis quoque notissimum est, in Italiam concessi Romamque deveni, ac domni et apostolici viri Iohannis colloquio simulque et benivolentia familiarissime usus, ab eo petere si quid optarem monitus sum. Ratusque petendum ut res domni ac patroni nostri Remigii suae auctoritatis privilegio contra quoslibet tirannos stabiliret et abbatiam sancti Timothei

30

Adalbero Has the Papal Privilege Confirmed by the Bishops at a Synod

Six months later Adalbero assembled a synod of bishops   972/973
at Mont-Notre-Dame in the diocese of Reims. After they had
taken their seats and addressed some matters of importance
to the synod and to the advantage of the holy church, the
archbishop spoke to them as follows: "Holy fathers, because
we have assembled here by the grace of the Holy Spirit to
make provision for those things that we have deemed beneficial for the condition of the holy church, there still remains
one thing that is dear to my heart, which will benefit many
sons of our church both now and in the future, a matter that
I think must be submitted to your authority to receive your
confirmation. Seven months ago, as you well know, I traveled to Italy and went to Rome, and after receiving an audience with Pope John and being treated with the most cor-
dial generosity, I was advised to present any request that I
might have to him. I decided to ask him to confirm the possessions of our lord and patron Remigius against the usurpa-
tions of any and all tyrants with a papal privilege, and to ask
that he include within it the abbey of Saint Timothy, which

martiris a me datam illis uniret, id absque refragatione obtinui. Scripsit ergo ac coram episcopis numero XII recitari iussit eisque roborandum porrexit. Quod et domni papae sigilli nota insignitum, vobis quoque roborandum attuli, ut plurimorum auctoritate subnixum, nullorum machinatione quandoque valeat dissolvi. Unde et a vobis idem roborari volo.' Sinodus dixit: 'Roboretur.' Prolatum igitur a metropolitano, in concilio recitatum est eisque porrectum, et ab eorum singulis manu imposita roboratum. Quod etiam a monachis qui ibi aderant exceptum, archivo monasterii relatum est.

31

Conquestio metropolitani de monachorum religione rituumque correctione

Inter hec quoque et alia utilia quae ibi constituta sunt, de monachorum religione a metropolitano motu gravissimo conquestio habita est, eo quod ritus a maioribus constituti a

I had turned over to the monks as a gift, and I obtained this without any opposition. Consequently, he drew up the privilege, ordered it to be read out before twelve bishops, and gave it to them to confirm. I have brought you this document, which bears the mark of the papal seal, for you to confirm as well, so that after it has been reinforced by the authority of a great many men, it may never be invalidated through anyone's schemes. I hereby ask that you also confirm this document." The synod declared, "Let it be confirmed." The papal privilege was then brought forward by the archbishop, read out before the council, and presented to the bishops, after which each one of them placed his hand upon it to confirm it. Thereafter it was taken up by the monks who were in attendance there and brought back to the monastery's archives.

31

The Archbishop's Complaint Concerning the Observance of the Monks, and the Correction of Their Practices

In addition to this and the other useful business that was decided there, the archbishop delivered an impassioned complaint on the state of monastic observance, since it had become clear that the usages established by their forefa-

quibusdam depravati et immutati viderentur. Unde et sub episcoporum presentia ab eodem decretum est ut diversorum locorum abbates convenirent et inde utiliter consulerent. Huiusque habendae rationis tempus et locus mox constituta sunt, et sic sinodus soluta est.

32

Quod abbas Rodulfus abbatum primas fuerit

Interea tempus advenit. Abbates quoque ex diverso in unum collecti sunt. Quorum precipuus et primas constitutus est vir divae memoriae Rodulfus, ex coenobio sancti Remigii abbas. Quo presidente et prelaturae dignitatem tenente, alii circum dispositi sunt. Metropolitanus vero ex adverso in cliotedro resedit. Qui primatis aliorumque patrum hortatu concionatus, sic prelocutus est:

thers had been corrupted and altered by certain people. Thus, he decreed in the presence of the synod that abbots from different places should assemble to address this issue in a productive manner. Shortly thereafter a time and place was set for the meeting, and with that the synod was dissolved.

32

Rodulf Is Appointed Abbot Primate

When the time had come, abbots from all over assembled in one body.[42] Abbot Rodulf of Saint-Rémi of divine memory was established as first and foremost among them. He presided and held the position of authority, with the others arrayed around him. The archbishop sat across from him in the seat of honor. At the urging of the primate and the other abbots, the archbishop addressed them as follows:

33

Praelocutio metropolitani in sinodo abbatum

'Magnum est, patres sanctissimi, bonos quosque convenire, si fructum virtutis quaerere elaborent. Inde enim et bonorum utilitas et rerum honestas comparatur. Sicut econtra perniciosum, si pravi confluant ut illicita quaerant et expleant. Unde et vos, quos in dei nomine collectos arbitror, optima quaerere hortor atque ex malivolentia nihil moliri moneo. Amor secularis et odium apud vos locum nullum habeant, quibus enervatur iustitia, aequitas suffocatur. Vestri ordinis antiqua religio ab antiquitatis honestate, ut fama est, supra modum aberravit. Dissidetis enim inter vos in ipsa regularis ordinis consuetudine, cum aliter alter, alter aliter velit ac sentiat. Quapropter et sanctitati vestrae hactenus multum derogatum est. Unde et utile duxi ut vobis hic gratia dei in unum collectis suadeam idem velle, idem sentire, idem cooperari, ut eadem voluntate, eodem sensu, eadem cooperatione et virtus neglecta repetatur et pravitatis dedecus vehementissime propulsetur.'

33

The Archbishop's Address to the Synod of Abbots

"It is a great thing, most holy fathers, for good men to come together when they work to find the fruits of their virtue; for in that case what is expedient for the good and honorable in deed will be achieved. In just the same way, however, it is dangerous for wicked men to assemble for the purpose of seeking out and implementing what is unlawful. And so I urge you, who have gathered here, I believe, in the name of God, to seek out what is best, and I advise you to undertake nothing based upon malice. Neither worldly love nor hatred should have any place among you, for it is through these things that justice is enfeebled and equity stifled. The venerable devotion of your order, so it is said, has strayed far from its ancient virtue. You are at odds with each other over the very customs and habits of the monastic life, with different people wanting and thinking different things. As a result your sanctity has to this point been much diminished. For this reason I have deemed it worthwhile that you should assemble here by the grace of God so that I may persuade you to have the same desires and the same opinions, and to work together toward the same goals, so that united in will, in feeling, and in common effort you may both recover your neglected virtue and forcefully reject the disgrace of immoral conduct."

34

Responsio primatis et in pravos indignatio

Ad haec abbatum primas: 'Quod hic,' inquit, 'a te promulgatum est, pater sanctissime, alta memoria condendum est, eo quod et corporum dignitatem et animarum salutem affectes. Constat enim ad habitum virtutis neminem pervenisse, nisi quem talis animus munivit quo et appetenda peteret et vitanda refelleret. Unde et patet nos aliquid dedecoris contraxisse, quod ab appetendis[7] aberravimus. Quod etiam multa obiurgatione reprehendendum est, cum nec ignavia nos precipitaverit, nec inopia ad id impulerit.'

35

Item indignatio primatis

'Quae enim vis impulit ut monachus intra claustra monasterii dominicis servitiis mancipandus compatrem habeat et compater dicatur? Et o, quantum nostro ordini dissentiat

34

The Primate's Reply and His Outrage at the Perverse

In response the abbot primate, declared: "Everything you have said here, most holy father, should be preserved deep within our memories, because your words touch upon both the dignity of our bodies and the salvation of our souls. It is clear that no one can achieve a virtuous disposition unless he steels his mind to pursue those things that he ought to desire and to reject the things which ought to be shunned. Thus, it is clear that we have acquired some taint of dishonor because we have strayed from that which we ought to seek. This is all the more deserving of reproach because idleness has not been the cause of our downfall, nor has poverty driven us to it."

35

More Outrage from the Abbot Primate

"For indeed, what power has brought it about that a monk who ought to be devoted to the service of the Lord within the cloister should keep a companion and himself be

considerate. Si, inquam, compater est, ut a verisimili probabile efferam, cum eo qui pater est ipse est pater. Si vero pater est, filium vel filiam habere dubium non est. Unde et
scortator potius quam monachus dicendus est. Sed quid de
commatre? Quid in hoc nomine a secularibus perpenditur
nisi turpitudinis consentanea? Hoc licet verisimile dicens,
secularibus non preiudico, sed nostro ordini illicita repre-
hendo. Quod quia ineptum videtur, vestra interminatione
inhibendum est.' His venerandus metropolitanus subiun-
gens, 'Si,' inquit, 'placet sinodo, interdicetur.' Sinodus dixit,
'Interdicatur.' Metropolitani itaque auctoritate, omnium
consensu inhibitum est.

36

Alia[8] primatis obiectio

Rursusque primas exorsus: 'Adhuc,' inquit, 'nostro ordini
inimica proferam. In quo quidam dinoscuntur quibus mos
inolevit ut soli a monasteriis egrediantur,[9] soli foris nullo sui
operis teste maneant, et quod pessimum est, absque fratrum

called a companion? Consider—alas!—how much this is at odds with our order. And if he is a companion *(compater)*, then to draw a plausible conclusion from the appearance of truth, he is himself a father *(pater)* with *(cum)* one who is also a father.[43] Yet if he is a father, he assuredly has a son or daughter, whence he is rather to be called a fornicator than a monk. And what of the *commater?* What does this word signify among worldly men except a woman who consents to what is base and shameful? Although what I say rings true, my purpose is not to cast aspersions on the laity, but to reprove that which is forbidden to our order, and which, because of its impropriety, must be prohibited by your sanctions." To this the venerable archbishop added, "If it is the will of the synod, it shall be forbidden." The synod declared, "Let it be forbidden." And so by virtue of the archbishop's authority it was prohibited with unanimous consent.

36

Another Charge from the Abbot Primate

The abbot primate spoke once more. "I have still more unwelcome words to pronounce against our order. For it is known that certain among us have grown accustomed to leave their monasteries by themselves and remain outside on their own, without anyone to bear witness to what they are

benedictione et exeant et sine ea redeant. Unde non dubium est eos facilius posse falli quos fratrum orantium benedictio non munit. Inde est quod turpitudo vitae, morum pravitas, proprietatis peculium nobis a calumniantibus intenduntur. Unde etiam necesse est ut his calumniis subdamur, cum repulsioni testes habere non possimus. Hoc quoque vestra censura prohibeat.' Sinodus dixit, 'Prohibeatur.' Et memorabilis metropolitanus, 'Hoc quoque,' inquit, 'nostra auctoritate prohibemus.'

37

Tertia primatis indignatio

His quoque primas alia adiungens: 'Quoniam,' inquit, 'de vitiis nostri ordinis dicere coepi, nihil relinquendum putavi, ut his amotis, religio nostra acsi enubilata reluceat. Sunt enim, inquam, nostri ordinis quidam quibus curae est pillea aurita capiti manifeste imponere pellesque peregrinas pilleo regulari preponere, pro abiectae vestis habitu vestes lautissi-

doing. And what is worst of all, they depart and return without receiving the blessing of their brothers. Hence there is no doubt that they are more likely to fall into error, because they have not been fortified by the prayers of their fellow monks. As a result, slanderers accuse them of a shameful manner of life, moral depravity, and the possession of private property. And indeed we must endure these calumnies because we cannot produce witnesses to refute the charges. Let this also be prohibited by your censure." The synod declared "Let it be prohibited." And the eminent archbishop added, "We, too, prohibit this by virtue of our authority."

37

A Third Rebuke from the Abbot Primate

Continuing on in this vein, Rodulf said, "Since I have undertaken to speak about the vices of our order, I have decided not to leave anything out, so that once these errors have been rooted out, our devotion may shine forth brightly once more, as if reappearing from behind dark clouds. Now there are some members of our order who have taken to openly wearing hats with covered ears, who prefer exotic pelts to the cap of a monk, and who dress themselves in expensive garments instead of the humble garb of the monas-

mas induere.[10] Nam tunicas magni emptas plurimum cu-
piunt, quas sic ab utroque latere stringunt, manicisque et
giris diffluentibus diffundunt, ut artatis clunibus et proten-
sis natibus potius meretriculis quam monachis a tergo assi-
milentur.'

38

De superfluo vestium
colore

'Quid vero de colore vestium? Unde tantum decepti
sunt, ut dignitatis merita coloribus comparent. Nam nisi tu-
nica nigro colore[11] deceat, ea indui nullomodo placet. Quod
si etiam nigro albus laneficii opere intermixtus sit, hic quoque talis vestem abiectam facit. Fulvus quoque abicitur. Nec
minus niger nativus non sufficit, nisi etiam corticum inficia-
tur sucis. Atque haec de vestibus.'

tic habit. They have a great fondness for costly tunics, which they cinch up on both sides, while their sleeves and folds hang down in profusion, so that with their haunches pressed close together and their buttocks clenched tight, from behind they give the appearance of harlots rather than monks."

38

On the Superfluous Color of Their Clothing

"What then of the color of their clothes? Here they are so deluded that they equate colors with the merits of worthiness. If a tunic is not the appropriate shade of black, they absolutely refuse to wear it. If, in the process of weaving, some white has become intermixed with the black, then this by itself makes the clothing worthless. A tawny color is rejected out of hand, nor are they satisfied with a natural shade of black unless it has been dyed with the juice of tree bark. But enough about clothing."

39

De calciamentis superfluis[12]

'De calciamentorum vero superfluitate quid referam?
Tantum enim in his insaniunt, ut commoditatem sibi plurimam per ea auferant. Ea enim sic arta induunt, ut cippati
pene impediantur. In quibus etiam rostra componunt, aures
hinc inde erigunt. Et ne folleant, magnopere elaborant. Ut
luceant quoque, famulis consciis indicunt.'

40

De linteis et operimentis[13] superfluis

'An lintea operosa atque pellicea operimenta sileam?
Cum, inquam, a maioribus clementiae gratia pro lenis indui
pellibus mediocribus concessum sit, vitium superfluitatis irrepsit. Unde et nunc peregrinis operimentis limbos bipal-

39

On the Extravagance of Their Shoes

"What then shall I say about the unnecessary extravagance of their shoes? They are so crazy in this regard that through them they detract greatly from their own comfort. For they wear shoes that are so tight that they walk as if they were hindered by fetters, and they adjust them to have pointed toes and ears that stick out on either side. They go to great lengths to make sure that they do not puff out, and they instruct trusted servants to make them shine."

40

On Extravagant Linens and Robes

"Shall I remain silent about their costly linens and fur garments? Although our forefathers, in the grace of their mercy, gave us permission to dress in modest fleeces instead of woolen cloaks, the vice of excess has gradually introduced itself, so that now they trim their exotic robes with fringes

mos circumducunt atque pannis Noricis ea desuper dupli-
cant. Linteis vero pro stragulis minime uti concessum est,
sed a quibusdam minus religiosis caeteris superfluis id additum est. Quorum numerus cum ex locis diversis plurimus
esset, a pluralitate malorum bonorum paucitati id persuasum est.'

41

De femoralibus iniquis

'Sed quid femoralia iniqua referam? Horum etenim tibia-
les quater sesquipede patent atque ex staminis subtilitate
etiam pudenda intuentibus non protegunt. In quorum com-
positione id uni non sufficit quo duo contenti ad plenum
esse valerent. Haec coram hic relata an prohiberi velitis indicate. Caetera vero nostris conciliis in privato corrigenda
sunt.'[14] Sinodus dixit, 'Et prohibeantur.'

two palms in width and double them over with Bavarian cloth. The use of linens for bed coverings is strictly forbidden, but this has been added to the list of other excesses by some of the less observant brothers. And because their numbers are everywhere so great, the wicked majority have inculcated their own bad habits among the few good men who remain."

41

On the Impropriety of Their Breeches

"What shall I say about the impropriety of their breeches? The leggings thereof measure four times one-and-a-half feet, but because of the fineness of the thread, they do not even shield the private parts from the gaze of onlookers. In their construction an amount of material that ought to be enough for two people does not even suffice for one. Signify whether you wish the things that have been recounted here to be forbidden. What remains must be corrected in our own private councils." The synod declared, "Let these things too be prohibited."

42

Responsio metropolitani
ad primatem

Ad haec quoque metropolitanus subiunxit: 'Gravitatis quidem vestrae fuit pauca dicendo pluribus parcere. Sed quoniam horum[15] quae reprehensioni in vestro ordine subiacent, alia nobis, alia vero privatis conciliis corrigenda iudicatis, idem sentio, idem laudo. Unde et quae hic inhiberi vestra gravitas petit, nostra auctoritas interdicit. Quae vobis silendo reservastis, vestris relinquimus inmutanda iuditiis.' His quoque dictis, sinodus soluta est. Quo tempore monachorum religio admodum floruit, cum eorum religionis peritissimus metropolitanus huius rei hortator esset et suasor. Et ut nobilitati suae in omnibus responderet, aecclesiae suae filios studiis[16] liberalibus instruere utiliter quaerebat.

42

The Archbishop's Reply to the Abbot Primate

In response to this the archbishop added, "It was characteristic of your gravity that by saying little you should spare many. But since it is your judgment that some of the practices that warrant reproach among your order should be corrected by us and others should be corrected by you in your private councils, I fully agree with and applaud this proposal. Consequently, our authority forbids those things that you have asked to be prohibited. As for those things that you have reserved for yourself by passing over them in silence, we leave it to you to reform them according to your own judgment." After this speech the synod was dissolved. At that time the religious life of the monks flourished due to the encouragement and exhortations of the archbishop, who was exceedingly knowledgeable about their practices. And in order to satisfy in all respects his own nobility of character, he sought to have the sons of his church instructed in the liberal arts for their own benefit.

43

Adventus Gerberti Romam[17]

Cui etiam cum apud sese super hoc aliqua deliberaret, ab ipsa divinitate directus est Gerbertus, magni ingenii ac miri eloquii vir, quo postmodum tota Gallia acsi lucerna ardente vibrabunda refulsit. Qui Aquitanus genere, in coenobio sancti confessoris Geroldi a puero altus et grammatica edoctus est. In qua[18] utpote adolescens cum adhuc intentus moraretur, Borrellum citerioris Hispaniae ducem orandi gratia ad idem coenobium contigit devenisse. Qui a loci abbate humanissime exceptus, post sermones quotlibet an in artibus perfecti in Hispaniis habeantur sciscitatur. Quod cum promptissime assereret, ei mox ab abbate persuasum est ut suorum aliquem susciperet secumque in artibus docendum duceret. Dux itaque non abnuens, petenti liberaliter favit. Ac fratrum consensu Gerbertum assumptum duxit atque Hattoni episcopo instruendum commisit. Apud quem etiam

43

Gerbert's Arrival in Rome

As Adalbero was thinking this matter over, God himself sent to him Gerbert, a man of great intellectual talent and marvelous eloquence, through whose agency all of Gaul later shone resplendent, like a blazing lamp. He was an Aquitainian by birth, raised from boyhood and instructed in grammar at the monastery of the holy confessor Gerald.[44] During his youth, while he was still deeply ensconced in his studies, it so happened that Borrell, the duke of nearer Spain,[45] came to the monastery of Saint-Gerald to pray. He was warmly received by the abbot, and after they had talked for some time, the abbot asked him whether there were men in Spain who were completely proficient in the liberal arts. When Borrell affirmed that there were, the abbot urged him to take one of his charges and bring him back with him to be educated in this subject matter. The duke did not refuse what was asked of him, but generously complied with this request. And with the agreement of the brothers, he took Gerbert and entrusted him to Bishop Hatto[46] for instruc-

in mathesi plurimum et efficaciter studuit. Sed cum divinitas Galliam iam caligantem magno lumine relucere voluit, predictis duci et episcopo mentem dedit ut Romam oraturi peterent. Paratisque necessariis, iter carpunt ac adolescentem commissum secum deducunt. Inde urbem ingressi, post preces ante sanctos apostolos effusas, beatae recordationis papam . . . adeunt, ac sese ei indicant, quodque visum est de suo iocundissime impertiunt.

44[19]

Nec latuit papam adolescentis industria simulque et discendi voluntas. Et quia musica et astronomia in Italia tunc penitus ignorabantur, mox papa Ottoni regi Germaniae et Italiae per legatum indicavit illuc huiusmodi advenisse iuvenem, qui mathesim optime nosset suosque strenue docere valeret. Mox etiam ab rege papae suggestum est ut iuvenem retineret, nullumque regrediendi aditum ei ullomodo preberet. Sed et duci atque episcopo qui ab Hispaniis convenerant a papa modestissime indicatur[20] regem velle sibi iuve-

tion. Under Hatto's tutelage Gerbert made great strides in
the study of the mathematical arts.[47] But when God desired
that Gaul, which at that time lay mired in darkness, should
shine forth once more with a great light, he put it in the
mind of Borrell and Hatto to go to Rome to pray. After get-   970–971
ting together the necessary provisions, they set out, taking
with them the young man who had been entrusted to their
care. They entered the city of Rome, and after pouring out
prayers to the holy apostles, they went before Pope [John][48]
of blessed memory, announcing their arrival and joyfully
sharing with him their intentions regarding their companion.

44

The young man's diligence and love of learning did not escape the notice of the pope. And because hardly anything
was known of music or astronomy in Italy at the time, he
sent an envoy to inform King Otto of Germany and Italy
that a young man had arrived who possessed a complete understanding of the mathematical arts and was capable of
providing vigorous instruction for his students. King Otto
straightaway sent word to the pope that he should keep the
young man with him and under no circumstances allow him
an opportunity to go home. The pope discreetly informed
the duke and the bishop who had come from Spain to meet
with him that the king wanted to keep Gerbert with him for
the time being, but that he would send him back shortly

nem ad tempus retinere, ac non multopost eum sese cum
honore remissurum; insuper etiam gratias inde recompensaturum. Itaque duci ac episcopo id persuasum est, ut hoc
pacto iuvene dimisso, ipsi in Hispanias iter retorquerent.
Iuvenis igitur apud papam relictus, ab eo regi oblatus est.
Qui de artibus[21] interrogatus, in mathesi se satis posse, logicae vero scientiam se addiscere velle respondit. Ad quam
quia pervenire moliebatur, non adeo in docendo ibi moratus
est.

45

Quod ab Ottone rege G. logico commissus sit

Quo tempore G. Remensium archidiaconus in logica clarissimus habebatur. Qui etiam a Lothario Francorum rege
eadem tempestate Ottoni regi Italiae legatus directus est.
Cuius adventu iuvenis exhilaratus, regem adiit atque ut G.

with great honor; and in addition to this he would repay them with tokens of his gratitude. The duke and the bishop were persuaded to leave the young man behind under these terms and they bent their steps back to Spain. Gerbert was left behind with the pope, who brought him before the king. When he was asked about the liberal arts, he replied that he had a satisfactory knowledge of mathematics but that he still wished to study the arts of logic.[49] And because he was eager to purse this branch of knowledge, he did not stay there to teach for very long.

45

King Otto Entrusts Gerbert to G[erannus],[50] a Teacher of Logic

At that time G[erannus], the archdeacon of Reims, was famed for his knowledge of logic, and on this particular occasion King Lothar of the Franks sent him as his envoy to King Otto in Italy. Delighted by the arrival of G[erannus], Gerbert went before the king and obtained permission to study with him. He remained by his side for some period of time and went back to Reims with him. There he studied

972

committeretur optinuit. Ei ergo per aliquot tempora haesit, Remosque ab eo deductus est. A quo etiam logicae scientiam accipiens, in brevi admodum profecit. G. vero, cum mathesi operam daret, artis difficultate victus, a musica reiectus est. Gerbertus interea studiorum nobilitate predicto metropolitano commendatus, eius gratiam pre omnibus promeruit. Unde et ab eo rogatus, discipulorum turmas artibus instruendas ei adhibuit.

46

Quem ordinem librorum in docendo servaverit[22]

Dialecticam ergo ordine librorum percurrens, dilucidis sententiarum verbis enodavit. Inprimis enim Porphirii ysagogas, id est introductiones, secundum Victorini rhethoris translationem, inde etiam easdem secundum Manlium explanavit, Cathegoriarum, id est predicamentorum, librum Aristotelis consequenter enucleans. Periermenias vero, id

the arts of logic with him, making great progress in a short amount of time. But although G[erannus] applied himself to the mathematical arts, the difficulty of music was too great for him, and he gave it up. In the meantime the advanced nature of Gerbert's studies recommended him to the archbishop, whose favor he won above all others. As a result, at Adalbero's request he brought in throngs of students to be instructed in the liberal arts.

46

The Sequence of Books That He Maintained in Teaching

Gerbert proceeded through the whole of the art of dialectic according to a fixed sequence of texts, elucidating the subtleties of this art with clearly formulated pronouncements. In the first place he explicated Porphyry's *Isagoge* (that is, "Introduction") according to the translation of the rhetorician Victorinus and the commentary by Boethius.[51] Next he explained the book of Aristotle called the *Categories* (that is, "Predications") and he skillfully demonstrated the

est de interpretatione librum, cuius laboris sit aptissime monstravit. Inde etiam topica, id est argumentorum sedes, a Tullio de Greco in Latinum translata et a Manlio consule sex commentariorum libris dilucidata, suis auditoribus intimavit.

· 47 ·

Quid provehendis rhethoricis providerit

Necnon et quatuor de topicis differentiis libros, de sillogismis cathegoricis duos, de ypotheticis tres, diffinitionumque librum unum, divisionum aeque unum utiliter legit et expressit. Post quorum laborem, cum ad rhethoricam suos provehere vellet, id sibi suspectum erat, quod sine locutionum modis, qui in poetis discendi sunt, ad oratoriam artem ante perveniri non queat. Poetas igitur adhibuit quibus assuescendos arbitrabatur. Legit itaque ac docuit Maronem et Statium Terentiumque poetas, Iuvenalem quoque ac Persium Horatiumque satiricos, Lucanum etiam historiographum. Quibus assuefactos locutionumque modis compositos, ad rhethoricam transduxit.

difficulty of the *Peri hermeneias* ("On Interpretation"). After that he introduced his students to the *Topics* (that is, the "Sources of Arguments"), as translated from Greek into Latin by Cicero and expounded in the six books of commentaries written by the consul Manlius Boethius.

47

The Measures He Took to Advance Them to the Art of Rhetoric

He also lectured on and effectively expounded four books on differential topics, two books on categorical syllogisms, three on hypothetical syllogisms, and one book each on definition and division.[52] After his students had labored over these texts, he wanted to promote them to the study of rhetoric, but he was concerned that they would not be able to learn the art of oratory without prior knowledge of the modes of expression,[53] which are learned in the works of the poets. For this reason he introduced them to the poets with whom he thought they ought to be made acquainted, expounding and teaching the poets Virgil, Statius, and Terence, the satirists Juvenal, Persius, and Horace, and the historian Lucan.[54] When they had been familiarized with these authors and trained in the modes of expression, he promoted them to the study of rhetoric.

48

Cur eis sophistam adhibuerit

Qua instructis, sophistam adhibuit apud quem in contro-
versiis exercerentur, ac sic ex arte agerent, ut preter artem
agere viderentur, quod oratoris maximum videtur. Sed haec
de logica.

49

Qui labor ei in mathematicis
impensus sit

In mathesi vero quantus sudor expensus sit, non incon-
gruum dicere videtur. Arithmeticam enim, quae est mathe-
seos prima, inprimis dispositis accommodavit. Inde etiam
musicam, multo ante Galliis ignotam, notissimam effecit.
Cuius genera in monocordo disponens, eorum consonantias

48

Why He Brought a Sophist Before Them

When they had been instructed in this art, he brought in a sophist with whom they engaged in practice disputations, conducting themselves according to the principles of this art in such a way that they seemed to act without any art at all, which is the greatest achievement for an orator.[55] But this is enough about logic.

49

The Labor He Expended on the Mathematical Arts

I do not think it would be out of place to mention how much effort he expended on the mathematical arts. In the first place, he introduced those who were ready for it to the study of arithmetic, which is the first element of mathematics. Next he established the knowledge of music, which for a long time had been unknown in Gaul. By demonstrating the arrangement of the different musical genera[56] on the monochord, by separating their consonances or harmonies into

sive simphonias in tonis ac semitoniis, ditonis quoque ac
diesibus distinguens, tonosque in sonis rationabiliter distribuens, in plenissimam notitiam redegit.

50

Sperae solidae compositio

Ratio vero astronomiae quanto sudore collecta sit dicere
inutile non est, ut et tanti viri sagacitas advertatur et artis
efficacia lector commodissime capiatur. Quae cum pene intellectibilis sit, tamen non sine admiratione quibusdam
instrumentis ad cognitionem adduxit. Inprimis enim mundi
speram ex solido ac rotundo ligno argumentatus, minoris si-
militudine maiorem expressit. Quam cum duobus polis[23]
obliquaret, signa septentrionalia polo erectiori dedit, aus-
tralia vero deiectiori adhibuit. Cuius positionem eo circulo
rexit qui a Grecis orizon, a Latinis limitans sive determinans
appellatur, eo quod in eo signa quae videntur ab his quae non
videntur distinguat ac limitet. Qua in orizonte sic collocata,

whole tones and semitones, major thirds and quarter-tones, and by methodically breaking down these tones into their constituent sounds,[57] he restored a complete understanding of this art.

50

The Construction of a Solid Sphere

It will not be inexpedient to mention the exertions by which he demonstrated the principles of astronomy, so that the ingenuity of such a great man may be appreciated and the reader may be duly convinced of the effectiveness of his methods. Although this subject is virtually inaccessible to the understanding, he nonetheless made it comprehensible in marvelous fashion by employing certain instruments. In the first place he fashioned a celestial globe out of a solid sphere of wood, using the smaller as a model of the larger. He then tilted it in alignment with the two poles, adding the northern constellations to the upper half and the southern constellations to the lower one. He regulated their position by means of the circle that the Greeks call the horizon and the Latins the *limitans* or *delimitans* because it divides and separates the visible constellations from those that cannot be seen. On the horizon, which was positioned to demon-

ut et ortum et occasum signorum utiliter ac probabiliter demonstraret, rerum naturas dispositis insinuavit instituitque in signorum comprehensione. Nam tempore nocturno ardentibus stellis operam dabat, agebatque ut eas in mundi regionibus diversis obliquatas tam in ortu quam in occasu notarent.

51

Intellectibilium circulorum comprehensio

Circuli quoque qui a Grecis paralleli, a Latinis aequistantes dicuntur, quos etiam incorporales esse dubium non est, hac ab eo arte comprehensi noscuntur. Effecit semicirculum recta diametro divisum. Sed hanc diametrum fistulam constituit, in cuius cacuminibus duos polos boreum et austronothum notandos esse instituit. Semicirculum vero a polo ad polum XXX partibus divisit. Quarum sex a polo distinctis, fistulam adhibuit per quam circularis linea arctici signaretur. Post quas etiam V diductis, fistulam quoque adiecit quae aestivalem circulationem indicaret. Abinde quoque quatuor divisis, fistulam identidem addidit unde aequinoctialis rotunditas commendaretur. Reliquum vero spatium usque ad notium polum eisdem dimensionibus distinxit.

strate effectively and accurately the rising and setting of the constellations, he imparted information about the properties of nature to his students and used it to aid them in recognizing the constellations.[58] At night he devoted his attention to the shining stars, helping his students to see how they moved in an oblique motion as they rose and set over the different regions of the world.

51

A Demonstration of the Invisible Circles[59]

He imparted an understanding of the circles which the Greeks call parallels and the Latins equidistants (which do not, of course, have a corporeal existence) through the following method: He fashioned a semicircle[60] with a straight diameter that consisted of a hollow tube, the ends of which he designated as the North and South Poles. He divided the semicircle into thirty parts from pole to pole. Six segments below the North Pole he placed another hollow tube that he used to signify the Arctic Circle. Five segments below that he inserted an additional tube to indicate the Tropic of Cancer. Four segments below that he added a tube to represent the equator. He marked off the rest of the distance down to the South Pole according to the same measurements. This

Cuius instrumenti ratio in tantum valuit, ut ad polum sua diametro directa, ac semicirculi productione superius versa, circulos visibus inexpertos scientiae daret atque alta memoria reconderet.[24]

52

Sperae compositio planetis cognoscendis aptissima

Errantiumque quoque siderum circuli cum intra mundum ferantur et contra contendant, quo tamen artificio viderentur scrutanti non defuit. Inprimis enim speram circularem effecit, hoc est ex solis circulis constantem. In qua circulos duos qui a Grecis coluri, a Latinis incidentes dicuntur, eo quod in sese incidant, complicavit; in quorum extremitatibus polos fixit. Alios vero quinque circulos, qui paralleli dicuntur, coluris transposuit, ita ut a polo ad polum XXX partes sperae medietatem dividerent, idque non vulgo neque confuse. Nam de XXX dimidiae sperae partibus a polo ad primum circulum sex constituit; a primo ad secundum, quinque; a secundo ad tertium, quatuor; a tertio ad quartum, itidem quatuor; a quarto ad quintum, quinque; a quinto us-

instrument was so efficacious in design that if the diameter were pointed toward the North Pole and the curved part of the semicircle were rotated, it would reveal those circles that are invisible to the eye and store them deep within the memory.

52

The Construction of a Sphere for Use in Studying the Planets

Nor did he lack the means to demonstrate to the observer the orbits of the planets as they moved with and against the rotation of the heavens.[61] First he fashioned an armillary sphere, which is a sphere made up entirely of circles. He wound around it the circles that the Greeks call *colures* and the Latins "incidents" because they intersect one another, and at their ends he fixed the poles.[62] He extended the five other circles[63] called parallels across the *colures,* so that from pole to pole they divided half of the sphere into thirty parts. Nor did he do this in a random or haphazard manner. Of the thirty parts of the hemisphere, he assigned six to the area from the North Pole to the first circle, five from the first circle to the second circle, four from the second to the third circle, another four from the third to the fourth circle, five from the fourth to the fifth circle, and six

que ad polum, sex. Per hos quoque circulos eum circulum obliquavit qui a Grecis loxòs vel zoe, a Latinis obliquus vel vitalis dicitur, eo quod animalium figuras in stellis contineat. Intra hunc obliquum errantium circulos miro artificio suspendit, quorum absidas et altitudines, a sese etiam distantias, efficacissime suis demonstravit. Quod quemadmodum fuerit, ob prolixitatem hic ponere commodum non est, ne nimis a proposito discedere videamur.

53

Aliae sperae compositio signis cognoscendis idonea

Fecit preter haec speram alteram circularem, intra quam circulos quidem non collocavit, sed desuper ferreis atque aereis filis signorum figuras complicavit. Axisque loco fistulam traiecit per quam polus caelestis notaretur, ut eo perspecto, machina caelo aptaretur. Unde et factum est ut singulorum signorum stellae singulis huius sperae signis clauderentur. Illud quoque in hac divinum fuit, quod cum

from the fifth circle to the South Pole.[64] Through these parallels he extended the slanted band that the Greeks call *loxos* or *zoe* and the Latins "oblique" or "life-sustaining" because it contains the shapes of animals within the stars.[65] With remarkable ingenuity he suspended the planetary circles inside this oblique band, effectively demonstrating to his students their apogees, altitudes, and distances from one another.[66] This is not the place to describe how he did this, because it would take too long and I would be straying too far from the topic I have set for myself.

53

The Construction of Another Sphere for Use in Demonstrating the Constellations

In addition to this he fashioned another circular sphere. He did not place circles in the interior of this one,[67] but instead wound images of the constellations made out of iron and brass wires to the surface. He passed a hollow tube through the axis through which the celestial pole could be seen, so that when the polestar was sighted the device would be in alignment with the heavens. In this way the stars that belonged to each individual constellation were included on the constellations that were represented on the sphere. There was also something miraculous about this instru-

aliquis artem ignoraret, si unum ei signum demonstratum foret, absque magistro cetera per speram cognosceret. In qua etiam suos liberaliter instruxit. Atque haec actenus de astronomia.

54

Confectio abaci

In geometria vero[25] non minor in docendo labor expensus est. Cuius introductioni abacum, id est tabulam dimensionibus aptam, opere scutarii effecit. Cuius longitudini in XXVII partibus diductae, novem numero notas omnem numerum significantes disposuit. Ad quarum etiam similitudinem mille corneos effecit caracteres, qui per XXVII abaci partes mutuati, cuiusque numeri multiplicationem sive divisionem designarent, tanto compendio numerorum multitudinem dividentes vel multiplicantes, ut pre nimia numerositate potius intelligi quam verbis valerent ostendi. Quorum scientiam qui ad plenum scire desiderat, legat eius librum quem scribit ad Constantinum[26] grammaticum. Ibi enim haec satis habundanterque tractata inveniet.

ment, for if someone who knew nothing of astronomy were shown one constellation with this sphere, he could then use it to identify all of the other constellations without the need for a teacher. Gerbert made generous use of it in teaching his students. That will suffice for astronomy.

54

The Construction of an Abacus

He expended no less effort in teaching geometry. As an introduction to this subject he had a shield maker fashion an abacus, which is a board designed with particular measurements. It was divided into twenty-seven columns, and nine symbols could be arranged upon it to signify any number.[68] He had a thousand markers with these symbols on them made out of horn. These could then be taken in and out of the twenty-seven columns of the abacus to represent the multiplication or division of any number, and by employing this shortcut one could multiply and divide a great many numbers so large that they could be perceived by the mind more easily than they could be represented in words. Whoever wishes to acquire a more complete knowledge of this body of knowledge should read the book that Gerbert wrote for Constantine the Grammarian.[69] There he will find a very thorough treatment of the subject.

55

Fama Gerberti per Gallias et Italiam diffusa

Fervebat studiis, numerusque discipulorum in dies accrescebat. Nomen etiam tanti doctoris ferebatur non solum per Gallias, sed etiam per Germaniae populos dilatabatur. Transiitque per Alpes ac diffunditur in Italiam usque Thirrenum et Adriaticum. Quo tempore Otricus in Saxonia insignis habebatur. Hic cum philosophi famam audisset adverteretque quod in omni disputatione rata rerum divisione uteretur, agebat apud suos ut aliquae rerum divisarum figurae ab scolis philosophi sibi deferrentur, et maxime philosophiae, eo quod in rata eius divisione perpendere ipse facilius posset an recte is saperet qui philosophari videbatur, utpote in eo quod divinarum et humanarum scientiam profitetur. Directus itaque est Remos Saxo quidam, qui ad haec videbatur idoneus. Is cum scolis interesset et caute generum divisiones a Gerberto dispositas colligeret, in ea tamen maxime divisione quae philosophiam ad plenum dividit plurimum ordine abusus est.

55

Gerbert's Fame Spreads Throughout Gaul and Italy

Gerbert pursued his studies with tremendous energy, and the number of his students increased every day. His fame as a great teacher was not only carried throughout Gaul, but also circulated among the peoples of Germany, and it crossed the Alps and spread into Italy all the way to the Tyrrhenian and Adriatic seas. At that time Otric[70] was held in high regard in Saxony. When he heard about Gerbert's reputation as a philosopher and learned that in every disputation Gerbert employed a particular taxonomy, he asked his students to bring to him some taxonomical diagrams from the school of this philosopher. He was particularly interested in Gerbert's taxonomy of the parts of philosophy, because it would help him to determine whether this man who gave the appearance of being a philosopher (inasmuch as he taught the knowledge of divine and human affairs) was correct in his understanding. And so a certain Saxon who was deemed suitable for the task was sent to Reims. He attended the school there and carefully collected divisions of genera as they had been drawn up by Gerbert. In the case of the particular taxonomy wherein Gerbert made a complete division of philosophy, however, he got the arrangement completely wrong.

ca. 979/
980

56

Figura Gerberti philosophica per malivolos depravata, ab Otrico reprehenditur

Etenim cum mathematicae phisica par atque coaeva a Gerberto posita fuisset, ab hoc mathematicae eadem phisica ut generi species subdita est. Incertumque utrum industria an errore id factum sit. Sicque cum multiplici diversarum rerum distributione Otrico figura delata est. Quam ipse diligentissime revolvens, Gerbertum male divisisse apud suos calumniabatur, eo quod duarum aequalium specierum alteri alteram substitutam ut generi speciem figura mentiebatur. Ac per hoc nihil eum philosophiae percepisse audacter astruebat, illudque eum penitus ignorare dicebat, in quo divina et humana consistunt, sine quibus etiam nulli sit philosophandum. Tulit itaque ad palatium figuram eandem et coram Ottone augusto iis qui sapientiores videbantur eam explicavit. Augustus vero, cum et ipse talium studiosissimus haberetur, an Gerbertus erraverit admirabatur. Viderat ete-

56

Gerbert's Philosophical Diagram Is Distorted by the Spiteful and Criticized by Otric

For although Gerbert had arranged physics as part of the same genus as mathematics,[71] in the version that this man brought back physics was subordinated to mathematics as species to genus (it is not known whether he did this deliberately or if it was a mistake). And so the diagram was brought to Otric with a manifold division of different terms. After examining it very carefully, Otric criticized Gerbert in front of his students for having made an incorrect division, since the diagram took two species of the same genus and wrongly subordinated one to the other as species to genus. For this reason Otric had the temerity to assume that Gerbert had no understanding of philosophy at all, and he claimed that he was wholly ignorant of the composition of things divine and human, without the knowledge of which no one ought to practice philosophy. And so he took this same diagram to the palace, where he proceeded to describe it to those men of Otto's court who were deemed to be learned.[72] The emperor, however, since he himself was considered to be very interested in these sorts of things, wondered whether Gerbert had really made such an error, for he

nim illum et non semel disputantem audierat. Unde et ab eo predictae figure solutionem fieri nimium optabat. Nec defuit rei occasio.

57

Nam venerandus Remorum metropolitanus Adalbero post eundem annum Romam cum Gerberto petebat ac Ticini augustum cum Otrico repperit. A quo etiam magnifice exceptus est ductusque per Padum classe Ravennam. Et tempore oportuno imperatoris iussu omnes sapientes qui convenerant intra palatium collecti sunt. Affuit predictus reverendus metropolitanus; affuit et Adso abbas Dervensis, qui cum ipso metropolitano advenerat. Sed et Otricus presens erat, qui[27] anno superiore Gerberti reprehensorem sese monstraverat. Numerus quoque scolasticorum non parvus confluxerat, qui imminentem disputationis litem summopere prestolabantur. Haerebant etenim an Otrico[28] quispiam resistere auderet. Necnon et augustus huiusmodi certamen habendum callide pertractabat. Nitebatur autem Gerbertum incautum Otrico opponere, ut si incautus appeteretur, maiorem controversandi animum in contrarium moveret.

had seen and heard him engaging in disputations on more than one occasion. For this reason he was most eager to get an explanation of this diagram from Gerbert himself—nor did he lack an opportunity to do so.

57

For a year later, Adalbero, the venerable archbishop of Reims, was traveling to Rome with Gerbert and found the emperor at Pavia with Otric. He received a splendid reception there, after which he was taken by ship via the Po to Ravenna. At the appropriate time the emperor instructed all of the learned men who had accompanied him there to assemble in the palace. Among them were the reverend archbishop Adalbero, and Adso,[73] the abbot of Montier-en-Der, who had come with him. Also present was Otric, who had shown himself to be a critic of Gerbert the previous year. In addition, a considerable number of scholars had come, and they were eagerly awaiting the contest in disputation that was soon to take place. For they were anxious to see if there was anyone who would dare to contend with Otric. Otto handled the staging of this sort of contest very cleverly. He strove to pit Gerbert against Otric without giving him any advance notice, so that if Gerbert were unexpectedly attacked, he would then pursue his opponent with

980

980/981

Otricum vero multa proponere nihilve solvere hortabatur. Atque his omnibus ex ordine considentibus, augustus eorum medius sic e sublimi coepit:

58

Allocutio augusti Ottonis in conventu sapientium pro emendatione figurae

'Humanam,' inquiens, 'ut arbitror, scientiam crebra meditatio vel exercitatio reddit meliorem, quotiens rerum materia competenter ordinata sermonibus exquisitis per quoslibet sapientes effertur. Nam cum per otium sepissime torpemus, si aliquorum pulsemur questionibus, ad utillimam mox meditationem incitamur. Hinc scientia rerum a doctissimis elicita est. Hinc est quod ab eis prolata, libris tradita sunt nobisque ad boni exercicii gloriam derelicta. Afficiamur igitur et nos aliquibus obiectis, quibus et animus excellentior ad intelligentiae cerciora ducatur. Et eia, inquam, iam nunc revolvamus figuram illam de philosophiae partibus

more vigor in the disputation. As for Otric, he encouraged him to introduce a great many propositions, but not to answer any of them. After everyone in the audience had been seated according to his rank, the emperor, who was in their midst, addressed them from on high:

58

The Emperor Otto's Address to the Assembly of Learned Men Concerning the Correction of Gerbert's Diagram

"It is my belief that human knowledge is improved by frequent contemplation and regular practice whenever its subject matter is properly organized and given expression by any learned men in carefully formulated language. For when, as is often the case, we grow listless through idleness, if other people provoke us with questions we are immediately roused to start thinking productively. Thus it is that knowledge has been drawn forth from learned men. Thus it is that what they have produced has been committed to writing and passed down to us to glorify it by putting it to good use. Let us therefore apply ourselves to some problems by means of which the higher part of our intellectual faculties may be led to greater certainty of understanding.[74] And so, I say, let us all now consider the diagram of the parts of

quae nobis anno superiore monstrata est. Omnes diligentissime eam advertant, dicantque singuli quid in ea aut contra
eam sentiant. Si nullius extrinsecus indiget, vestra omnium
roboretur approbatione. Si vero corrigenda videbitur, sa-
pientium sententiis aut improbetur aut ad normam rediga-
tur. Coramque deferatur iam nunc videnda.' Tunc Otricus
eam in aperto proferens, a Gerberto sic ordinatam et a suis
auditoribus exceptam scriptamque respondit, et sic domno
augusto legendam porrexit. Quae perlecta, ad Gerbertum
delata est. Qui diligenter eam percurrens, in parte approbat
et in parte vituperat, simulque non sic eam sese ordinasse
asseruit.

59

Divisio theoreticae philosophiae
in species

Rogatus autem ab augusto corrigere, ait: 'Quoniam, o
magne caesar auguste, te his omnibus potiorem video, tuis,
ut par est, iussis parebo. Nec movebit me malivolorum livor,

philosophy that was shown to me last year. Let everyone examine it carefully, and let each person say what he thinks about it or what he has to say against it. If nothing more needs to be added to it, then let it be confirmed by all of your approval. But if it appears to stand in need of correction, then let it either be rejected or else restored to the correct standard based upon the opinions of learned men. Let it now be brought out in public so that it may be examined." Then Otric, bringing the diagram out into the open, replied that this was the way that Gerbert had drawn it up, and this was the way it had been understood and copied down by his audience. And with that he handed it over to the emperor to read. After Otto had perused it, the diagram was taken over to Gerbert. Scrutinizing it carefully, he accepted it in part and critiqued it in part, while at the same time asserting that he had not drawn it up in this way.

59

The Division of Theoretical Philosophy into Species

When he was asked by the emperor to correct it, he replied: "Because, most eminent Caesar Augustus, I can see that you rank supreme among all those who are here, it is only proper that I comply with your orders. Nor will I be in-

quorum instinctu id factum est, ut rectissima philosophiae divisio, probabiliter dilucideque a me nuper ordinata, unius speciei suppositione vitiata sit.[29] Dico itaque mathematicam, phisicam, et theologicam aequaevas eidem generi subesse. Earum autem genus eis aequaliter participare. Nec fieri posse unam eandemque speciem una eademque ratione eidem speciei et parem esse et ut inferiorem acsi generi speciem subiacere. Et ego quidem de his ita sentio. Caeterum si quis contra haec contendat, rationem inde affectet, faciatque nos intelligere quod fortassis naturae ipsius ratio nemini adhuc contulisse videtur.'

60

Philosophiae divisio

Ad haec Otricus, innuente augusto, sic ait: 'Quoniam philosophiae partes aliquot breviter attigisti, ad plenum oportet ut et dividas et divisionem enodes. Sicque fieri poterit ut ex probabili divisione vitiosae figurae suspicio a te removeatur.' Tunc quoque Gerbertus, 'Cum hoc,' inquit,

fluenced by the envy of spiteful men, who are responsible for the fact that the wholly accurate division of philosophy that I recently demonstrated in clear and convincing fashion was invalidated by the improper subordination of one species. Thus, I declare that mathematics, physics, and theology are all coequal species of the same genus, in which they participate equally. Nor is it possible that one and the same species could at the same time be equal to another species and also subordinated to it as species to genus. This is my opinion on the matter. If anyone wishes to argue the opposite case, let him attempt an explanation and make us understand that which the law of nature itself seems not to have granted anyone else yet."

60

The Division of Philosophy

At a nod from the emperor, Otric offered his response: "Since you have briefly touched upon several of the parts of philosophy, you ought now to make a complete division and to explain your classification. For by providing a credible division of philosophy you will eliminate any suspicion that you were responsible for producing an incorrect diagram." To this Gerbert responded, "Although this is a very serious matter, encompassing as it does a true understand-

'magni constet, utpote divinarum et humanarum rerum comprehensio veritatis, tamen ut nec nos ignaviae arguamur, et auditorum aliqui proficere possint, secundum Vitruvii[30] atque Boetii divisionem dicere non pigebit. Est enim philosophia genus cuius species sunt practice et theoretice. Practices vero species dico dispensativam, distributivam, civilem. Sub theoretice vero non incongrue intelliguntur phisica naturalis, mathematica intelligibilis, ac theologia intellectibilis. Rursusque mathematicam sub phisica non preter rationem collocamus.'

61

Reprehensio divisionis ab Otrico inutilis, ac Gerberti responsio

Nisusque quod reliquum erat prosequi, Otricus subintulit: 'Miror,' inquiens, 'vehementissime quod phisicae mathematicam sic de propinquo subdidisti, cum inter utramque subalternum genus intelligi possit phisiologia. Vitiosum etenim valde videtur, si nimis longe petita pars ad generis conferatur divisionem.' Ad haec Gerbertus, 'Inde,' inquit, 'vehe-

ing of things divine and human, nonetheless, so that I will not be accused of idleness, and so that some of those who are listening may derive profit from it, I will not shrink from making a division of philosophy according to Vitruvius[75] and Boethius. Philosophy, therefore, is a genus whose species are the practical and the theoretical. The species of practical philosophy are economics, ethics, and politics. Under the heading of theoretical philosophy are to be understood physics, which is natural, mathematics, which is intelligible, and theology, which is intellectible.[76] And so once again I have not made the mistake of placing mathematics beneath physics.[77]

61

Otric's Ineffective Critique of Gerbert's Division, and Gerbert's Reply

In an effort to pursue what Gerbert had neglected to mention, Otric responded, "I am astonished that you have placed mathematics directly beneath physics, since the subaltern genus of physiology may be understood to exist between them. Indeed, it would be erroneous if one had to go so far afield to find a part of philosophy that would serve to divide the genus." To this Gerbert replied, "It is even more astonishing to me that I should be thought to have subordi-

mentius mirandum videtur quod mathematicam phisicae, suae videlicet coaevae, ut speciem subdiderim. Cum enim coevae sub eodem genere habeantur, maiore inquam admiratione dignum videtur, si alteri altera subdatur. Sed dico phisiologiam phisicae genus non esse quemadmodum proponis, nullamque earum differentiam aliam assero, nisi eam quam inter philosophiam et philologiam cognosco. Alioquin philologia philosophiae genus conceditur.' Ad haec scolasticorum multitudo philosophiae divisionem interruptam indignabatur eamque repeti apud augustum petebat. Otricus vero post paululum idem repetendum dicebat, prius tamen habita ratione de causa ipsius philosophiae. Intendensque in Gerbertum, quae esset causa philosophiae sciscitabatur.

62

Quae sit causa conditi mundi

Qui cum a Gerberto ut apertius quid vellet ediceret rogaretur, utrum videlicet causam qua inventa est an causam cui inventa debetur, ille mox, 'Ipsam,' inquit, 'causam dico propter quam inventa videtur.' Tunc vero Gerbertus, 'Quoniam,' inquit, 'nunc patet quid proponas, ideo inquam inventa est, ut ex ea cognoscamus divina et humana.' Et Otri-

nated mathematics to physics as species to genus, when in fact they are coequal.[78] For since coequal species are found under the same genus, it would be surprising if one were subordinated to the other. In fact, physiology is not the genus of physics, as you propose, and the difference between these two terms is the same as that between philosophy and philology.[79] Otherwise one would have to grant that philology is a genus of philosophy." At this the crowd of scholars became annoyed that the division of philosophy had been left incomplete, and they asked the emperor to have them revisit this subject. Otric said that he would return to it very shortly, but only after the cause of philosophy itself had been explained. He then turned to Gerbert and asked him what the cause of philosophy was.

62

The Cause of the Creation of the World[80]

Gerbert asked him to explain more clearly what it was that he wanted: was it the cause by which it had been devised or the reason to which it owed its devising? Otric replied, "I am speaking of the reason for which it was devised." Gerbert then said, "Since what you are asking is now clear, I will tell you that it was devised so that as a result of it we might recognize things divine and human." In response

cus, 'Cur,' inquit, 'unius rei causam tot dictionibus nominasti,
cum ex una fortassis nominari potuit, et philosophorum sit
brevitati studere?'

63

Quod non omnia nomina causarum singulis dictionibus efferuntur

Gerbertus quoque, 'Non omnes,' inquit, 'causae uno valent nomine proferri. Etenim cum a Platone causa creati
mundi non una sed tribus dictionibus 'bona dei voluntas' de-
clarata sit, constat hanc creati mundi causam non aliter
potuisse proferri. Nam si dixisset voluntatem causam esse
mundi, non id esset consequens; quaelibet enim voluntas id
esse videretur, quod non procedit.' Atque hic Otricus, 'Si,'
inquit, 'dei voluntatem causam conditi mundi dixisset, brevius quidem et sufficienter dictum foret, cum numquam nisi
bona fuerit dei voluntas. Non enim est qui abnuat bonam
esse dei voluntatem.' Et Gerbertus, 'In hoc,' inquit, 'penitus
non contradico. Sed vide, quia constat deum substantia solummodo bonum, quamlibet vero creaturam participatione

Otric asked him, "Why is it that you used so many words to name the cause of a single thing, when it could have been designated with one word, and philosophers ought to strive for brevity?"

63

The Names of All Causes Cannot Be Expressed in a Single Word

"Not all causes," said Gerbert, "can be denominated with a single word. Indeed, because Plato used not one word but three—'God's good will'—to explain the cause of the world's creation, it is clear that it cannot be expressed in any other way. For it would not have made sense if he had said that 'will' was the cause of the world, because this could have been a reference to any kind of will whatsoever, and this will not do." To this Otric replied, "He could have said the same thing just as well and more concisely by saying that 'God's will' was the cause of the world, because God never wills anything that is not good, and there is no one who would deny that the will of God is good." Gerbert responded, "Here we are in complete agreement. But note that while it is agreed that God is necessarily good with respect to substance, anything that he creates is only good by participa-

bonam, ad eius naturae qualitatem exprimendam 'bona' additum est, quod id eius proprium sit, non etiam cuiuslibet creaturae. Tandem quicquid illud sit, id sine dubio constat, non omnia causarum nomina una dictione proferri posse.'

64

Quae sit causa umbrae

'Quae enim tibi umbrae causa videtur? An haec una dictione indicari valet? Sed dico umbrae causam esse 'corpus luci obiectum.' Atque haec brevius nullomodo dici valet. Si enim corpus umbrae causam dixeris, nimis commune protulisti. Quod si corpus obiectum volueris, id quoque tantum non procedit quantum ab hac parte relinquitur. Sunt enim corpora nonnulla, atque etiam diversis obiecta, quae umbrae causa esse non possunt. Nec abnuo multarum rerum causas singulis dictionibus efferri, veluti sunt genera quae specierum causas nemo ignorat, velut est substantia, quantitas, qualitas. Alia vero non simpliciter proferuntur, ut rationale ad mortale.'

tion. So in order to express this quality of his nature, we add the word 'good,' because this is a property that belongs to him, but not to any of element of his creation. Ultimately, whatever the case may be, one thing is certain: the names of all causes cannot be expressed in a single word."

64

An Inquiry into the Cause of Shadows

"For what do you think is the cause of a shadow? Can it be designated by a single word? On the contrary, I would say that the cause of a shadow is 'a body interposed with light.' Nor is there any way to state this more concisely. For if you say that 'body' is the cause of shadow, then you have offered too general a definition. But if you instead prefer 'an interposed body,' then this definition, too, is inadequate insofar as it is deficient in this respect: namely, there are some bodies that cannot cause shadows, even when they are put in front of different things. Now I do not deny that there are many things whose causes can be expressed in a single word, just as there are genera such as substance, quantity, and quality that are universally acknowledged to be the causes of species. But other things cannot be defined so simply, as for example the rational as it applies to the mortal."

65

Quod continentius sit,
rationale an mortale[31]

Tunc vehementius Otricus admirans ait, 'An mortale rationali supponis? Quis nesciat quod rationale deum et angelum hominemque concludat, mortale vero utpote maius et continentius omnia mortalia et per hoc infinita colligat?' Ad haec Gerbertus, 'Si,' inquit, 'secundum Porphirium atque Boetium substantiae divisionem usque ad individua idonea partitione perpenderes, rationale continentius quam mortale sine dubio haberes. Idque congruis rationibus enucleari in promptu est. Etenim cum constet substantiam, genus generalissimum, per subalterna posse dividi usque ad individua, videndum est an omnia subalterna singulis dictionibus proferantur. Sed liquido patet alia de singulis, alia de pluribus nomen factum habere. De singulis, ut corpus; de pluribus, ut 'animatum sensibile.' Eadem quoque ratione subalternum, quod est animal rationale, predicatur de subiecto, quod est animal rationale mortale. Nec dico quod rationale

65

Whether the Rational or the Mortal Is the Larger Category

At this Otric expressed even greater astonishment: "Are you subordinating the mortal to the rational?" he asked. "Who could be unaware that the rational encompasses God, the angels, and man, whereas the mortal, inasmuch as it is a larger and more inclusive category, includes everything that is mortal, which makes it infinitely large?" To this Gerbert replied, "If you were to consider an appropriately partitioned division of substance down to its individual parts, as is found in Porphyry and Boethius, you would assuredly discover that the rational is a broader category than the mortal. It is easy to demonstrate this through proper reasoning. For since it is agreed that substance, the most general of all genera, can be divided through subaltern genera into individual terms, we must examine whether all subaltern genera can be denominated in a single word. But it is perfectly clear that some of these have names made up of a single word, and others of multiple words. For example, in the former category we have 'body' and in the latter 'animate sensible.' In the same way, the subaltern genus 'rational animal' is predicated of the subject 'mortal rational animal.' I am not

simplex predicetur de simplici mortali; id enim non procedit. Sed rationale inquam animali coniunctum predicatur de mortali, coniuncto animali rationali.' Cumque verbis et sententiis nimium flueret et adhuc alia dicere pararet, augusti nutu disputationi finis iniectus est, eo quod et diem pene in his totum consumserant, et audientes prolixa atque continua disputatio iam fatigabat. Ab augusto itaque Gerbertus egregie donatus, cum suo metropolitano in Gallias clarus remeavit.

66

Sinodus apud sanctam Magram habita

Eodem tempore Emma regina et Adalbero Laudunensis episcopus infames stupri criminabantur. Id tamen latenter intendebatur, nullius manifesto intentionis teste. Sed quia suppresse dictum ad omnium aures devenerat, episcopis visum est id esse discutiendum, ne frater et coepiscopus eorum infamiae tantae subderetur. A supradicto ergo metropolitano collecta est episcoporum sinodus apud sanctam

claiming that 'rational' by itself is predicated of 'mortal' by itself, because that is not valid, but I am saying that 'rational,' when joined to 'animal,' is predicated of 'mortal,' when it is joined to 'rational animal.'" Because he was producing a steady stream of words and sentences, and preparing to address still other topics, the emperor gave the sign to bring the disputation to an end, since it had taken up most of the day, and the audience was worn out from the lengthy and uninterrupted debate. After receiving a handsome reward from the emperor, Gerbert returned to Gaul with his metropolitan, covered in glory.

66

The Synod of Saint-Macre

At that time[81] Queen Emma and Bishop Adalbero of Laon were being accused of adultery. These allegations were only made in private, however, since no one was prepared to bring a charge openly. But because the rumors had reached everyone's ears, the bishops decided to adjudicate the matter so that their brother and fellow bishop would not have to endure such a scandalous allegation. A synod of bishops

Magram, locum Remorum diocesaneum. Considentesque et quaeque utilia pertractantes, postquam metropolitanus. . . .

67

Ottonis promotio per Germanos et Belgas[32]

Post obitum domni Ottonis Germanorum regis, eius filius Otto, a Germanis Belgisque rex creatus, rem publicam strenue atque utiliter amministravit, vir magni ingenii totiusque virtutis, liberalium litterarum scientia clarus, adeo ut in disputando ex arte et proponeret et probabiliter concluderet. Penes quem regnum Germaniae cum Galliarum aliqua parte usque ad diem vitae eius supremum mansit, sed aliquando dubio statu. Nam inter ipsum et Lotharium Gallorum regem quandoque et odium immane et anceps victoria fuit. Etenim cum ab Ottone Belgica teneretur, et a Lothario im-

therefore assembled at Saint-Macre,[82] in the diocese of Reims, at the behest of Archbishop Adalbero. They took their seats and discussed some preliminary matters of importance, and after the archbishop <. . .>[83]

67

The Elevation of Otto by the Men of Germany and Belgica

After the death of King Otto of the Germans, his son   973
Otto, who had been raised to the throne by the Germans and the men of Belgica, governed the realm energetically and capably. He was a man characterized by great intellectual ability and the possession of every virtue, and he was conspicuous for his knowledge of the liberal arts, so much so that when engaging in a disputation he could state propositions and draw convincing conclusions in accordance with the rules of this art. During his reign and down to the end of his life the kingdom of Germany exercised control over a portion of Gaul, but this was periodically disputed. For a passionate hatred flared up intermittently between Otto and Lothar, king of the Gauls, and neither man was able to prevail over the other.[84] For since Belgica was controlled by

peteretur, contra se dolos aut vires moliebantur, eo quod uterque et suum patrem eam tenuisse contenderet, et exercituum multitudine uterque eam se defensurum non diffideret. Nam et Ludovici patris Lotharii fuit, et eius post dono huius Ottonis pater Otto obtinuit. Horum ergo discordiae incentivum principium Belgica fuit.

68

Indignatio Lotharii in Ottonem

Igitur in Aquensi palatio Ottone commorante cum coniuge Teuphanu gravida, Lotharius illum propius accessisse acerrime motus indignabatur. Ergo Francorum ducem Hugonem reliquosque regni primates consilium petiturus Lauduni collegit. Dux itaque processit; reliqui etiam quibus quoque consulendum erat ante regem consequenter admissi sunt. Quibus residentibus, rex duplicem iniuriam sibi illatam esse commemorat, cum regni sui pars ab hoste usurpata

Otto but contested by Lothar, they vied against one another through cunning and force of arms, each one of them maintaining that his own father had previously held this territory, and neither showing any hesitation about using a host of armies to defend his claim. In reality Belgica had previously belonged to Lothar's father, Louis, but Otto, the father of the present Otto, later obtained it by a grant from him. Belgica, then, was the origin and source of the discord between them.[85]

68

Lothar's Resentment against Otto

Otto had taken up residence in his palace at Aachen with his pregnant wife Theophanu, and the fact that he had moved into such close proximity provoked a furious reaction from Lothar. Consequently, he summoned Duke Hugh of the Franks and the other chief men of the realm to Laon to seek their counsel. After Duke Hugh had made his entrance, the rest of the men who were to take part in the council were admitted before the king. Once they were seated, the king declared to them that he had been the victim of a twofold injury, inasmuch as part of his kingdom had

978

fuerit, et ipse hostis ad fines suos temerarius accesserit. Nec maiori iniuriae esse quod tenuerit, quam quia tenens ad fines suos accedere non formidaverit. Se etiam id multa aviditate ulcisci velle, si consilio suo velint cedere. Nec posse se ab hoc animo temperari, si ad id agendum copia militum non defecerit. Gratias etiam sese quandoque redditurum, si id quod cupit aequo animo adoriantur.

69

Impetus Gallorum spontaneus in Ottonem

Mox dux et alii primates sine deliberandi consultatione sententiam regiam attollunt. Sese sponte ituros cum rege, et Ottonem aut comprehensuros aut interfecturos aut fugaturos pollicentur. Huius consilium negotii[33] dissimulatum, ad paucorum tunc notitiam pervenire potuit, adeo ut euntes quorsum nescirent. Tandem collectus, exercitus sic densus incedebat ut erecta hastilia lucum potius quam arma por-

been usurped by his enemy, and now that same enemy had had the audacity to approach the borders of his realm. The fact that Otto occupied this territory was no more of an affront to him than the fact that his control over this area had emboldened him to threaten the king's lands. He was determined to avenge this insult if they were willing to yield to his judgment. Nor would he be dissuaded from his intentions as long as there were sufficient troops available to him to put his plan into effect. Moreover, he would show his gratitude to them in the future if they would undertake what he asked without complaint.

69

The Surprise Attack of the Gauls on Otto

The duke and the other magnates gave their blessing to the king's proposal right away, without mutual deliberation. They promised that they would go with him willingly, and that they would either capture Otto, kill him, or force him to flee. The plan was kept secret and was only able to reach a very few, so that those who went on the campaign did not even know where they were going. When the army had at last assembled, the men marched forth in ranks so dense that their upright spears looked like a grove of trees rather

tenderent. Ibat ergo per cuneos simbolo distinctos. Cum vero vada Mosae transmisissent, centuriones constituti et dispositi per centurias Ottonem non sufficientem habere exercitum diligenter contemplati sunt. Itaque[34] accedebant, multamque inopiam rei militaris apud hostem predicabant.

70

Quae dum ad aures Ottonis referuntur, ille, utpote erat audaci animo, Lotharium numquam haec aggressum respondit. Nec vero in suas partes adventare potuisse, cum nec ei copia militum sufficeret, nec de suis satis spei haberet. At cum alii atque alii Lotharium iam adesse dicerent, et in eo perseverarent, Otto dixisse fertur se ad his credendum nullomodo posse allici,[35] nisi ipse quoque videndo per sese addisceret. Equis ergo inclamatis et adductis, Otto ad viden-

than arms. For this reason they marched in divisions distinguished by their standards. When they had crossed the ford over the River Meuse, the centurions who had been designated and assigned to the centuries learned from careful observation that Otto did not have a sufficient number of troops.[86] And so they drew near, declaring the enemy to be badly outnumbered.

70

When the news was reported to Otto, he replied with his customary bravado that Lothar had never before attempted this. Nor, for that matter, was he even capable of mounting a campaign into his territory, since he had insufficient troops available to him and he lacked confidence in his own men. But when more and more people kept coming to tell him that Lothar had already arrived, and when they persisted in their claims, Otto reportedly said that he could never under any circumstances be led to believe this unless he could confirm it with his own eyes. He called for horses, and after they had been brought to him, he set off to see for himself. He observed that Lothar was in the area

dum[36] processit. Lotharium cum $\overline{XX}$ instare advertit. Cogitabat itaque nunc reniti, nunc quoque ad tempus recedere, et post cum exercitu copioso reverti meditabatur.

71

Tandem quia Lotharius urgebat, stare non potuit. Abscessit ergo non sine lacrimis cum uxore Teuphanu regnique principibus, relicto palatio atque regio apparatu. Lotharius cum exercitu affuit, Ottonem se capturum ratus. Et certe cepisset,[37] si in itinere sese exercitus angariis non impedisset. Nam si ante eius discessum pridie advenisset, eum aut capere aut neci dare potuisset. Palatium igitur ab hostibus occupatur; regiae mensae evertuntur; ciborum apparatus per calones diripitur. Regia quoque insignia a penetralibus erepta asportantur. Aeream aquilam quae in vertice palatii a Karolo Magno acsi volans fixa erat in vulturnum converterunt. Nam Germani eam in favonium[38] converterant, subtiliter significantes Gallos suo equitatu quandoque posse devinci. Lotharius, frustra impetu facto, sine obside vel pace sequestra exercitum reduxit, postea se rediturum confidens.

with twenty thousand men. And so he vacillated between putting up a fight and making a temporary retreat, before deciding to return later with a substantial army.

71

At last because Lothar was upon him, Otto could not remain where he was. He therefore made a tearful departure with his wife, Theophanu, and the leading men of the realm, leaving behind the palace and all of the royal furnishings. Lothar arrived with his army, expecting to capture Otto. And he surely would have done so if the army had not been slowed down by its baggage train during the march. For if he had arrived the previous day, before Otto's departure, he would have been able to take him prisoner or put him to death. The palace was thus occupied by Lothar's forces. The royal tables were overturned, the tableware was stolen by the grooms, and the king's insignia were snatched from the inner chambers and carried off. The bronze eagle that Charlemagne had affixed to the top of the palace to appear as though it were in flight was turned to face eastward. For the Germans had previously pointed it to the west as a subtle reminder that the Gauls might be vanquished by their knights at any time. On the heels of this fruitless incursion, Lothar took his army home, having obtained neither hostages nor a truce, but confident that he would return in the future.

72

Otto, cui totum calamitatis pondus illatum fuerat, donis multiplicibus multisque favoribus suos sibi assciscebat. Et utpote vincendi cupidus, si quos leserat, revocabat, aut reddito quod sustulerat, aut dato quod spoponderat. Pacatis autem omnibus, atque sibi revocatis si qui forte abscesserant, regnorum principibus in unum collectis, coram sic locutus est:

73

Oratio Ottonis ad suos

'Non ab re, viri clari, huc vos convenisse volui. Virtus vestra suggessit a vobis consilium expetere, quos et ingenium decorat, et animi virtus informat. Nec dubitavi me suscepturum a vobis optimi consilii rationem, cum ab animo non excesserit quanto animo, quanta virtute in fide hactenus perstitistis. Ante hac, viri clari,[39] ingenti virtute pro egregiae laudis honore et gloria sategistis, cum et consilio

72

Now that the whole weight of the disaster had been brought home to him, Otto used all sorts of gifts and many favors to win his men back to his side. In his eagerness for victory he sought to recall anyone whom he had injured by returning what he had taken or by giving them what he had promised. After appeasing everyone and reconciling those who chanced to have become estranged from him, he gathered the leading men of the realm together and addressed them as follows:

73

Otto's Speech to His Men

"It is not without cause, illustrious gentlemen, that I have asked you to assemble here. Your excellence has prompted me to seek your counsel, you who are graced with intelligence and molded by valor. Nor did I doubt that I would receive the best possible advice from you, since I have not forgotten the courage and determination with which you have heretofore remained loyal to me. In times past, illustrious gentlemen, you pursued the honor and glory of a noble reputation with tremendous courage, distinguishing

clari et bello invicti enituistis. Nunc quoque eadem virtute
nitendum est, ne laudi egregiae turpis infamia succedat. Eni-
timini ergo pro viribus, et si quid dedecoris contraxistis, a
tanta claritudine amoveatis. Non vos latet fugae ignominiam
a Lothario nuper nos pertulisse. Quam non solum bello sed
etiam morte repellere et vestram claritudinem decet, et
tempus exposcit, facultas etiam persuadet. Si igitur magis
imperare quam servire parati estis, dum aetas viget animus-
que valet, hoc facinus ne parvipendatis. Ingenti virtute effi-
cite ut sitis formidini quibus ignobiles et vulgus fuistis.' Hac
sententia id fieri omnibus persuasum est.

74

Equitatus Ottonis in Galliam

Interea Otto cum $\overline{\text{XXX}}$ equitum in Gallias ire parabat.
Nec moratus, premissis centurionibus, ibat. Galliam Celti-
cam exercitu implevit. Quam partim combussit, partim de-

yourselves for the brilliance of your counsel and your invincibility in battle. Now you must exercise the same courage lest your noble reputation give way to ignominy and disgrace. Exert yourselves to the utmost, therefore, and seek to free your distinguished name from any taint of dishonor that you may have acquired. You are not unaware that we recently endured the disgrace of fleeing before Lothar. Your noble reputation requires, the hour demands, and the means recommend that we banish this shame, not only through battle, but even through death. If, therefore, you are prepared to rule rather than be slaves,[87] then, while you are in the prime of life and your courage avails you,[88] do not consider this task trivial. Through your outstanding valor see to it that you now inspire fear in those to whom you have appeared ignoble and common."[89] With these sentiments he won everyone over to his purpose.

74

Otto's Mounted Incursion into Gaul

Otto subsequently assembled a force of thirty thousand knights to lead into Gaul. He set off without delay, after sending centurions out in advance. His army spread throughout Celtic Gaul, plundering some areas and putting others to the torch. Having thus turned the tables, he pursued

populatus est. Sic etiam versa vice Lotharium adurgens, eo quod militum copiam non haberet, fluvium Sequanam transire compulit, et gemebundum ad ducem ire coegit. Turbati ergo repentino hostium adventu, rex Stampas adiit, dux vero ad colligendum exercitum Parisii resedit. Dum haec aguntur, Otto cum exercitu properat, fiscumque regium Atiniacum diripit atque comburit. Et per fines urbis Remorum transiens, sancto Remigio multum honorem exhibuit. Urbem quoque Suessorum pretergressus et sanctum Medardum venerans, palatium Compendiense pene diripuit. Nec minus centuriones previi eo ignorante sanctae Baltildis monasterium apud Chelas penitus subruerunt atque combusserunt. Quod non mediocriter dolens, multa in eius restaurationem delegavit. Tandem ad fluvium Sequanam accessit ibique exercitus tentoria fixit, Parisium in prospectu habens, totamque pene regionem per triduum depopulatus est.

75

Ibant ergo equites cum lixis palantibus ad victum deferendum stadiis CLX circumquaque. Et quia Sequana interfluebat, neuter exercitus ad se accedebat. Dux enim in altera fluvii parte milites colligebat. At hoc triduum non sufficie-

Lothar, who, because he had insufficient troops, was forced to cross over the Seine and bewail his sorrows to the duke. Both of them were alarmed at the enemy's unexpected arrival, and while the king went to Étampes, the duke remained behind at Paris to muster an army. While this was going on, Otto moved quickly with his troops, plundering and burning the royal estate at Attigny. When he crossed through the territory around Reims he showed great reverence to Saint Remigius. And after passing by the city of Soissons and venerating Saint Medard, he almost completely despoiled the palace at Compiègne. In addition, the centurions who made up the advance party utterly demolished and burned down the monastery of Saint-Balthild at Chelles without his knowledge. Otto grieved deeply when he heard this and gave generously to rebuild it. At last he arrived at the Seine, and there his army pitched camp, within sight of Paris. Over the course of the next three days they plundered most of the surrounding area.

75

His knights and their camp followers ranged over the area for twenty miles in every direction to bring in provisions. Because the two armies were separated by the Seine, neither side approached the other. For the duke was assembling his troops on the opposite side of the river, but this

bat ad colligendorum sufficientiam militum, nec fieri potuit copia unde congrederetur.

76

Monomachia duorum

Cum[40] ergo uterque exercitus dubio esset statu, et de victoria altrinsecus tota mente quaereretur, Germanus quidam, animo simul et viribus fidens, singularis ad dimicandum cum armis processit seseque ad pontem, ubi portae erant repagulis et clavis ferreis munitae, congressurum solum cum solo obtulit. Hostem ut veniret singularis saepenumero inclamavit. Et cum iam in Gallorum contemptum quaedam maledicta effunderet, nec aliquis ei responderet, per custodes duci aliisque principibus qui iam pauci advenerant relatum est ad portas pontis huiusmodi esse hominem, qui sese ad dimicandum singulariter solum cum solo proponeret, illumque probris et contumeliis verborum principes lacessire; nec illum inde recessurum esse, nisi aut singulariter congrediatur, aut portis incisis, totus exercitus intromittatur. Dux cum principibus hanc contumeliam non ferens, tirones[41]

period of three days was not enough time for him to gather a sufficient number of fighting men, and he could not raise a force large enough to allow him to go into battle.

76

Single Combat between Two Men

With both armies therefore in a state of uncertainty and yet each side completely determined upon victory, one of the Germans, a man confident of his courage and prowess, came forward by himself under arms to do battle. He presented himself for single combat on the bridge, at the place where the gates had been fortified with bars and iron locks, calling out repeatedly for one of the enemy to come forward. When he began to let loose with a number of curses disparaging the Gauls, and no one would respond to him, some of the guards came to inform the duke and the few leading men who had come with him that a man of this sort was at the gates of the bridge proposing to fight by himself in single combat. This person was abusing the leading men with insults and invective, and he was not going to budge from that spot unless someone came out to fight him, or else the gates were cut down and the whole army was let in. The duke and the leading men would not stand for these insults, and they exhorted their recruits to drive off this madman and win

hortatur ut furentem repellant et a tanta ignominia purgati[42] nominis gloriam sibi affectent. Mox quam plures animo ardentes ad resistendum sese obtulerunt. Ergo de pluribus unus electus,[43] congressurus procedit. Premium viri fortis propositum est. Et ablatis repagulis, portae patefactae sunt. Procedit sibi obviam hostis uterque. Qui obiectis clipeis telisque obnitentes, mente furiata pauca admodum probra sibi obiecerunt. Germanus tandem telum iaculatus, Galli clipeum gravi ictu pertundit. Gladioque educto cum urgere instaret, a Gallo mox telo obliquato confixus atque vita[44] privatus est. Gallus victoria potitus, ab hoste rapta arma asportavit atque duci obtulit. Vir fortis praemium petiit et accepit.

77

Ottonis a Gallia digressio[45] suorumque fusio[46]

Otto Gallorum exercitum sensim colligi non ignorans, suum etiam tam longo itinere quam hostium incursu posse minui sciens, redire disponit. Et datis signis, castra amove-

the glory of clearing their reputations of such a terrible disgrace. Straightaway a great many men volunteered to fight him, ablaze with anger. From among them all one was chosen who went forth to do battle. A reward was offered for this brave man, after which the bars were removed and the gates opened. The two adversaries then went forth to meet one another. Holding their shields in front of themselves and brandishing spears, they directed a few choice insults at each other in their rage. At last the German hurled his spear and pierced the Gaul's shield with a heavy blow. He then drew his sword and set upon his adversary, but the Gaul struck him a crosswise blow with his spear, running him through and killing him. The victorious Gaul then stripped the arms from his foe, carried them to the duke, and presented them to him, whereupon this valiant man asked for and received his reward.

77

The Departure of Otto from Gaul and the Rout of His Men

Otto was not unaware that the army of the Gauls was growing steadily larger every day, and knowing that his men were as vulnerable to the long march ahead as they were to enemy attacks, he made the decision to return home. The

runt. Angarias quoque accelerare moliti sunt, amotisque omnibus, ibant non segniter, nec sine metu. Axonae fluvii vada festinantes, alii transmiserant, alii vero ingrediebantur, cum exercitus a rege missus a tergo festinantibus affuit. Qui reperti fuere mox gladiis hostium fusi sunt; plures quidem, at nullo nomine clari. Otto interea cum exercitu digressus, Belgicam petiit ibique procinctum solvit, tanto favore et benivolentia apud suos usus, ut sicut imminenti periculo, ita quoque et omnibus capita sese obiecturos pollicerentur.

78

Lotharius considerans Ottonem neque dolis falli, neque viribus posse devinci, sepe et multum apud se quaerebat utrum potius foret stare contra hostem an reconciliari hosti. Si staret contra, cogitabat possibile esse ducem opibus corrumpi et in amiciciam Ottonis relabi. Si reconciliaretur hosti, id esse accelerandum, ne dux presentiret et ne ipse quoque vellet reconciliari. Talibus in dies afficiebatur. Et ex-

signal was given and camp was struck. They took measures to speed up the baggage train, and after everyone had decamped, they marched forward briskly, but not without apprehension. Some of Otto's men had gone ahead and crossed the ford over the River Aisne, and others were just entering the water, when an army sent by the king came up from behind them. Those who were caught were struck down by the swords of their enemies—quite a few men, in fact, but no one of any distinction. Meanwhile Otto got away with his army and returned to Belgica, where he disbanded his troops. He treated his men with such affection and goodwill that they promised to risk their lives for him at any time in the future, just as they had done during this most recent danger.

78

When Lothar reflected upon the fact that Otto could 979/980 neither be deceived through cunning nor vanquished by force of arms, he thought long and hard about whether it would be better to remain at odds with his enemy or to be reconciled with him. He thought that if he continued to defy him, it was possible that the duke might be induced by bribes to go back to his alliance with Otto. If he himself were to be reconciled with Otto, however, then he would have to hurry so that the duke would not get wind of what he was doing and seek to be reconciled with Otto as well. Every day he became increasingly preoccupied with these

inde his duobus ducem suspectum habuit. A consultantibus tamen decretum[47] est Ottonem in amiciciam regis revocandum, eo quod ipse vir virtutis esset, et per illum non solum dux mansuesci posset, sed et aliarum gentium tiranni subiugari utiliter valerent. Legati igitur a Lothario directi ab Ottone liberalissime suscepti, de habenda utriusque amicicia duce ignorante elaborant.

79

Oratio Gallorum ad Ottonem

'Hactenus,' inquiunt, 'discordiae, invidiae, caedis amatores floruerunt, cum inter nobilissimos reges tantum locum habuerunt. Quibus pro deliciis erat discordia, quia apud reges discordes se multa adquirere posse arbitrabantur. Enimvero de communi labe cogitabant, ut maioris gloriae et honoris locum apud conturbatos vindicarent. Sed proderit plurimum rei publicae, si malignitas pravorum iam dudum reprimatur, et virtus bonorum luce purius enitescat. Redeat

thoughts. And from that time forward he regarded the duke with suspicion for these two reasons. In the end the king's counselors decided that he should resume his friendship with Otto, because he was a man of virtue, and through his agency not only could Hugh be kept under control, but the tyrants of other nations could be effectively brought to heel as well. Envoys were therefore dispatched by Lothar, and after receiving a warm reception from Otto, they set about trying to restore the friendship between the two parties, unbeknownst to the duke.

79

The Speech of the Gauls to Otto

"Up until now," they said, "lovers of strife, ill will, and violence have flourished, because they have found a ready home between the most noble kings. These men took delight in discord because they thought that they would have much to gain from dissension among the kings. Indeed, they sought to compass our communal destruction so that they could lay claim to positions of greater honor and glory for themselves amid the turmoil. The realm now stands to benefit greatly if the machinations of the wicked are curbed and the virtue of good men shines forth more purely than light. Therefore, let virtue return, and let it flourish between the

ergo virtus et floreat inter gloriosissimos reges, ut et vestra virtute tantorum malorum auctores abinde conquiescant, et res publica vestra virtute potius gubernetur quam cupidorum invidia dilabatur. Securius enim ambo regnabitis, cum in amicicia coniuncti duos exercitus pro uno habebitis. Quod si ex vobis alter in ultimas suorum regnorum gentes ire disposuerit, alterum acsi fratrem fidumque suarum rerum tutorem habebit. Placeat ergo serenissimis regibus pax et amicicia, quos coniunxit etiam sanguinis affinitas. Vinciantur amicicia, quorum dissidentia rei publicae labem infert, et concordia utilitatem accommodat viresque ministrat.'

80

Responsio Ottonis ad Gallos

Ad haec Otto, 'Novi,' inquit, 'quantam labem rei publicae discordia sepenumero intulit, cum regnorum principes contra se aliquando moliti sunt. Nec illud etiam ignoro, quanta salus per amiciciae virtutem rei publicae comparata sit. Fateor hactenus me plurimum coluisse pacem et concordiam;

most glorious kings, so that through the exercise of your virtue those responsible for such evils may henceforth cease from their activities, and the state may be governed by your excellence, instead of being undermined by the malice of covetous men. For you will both rule more securely when you are joined together in friendship and have two armies instead of one. If one of you decides to travel to the most distant peoples of his realm, he will have the other to act as a loyal brother and guardian of his possessions. Therefore, let peace and friendship find favor among the most serene kings, who are already united by blood kinship.[90] Let these men, whose quarreling spells disaster, and whose concord confers benefits upon the realm and gives it strength, be bound together in friendship."

80

Otto's Reply to the Gauls

In response Otto declared, "I know how much ruin discord has visited upon the realm on the many occasions when the leading men of these kingdoms have taken up arms against one another. Nor am I unaware of how much security has been achieved for the realm through the power of friendship. I declare to you that up until now I have striven to cultivate peace and harmony, and I have always hated the

invidias atque discordias malignantium odio semper habuisse. Componantur ergo per vos animi dissidentium. Nam
huic rei vos video aptissimos, qui antehac mutua lesione rei
publicae plurimum derogavimus. Consilii vestri rationem
approbo. Dictis tandem facta consentiant.' Legati persua-
sione habita redeunt, ambosque reges alterutrius benivolentiam ad alterutrum referentes, in amicicia componunt.
Constituitur tempus colloquendi. Locus utrique commodus
deputatur. Et quia circa fluvium Mosam regna amborum
conlimitabant, in locum qui Margolius dicitur eis sibi occurrere placuit.

81

Lotharii et Ottonis regum conciliatio

Convenerunt ergo. Datisque dextris, osculum sibi sine
aliqua disceptatione benignissime dederunt; amiciciam altrinsecus sacramento stabilierunt. Belgicae pars quae in lite
fuerat in ius Ottonis transiit. Otto, regni sui pace facta, Italiam petiit Romamque devenit, suos revisurus atque de regni
statu quaesiturus; compressurus etiam si qui forte essent tu-

rivalries and disagreements of spiteful men. Therefore, since I can see that you are eminently suited for this task, you should be the ones to restore peace between the two of us, who before now have done such harm to the state through our mutual feuding. I approve of the course of action that you recommend. Now at long last let words be matched by deeds." At the conclusion of this speech the envoys returned, and after relating to both of the kings the goodwill that each had expressed toward the other, they united them in friendship. A time was established for a meeting between them, and a location was agreed upon that was suitable to both parties. And because both of their kingdoms were bordered by the Meuse River, they agreed to meet at a place called Margut.

81

The Reconciliation of Lothar and Otto

And so they came together. Extending their right arms, they kissed one another affectionately and without any contentiousness, and they confirmed their friendship with a mutual oath. The disputed part of Belgica passed under Otto's control. Now that Otto had obtained peace in his kingdom, he left for Italy and traveled to Rome to pay a visit to his subjects and inquire into the condition of the realm, intending to stamp out any unrest and recall turbulent men

980

multus, et tumultuantes in pacem revocaturus, si qui principum forte dissiderent. Lotharius vero Laudunum veniens,
apud suos quaeque congrua sibi pertractabat. Nec iam quicquam spei ex duce habebat, cum propter pacem dolo quaesi-
tam non mediocriter eum suspectum haberet. Cum iam
haec omnia vulgo predicarentur, nonnulli quoque inde indignati pro duce fremerent; dux constanti animo tristitiam
dissimulans omnia ferebat. Et sicut moris ei erat consulto
omnia deliberare, primatibus[48] advocatis, declamaturus resedit.

82

Oratio ducis apud suos

Quibus coram sic orsus cepit: 'Non preter fructum utilis
et honesti consilium a doctis expetitur. Quibus solis et decenter acceditur, et ab eis fluctuanti rei consilii ratio aperi-
tur. Vos[49] in consulendo arbitror idoneos,[50] cum ab animo
non discedat quanta virtute et ingenio vestri saepenumero

to peace, if by chance any of the magnates had defected from him. For his part, Lothar arrived at Laon and discussed whatever matters needed his attention with his men. He could no longer expect anything from the duke, since he was more than a little mistrustful of him as a result of the peace agreement that he had surreptitiously forged with Otto.[91] All of these things were now being widely talked about, and although there were some men who took umbrage on the duke's behalf and grumbled about what had happened, the duke concealed his unhappiness and bore it all with equanimity. And because it was his custom to subject all matters to careful deliberation, he summoned his chief men and addressed them in council.

82

The Duke's Address to His Men

He proceeded to address them as follows: "It is not without profit that advice about the expedient and the useful is sought from learned men.[92] For they are the only ones whom it is fitting to approach, and it is they who are able to unfold a plan of action to deal with tumultuous circumstances. In my judgment you are ideally suited for giving advice, for I have not forgotten that it was through your great bravery and cleverness that I outshone my enemies on many occa-

adversariis prenituerim. Cumque vos[51] mihi manibus et sacramento addictos fidem quoque inviolabilem servaturos
non dubitem, indubitanter a fidelibus consilium peto. Quod
si mihi conceditur, vos etiam participabitis. Si non suggeri-
tur, forte non aberit dispendium cui indecores succumbatis.
Ergo quia pro vita agitur, consilium utile liberaliter expro-
mite. Non enim vos latet quanta subtilitate doli Lotharius
rex incautum me fefellerit, cum absque me Ottoni reconciliari voluerit feceritque. Cui a mente[52] penitus excessit quam
liberali animo quantum periculum aggressus sim, cum per
me hostem nuper fugaverit, Belgicam quoque insignibus
sublatis hostilibus subarraverit. Quid ergo spei ulterius ex-
pectem, cum dolo fidem abruperit?'

83

Declamatio qua usi sunt
apud ducem sui

Ad haec primates: 'Non solum novimus,' inquiunt, 'quantis periculis[53] nobiscum pro Lothario rege caput obieceris,
verum quoque quanto discrimini claritudo tua adhuc patens

sions. And because I have no doubt that you, my faithful men, who are bound to me both by your hands and by oaths, will also keep your trust inviolate, I do not hesitate to seek your counsel. If you will grant this to me, then you will share in my decision. But if you withhold it, then there may be negative consequences to which you, in your dishonor, will succumb. Therefore, because this is a matter of life and death, be generous in offering me useful counsel. It has not escaped your notice that King Lothar used a subtle piece of trickery to deceive me when I was not expecting it, inasmuch as he wished to be reconciled with Otto without me and achieved his goal. He has completely forgotten the generosity of spirit with which I exposed myself to grave danger, when, thanks to me, he recently put his foe to flight and laid claim to Belgica by carrying off the enemy's insignia. What further expectation can I have of him now that he has violated his trust through his deceitful behavior?"

83

The Speech Delivered to the Duke by His Men

In response the chief men said: "We are well aware not only of the serious risks to which you exposed yourself with us on behalf of King Lothar, but also of the danger to which

sit, si, ut fama est, duo reges contra te conspiraverint. Nam si contra alterum exercitum pro defensione moliaris, ambos contra te mox stare invenies. Si contra ambos nisus fueris, plurima incommoda incurrere necesse est: equitatum intolerabilem, insidias multiplices, incendia atque rapinas, et quod pessimum est, nefarios infidi vulgi rumores, qui non contra adversarios nos exercere defensionem loquetur, at in rebellione contra regem temerarios atque periuros stare calumniabitur. Sic etiam ad quoscumque accedere posse mencietur ut sine delicto, sine periurii sacrilegio a dominis recedant et contra illos arroganter cervices attollant. Huius periculi extremum et utile consilium nobis videtur, ut cum duo contra nos coniuncti sint, alteri alterum subtrahamus. Quod si alteri alter subtrahi nequit, saltem in amicicia nobis eorum alterum devinciamus, ut alter nobis addictus, alteri vires non prebeat animumque ministret. Hoc quoque fieri possibile est,[54] si Romae nunc positum Ottonem legatis premissis cautus et circumspectus adieris. Non enim sic parvi est ingenii Otto, ut te potiorem Lothario armis et opibus

your eminence is still exposed if, as it is reported, two kings have conspired together against you. For if you undertake to defend yourself against one or the other of their armies, then you will soon find both of them in arms against you. And if you try to oppose both, then you will necessarily meet with a great many difficulties: knights that cannot be resisted, multifarious plots against you, arson and rapine, and worst of all, the insidious rumors of the fickle mob, who will deny that we are defending ourselves against our enemies and will instead defame us as rebels and perjurers who have taken up arms against our king. And thus they will falsely claim that from now on it could happen to anyone that they might desert their lord and raise their necks in rebellion without incurring sin or the sacrilege of perjury. In the face of this danger, this would seem to be the only practical advice: since these two kings are united against us, let us detach one from the other. If that is not possible, then at the very least let us bind one of them to us in friendship, so that the one who is attached to us will not provide military support or encouragement to the other. This can be accomplished if you approach Otto, who is now at Rome, cautiously and discreetly through envoys. For Otto is not so foolish as to be unaware that you outstrip Lothar in both

ignoret, cum sepe et id audierit et per sese expertus sit.
Unde et facilius eius amiciciam adipisceris.[55] Proderit etiam
sanguinis vestri propinquitas, cum aeque ut Lotharius ei in
hoc coniungaris.'

84

Quae sententia prolata favoraliter duci habita est. Legatis igitur directis, dux animum huiusmodi Ottoni Rome indicavit. Otto mira benivolentia legatos excepit. De amicicia
quoque inter illos habenda se paratissimum non negavit.
Quod si ipse dux ad se veniret ut amplius uterque amiciciae
vim experiretur, eum cum suis se decenter et cum honore
excepturum. Legati reversi duci mandata retulerunt. Dux
igitur quosdam magnae prudentiae et astutiae assumens,
Arnulfum videlicet Aurelianensium episcopum atque Bur-
chardum necnon . . . reliquos quoque admodum necessarios
viros, Romam progreditur. Sanctos apostolos honorat atque
sic regem petit.

military might and wealth, as he has frequently been told and experienced for himself! Hence you will all the more easily obtain his friendship. The blood tie between you will also speak in your favor, since you are just as closely related to him as Lothar is."[93]

84

The advice that they offered was received favorably by the duke. Consequently, Hugh sent envoys to Rome to let Otto know what he had in mind. Otto received them with remarkable generosity, and he did not deny that he was very eager for there to be friendship between himself and the duke. To that end, he said that if the duke came to him in person so that they could each make further trial of the strength of their friendship, he would give him and his men a fitting and honorable welcome. The envoys returned and reported this message back to the duke. Therefore, taking with him certain men of cleverness and sound judgment, namely Bishop Arnulf of Orléans, Burchard[94] <. . .> and other indispensable men,[95] the duke proceeded to Rome. He venerated the holy apostles, and with that he went before the king.

981

85

Ottonis cum Hugone ratio[56]

O tto gloriam sibi parare cupiens, ex industria egit[57] ut omnibus a cubiculo regio emissis, eius gladius super sellam plectilem deponeretur. Dux etiam solus cum solo episcopo introduceretur, ut rege Latiariter loquente, episcopus Latinitatis interpres duci quicquid diceretur indicaret. Introgressi igitur, a rege ingenti favore excepti sunt. Rex iniuriarum querelam deponit. Et osculum dans, gratiam sui favoraliter amico impertit. Post multa colloquia de amicicia habenda, cum rex exiret gladiumque respiciens peteret, dux paululum a se discedens se inclinavit, ut gladium tolleret ac post regem ferret. Hac enim causa super sellam relictus fuit, ut dum dux cunctis videntibus gladium ferret, in posterum etiam se militaturum[58] indicaret. Episcopus vero duci consulens, gladium ab eius manu rapuit, et ipse deferens, post regem incessit. Cuius prudentiam simul et astutiam rex admiratus, apud suos postea non sine laude sepius frequenta-

85

Otto's Plan Concerning Hugh

Out of a desire to secure distinction for himself, Otto deliberately arranged it so that everyone would be sent out of the royal chamber and his sword would be set down upon an embroidered seat cushion. The duke would then be admitted with only the bishop to accompany him, so that he could serve as an interpreter (since the king would be speaking Latin) and explain what was being said to the duke. The duke and the bishop entered accordingly and were received with great favor by the king. Setting aside his irritation at the wrongs that had been done to him, Otto kissed Hugh and graciously bestowed his favor upon him as a friend. After they had spoken at length about their mutual friendship, the king was leaving, when he turned back and asked for his sword. Briefly stepping aside, the duke leaned over to pick it up and carry it behind the king. The sword had actually been left on the chair for precisely this reason, so that when the duke carried it in sight of everyone, he would be signaling that in consequence of this he would henceforward be Otto's vassal. The bishop, however, taking thought for the interests of the duke, snatched the sword out of his hand and carried it behind the king himself. Otto marveled at the bishop's cleverness and good sense and spoke of it to his men on many future occasions, not without admiration. As

vit. Ducem quoque in plurima amicicia susceptum, cum honore et pace pene usque ad Alpes deduci fecit.

86

Epistola Lotharii ad Chonradum

Lotharius rex necnon et Emma regina insidias ubique pa-
rabant, et ut in itinere redeuntem caperent, dolos pretende-
bant. Igitur Conrado Alemannorum regi epistolam legavit
hunc modum habentem: 'Lotharius Francorum gratia dei
rex, Conrado[59] Alemannorum regi quicquid sibi. Amiciciam
inter nos a multo tempore constitutam inviolabiliter con-
servare semper mihi gratum fuit. Cuius fructus cum a me
multiplex exire valeat, utile duxi quiddam vobis indicare et
ad votum mihi fieri id petere. Hugonem ducem sciatis me
hactenus pro amico habuisse. Comperto vero quod latenter
hostis mihi esset, ab eius familiaritate me remotiorem feci.
Unde nunc Romam iens, Ottonem adiit in mei contumeliam
regnique labem ei plurimum persuasurus. Quapropter
summa ope, summo ingenio nitimini, ne evadat. Valete.'[60]
Exploratores itaque circumquaque dispositi, per prerupta

for the duke, Otto received him as a close friend and had
him escorted honorably and peaceably as far as the Alps.

86

Lothar's Letter to Conrad

Meanwhile King Lothar and Queen Emma were preparing ambushes for Hugh at every turn and setting traps to try
to capture him on his way home. To that end, Lothar sent a
letter to King Conrad of Burgundy, of which this was the
tenor: "Lothar, King of the Franks by the grace of God, to
Conrad, King of Burgundy, wishing him whatever he would
wish for himself. It has always pleased me to preserve inviolate the long-standing friendship between us. Since so many
of the fruits of this relationship derive from me, I have
deemed it appropriate to bring something to your attention
and ask that you act in accordance with my wishes. You
should know that up until now I have treated Duke Hugh as
a friend. But when I discovered that he had secretly become
my enemy, I removed myself from familiar acquaintance
with him. Consequently, he has now gone to Rome and
approached Otto to disparage me and urge him to bring
about the destruction of my kingdom. For this reason, you
must use all of your resources and ingenuity to make sure
that he does not escape. Farewell." After this, scouts were

montium et scopulorum, per viarum exitus, eius adventum opperiebantur.

87

Item epistola Emmae reginae ad matrem

Nec minus Emma regina matri suae in hunc modum epistolam direxit: 'Adelaidi matri, imperatrici semper augustae, Emma Francorum regina salutem. Licet multo terrarum interstitio semota, tamen a matre auxilii rationem filia peto. Hugo dux insidiis non solum regni nostri principes a nostra fidelitate amovit, sed et fratrem meum Ottonem a nobis conatur avertere, unde et Romam illum adiit. Ne ergo penitus sui voti compos glorietur, peto supplex filia matrem, ut in revertendo tantus hostis impediatur. Et si fieri potest, aut captus teneatur aut impunis non redeat. Sed ne vos suis dolis tergiversator evadat, totius formae illius inseparabilia accidentia vobis indicari curavi.' Tunc prosecuta oculorum, aurium, labiorum, dentium quoque et nasi, necnon et reli-

stationed all around, amid the rugged mountains and cliffs,
and at the mouths of the passes, to wait for Hugh's arrival.

87

A Letter from Queen Emma
to Her Mother

In like fashion Queen Emma sent her mother a letter to
this effect: "Emma, Queen of the Franks, sends greetings to
her mother, the ever august Empress Adelaide.[96] Although
we are separated from one another by a vast distance, nonetheless, as your daughter, I am asking for your help. Duke
Hugh, through his treachery, has not only detached the leading men of the realm from their allegiance to us, but he is
also trying to turn my brother Otto against us, for which
reason he approached him at Rome. Lest he should be able
to boast of having completely succeeded in his mission, I
beseech you, mother, as a suppliant daughter, to see to it
that so great an enemy is held up during his journey home.
And if it is possible, let him be seized and held captive, or
else prevented from returning unharmed. So that this turn-
coat does not employ trickery to escape from your grasp, I
have taken care to have the distinguishing features[97] of his
person set down for you." She then acquainted them with
this unfamiliar person by appending a description of his

quarum corporis partium accidentia, verborum quoque tenorem sic ignotum declaravit, ut his signis detegeret atque ignorantibus indicaret.

88

Hugo inmutato habitu insidias evadit

Dux horum non nescius, reditum accelerat. Dolisque premetuens, vestem mutat, seseque unum de clientibus simulat. Equos onera ferentes ipse regit atque exagitat. Onera imponit et deponit, omnibus se serviturum accommodat. Tantaque industria in abiecta veste et inculto habitu se ducem dissimulavit, ut et per insidiarum loca transiret quae nec vitare poterat, et insidiantes efficaciter falleret. Uno tantum hospitio pene deprehensus fuit. Nam dum eundum esset cubitum, ei lectus cum diligenti apparatu compositus est. Eique circumfusi se omnes ad serviendum obtulerunt. Alii enim genu flexo caligas extrahebant, extractasque alii excipiebant. Alii vero nudatos pedes sedentis subsidendo confricabant et giris vestium emundabant. Haec hospes per

eyes, ears, lips, teeth, and nose, and the other parts of his body, as well his manner of speaking, so that she might reveal his identity through these characteristics and make him recognizable to those who were unfamiliar with him.

88

Hugh Evades the Traps Set for Him by Adopting a Disguise

The duke was not unaware of this, and he made haste to return home. To guard against the possibility of being betrayed, he changed his clothes and disguised himself as one of his own attendants. He himself drove the packhorses and goaded them on. He loaded and unloaded the baggage and adapted himself to be everyone else's servant. And he took such pains to disguise his identity, that with his shabby clothes and unkempt appearance he was able to pass through the places where traps had been set for him (places that could not be avoided) and successfully elude those lying in wait for him. There was only one place of lodging where he came close to being caught. In this case, when it was time for him to go sleep, a bed was carefully made up for him, and all of his men positioned themselves around him to minister to his needs. Some got down on their knees and removed his boots, while others took the boots from them. Some crouched beside him as he sat, rubbing his bare feet

ostii rimas contemplatus est. Deprehensusque explorasse, mox ne rem detegeret vocatus est et intromissus. Strictisque mucronibus postquam ei necem minati sunt si vocem emitteret, comprehensum ligatis manibus et pedibus in ergastulum detruserunt. Qui voce suppressa ibi usque crepusculum convexus iacuit. Post nocte abscedente, in ipso crepusculo surrexerunt. Hospitem assumptum et equo invectum tandiu asportaverunt, donec loca suspecta transmitterent. Quibus transmissis, depositum dimiserunt reliquumque itineris celeres confecerunt. Nec minus Conradi regis dolos sepe simulando et dissimulando evasit, cum in dolis componendis insidiatores studio et hic niterentur. Tandem tantorum malorum securus, Gallia receptus est.

89

Lotharii et Hugonis reconciliatio

Cognitis autem utrorumque dolis ab utroque, tanta crudelitate in se non armis sed insidiis latentibus debacchati sunt, ut aliquot annis res publica principibus dissidentibus

and wiping them clean with their clothes. Their host observed all of this through the cracks in the door. He was de-
tected in the act of spying, however, and to prevent him
from revealing anything Hugh's men immediately called to
him and invited him in. Thereupon they drew their swords,
and after threatening to kill him if he made a sound,[98] they
seized him, bound his hands and feet, and threw him into a
tiny chamber, where he lay curled up until daybreak without
uttering a word. The night passed, and Hugh's men arose at
daybreak. They took their host, put him on a horse, and
took him along with them until they had passed through the
places that they were worried about. After they had made it
through, they set him down and let him go, whereupon they
made haste to finish their journey. Using a similar combina-
tion of bluff and disguise, Hugh was able to evade the traps
that had been set for him by King Conrad. For in Burgundy,
too, there were men lying in ambush for him and devoting
all of their efforts to catching him. At last he arrived back in
Gaul, safe from such grave dangers.

89

Lothar and Hugh Are Reconciled

When Lothar and Hugh became aware of the plots that
each had directed against the other, they raged against one
another with such savagery (through stealth and trickery

multum lederetur. Tunc etiam multarum rerum usurpatio-
nes, miserorum quoque oppressiones, et circa minus potentes calamitates nefariae a quibusdam pravis exercitae sunt.
Cum utriusque sapientiores in unum consulturi convenien-
tes, principes dissidere plurima commiseratione conquesti
sunt.

90

Statueruntque ut alterius fautores ad alterum suasuri de
reconciliatione transirent, ut alteruter benivolentia alterutrius captus, facilius sibi condescenderet, eumque pro lesa
amicicia utilius peniteret. Quod consultum[61] non multopost
effectum habuit. Nam et eis efficacissime persuasum est, ac
plurima dilectione sibi annexi sunt. Sic etiam in utrisque vis
amiciciae firmata visa est.

rather than force of arms) that for several years the realm was grievously afflicted by factional strife among the magnates.[99] There followed widespread appropriations of property, the oppression of the downtrodden, and the perpetration of terrible calamities against the less powerful by certain wicked people. When the wiser supporters of both parties met to consider the matter, they bitterly lamented the dissension among the leading men.

90

They decided that supporters of each party should go to the other side to persuade them of the need for reconciliation. In this way Lothar and Hugh would each be won over by the other's goodwill, and they would be more willing to swallow their pride and show genuine repentance for the damage that they had done to their friendship. Not long after this, their plan was brought to fruition, and both men were successfully persuaded to bind themselves to one another with great affection. In this way it was also made clear that the bonds of friendship had been strengthened between them.

91

Promotio Ludovici[62] in regnum Francorum

Etenim cum rex filium suum Ludovicum in regno sibi succedere vellet, ipsum quoque a duce ordinandum quaereret, dux hanc ordinationem mox liberali animo se administraturum respondit. Et legatis directis, regnorum principes Compendii collegit. Ibique a duce reliquisque principibus Ludovicus rex adclamatus, per metropolitanum episcopum Remorum, dignae videlicet memoriae Adalberonem, sancta die pentecostes in regnum Francorum promotus est. Duobus ergo regnantibus dux multa affabilitate ac famulatu multiplici per dies plures sese commendabat, adeo regiam dignitatem per omnia extollens et sese[63] eis supplicem[64] monstrans; se etiam facturum pollicens ut ambo gentibus iam domitis potenter imperarent, indomitas quoque efficaciter[65] mansuescerent. Id etiam meditabatur, ut in diversis regnis positi, regiam dominationem exercerent, ne unius regni angustia duorum regum maiestati nimium derogaret.

91

The Elevation of Louis to the
Throne of the Franks

And indeed, when the king desired that his son Louis   979
should be designated as his successor, he asked the duke to
arrange the coronation. The duke replied that he would be
happy to see to it at once, and he sent out envoys to assemble the leading men of the realm at Compiègne. There, after
Louis had been proclaimed king by the duke and the rest of
the leading men, he was elevated to the throne of the Franks
by the archbishop of Reims, namely Adalbero of worthy
memory, on the feast of Pentecost.[100] Over the course of
many days the duke commended himself to the two kings
with great courtesy and manifold devotion, exalting the
royal office in all respects and presenting himself to them as
a supplicant. Moreover, he promised to see to it that both
men would exercise effective rule over the peoples now under their dominion and successfully pacify those who were
not yet subject to them. His intention was that they should
both exercise royal authority while having their seats in different kingdoms, so that the sovereignty of the two kings
would not be diminished too much by being restricted
within the narrow confines of a single realm.

92

Item promotio Ludovici in regnum Aquitaniae, eiusque uxoratio

Dum haec multo conatu disponeret, alii quidam nimis callidi, hoc comperto, cum huiusmodi gloriam in sese transfundere vellent, Emmam reginam adeuntes, super maxima re se consulturos dixerunt. Qui suscepti a regina, id sibi videri optimum dixerunt, Ludovico regi assciscendam coniugem Adelaidem, Ragemundi nuper defuncti ducis Gothorum olim uxorem. Et non magis potentiam regnandi ex hoc posse augeri quam sibi nonnulla commoda adquiri. Enimvero possibile fieri totam Aquitaniam simulque et Gothiam suo imperio asstringi posse, postquam ex iure ductae uxoris oppida munitissima ad suum ius retorqueret. Magnum etiam quiddam in hac re et utile comparari, si patre hinc posito, et illinc filio, dux ceterique hostes in medio conclusi perpetuo urgeantur.

92

The Elevation of Louis to the Throne of Aquitaine, and His Marriage

While the duke was devoting all of his effort to these arrangements, some very cunning men found out what he was doing, and out of a desire to usurp this sort of distinction for themselves, they went to Queen Emma and declared that they had come to speak to her about a matter of utmost importance. Once they had been received by the queen, they told her that in their opinion the best course of action would be for Louis to be joined in marriage to Adelaide,[101] the wife of the recently deceased Duke Raymond of Gothia.[102] Not only would this potentially increase his power as king, but he would realize a number of benefits as well. For in fact it would be possible for all of Aquitaine and Gothia to be brought together under his dominion if he used his rights by marriage to turn the most heavily fortified strongholds over to his authority. There was a great advantage waiting to be realized here, for if his father were on one side, and he himself were on the other, then the duke and the rest of their enemies would be caught in between them and under constant threat.

93

Huius rationis consilium postquam regi suggestum est, apud Gozfredum comitem, qui aderat, ordinatum valuit. Haec duce ignorante parabantur. Quae cum post animadvertisset, ne regibus fieri videretur iniurius, contumeliam dissimulans, nihil penitus refragratus est. Interea, collectis regni principibus, equitatus regius disponitur; insignia regia invehuntur; cibi multiplices apparati vehiculis imponuntur. Quibus actis, reges utrique cum multo equitatu in Aquitaniam profecti sunt, castrumque Briddam quod vetus dicitur devenerunt.

94

Adelaidis a Ludovico reginae in Aquitania promotio, eorumque divortium

Quo a praefata Adelaide multo apparatu excepti sunt. Et die constituta, rationibus decentissime habitis et ex iure datis dotalibus, Ludovicus rex eam sibi uxorem copulavit at-

93

After this proposal had been made to the king, arrangements were undertaken by Count Geoffrey,[103] who was present there. The preparations were made without the duke's knowledge, and when he later got wind of them, he pretended not to be insulted and offered no opposition, so as not to appear to be giving offense to the kings. In the meantime, the leading men of the kingdom were gathered together, the king's knights were drawn up in order, and the royal insignia were brought forward. Many different types of foodstuffs were procured and loaded onto wagons. When the preparations were complete, both kings proceeded into Aquitaine with a large force of knights and came to the fortress of Vieille-Brioude.

980

94

The Elevation of Adelaide as Queen of Aquitaine by Louis, and Their Divorce

Here they were received by the aforementioned Adelaide in magnificent style. And on the appointed day, after the negotiations had been conducted in a fitting and ap-

que secum coronatam per episcopos in regnum promovit. Non tamen regium nomen sic in eis valuit ut ullatenus regnandi dominationem in principibus exercere valerent. Amor quoque coniugalis eis pene nullus fuit. Nam cum ille adhuc pubesceret, illa vero anus foret, contrariis moribus dissentiebant. Cubiculum commune sibi non patiebantur. Requieturi quoque diversis hospitiis potiebantur. Si quando colloquendum erat, locum sub divo habebant. Pro sermonibus producendis paucissima dicere sat erat. Et hoc apud eos fere erat per biennium. Quorum mores usque adeo discordes fuere, ut non multopost sequeretur et divortium.

95

Ludovicus vero, quia morum informatorem non habebat, utpote adolescens levium rerum vanitatibus insistebat. Habitum[66] patriae gentis pro peregrinis penitus deposuerat. Itaque in miserandam fortunam res penitus dilapsa est, ut et moribus degener et regnandi impotentia inglorius esset. Et qui paulo ante rex genere, fama, atque copiis potens, nunc

propriate manner, and the dowry had been transferred in accordance with the law, King Louis joined her to himself in marriage and had her crowned with him by the bishops and elevated to the throne.[104] The royal title, however, did not avail them enough to allow them to exercise any of the prerogatives of kingship over the magnates of the region. Nor was there much in the way of marital affection between them. For while Louis was still in the bloom of youth, Adelaide was an old woman, and their lifestyles were completely at odds with one another. They would not consent to share a bedroom, and when it was time to sleep they occupied different lodgings. If they ever needed to speak to one another, they did so outside in the open air. Instead of long discussions, they were content to say very little to one another. This state of affairs between them continued for almost two years. They differed so greatly in their habits that not long afterward a divorce followed.

95

Because Louis had no one around him to shape his character, he devoted himself to worldly vanities and trifles, as young men are wont to do. He had completely set aside the garb of his native country in favor of foreign clothes. From there his affairs devolved into a lamentable state, so that he became morally corrupt, without any honor to his name, and incapable of ruling. He who a short time earlier had ruled effectively by virtue of his blood, his reputation, and

erumnosus et inops, rei familiaris simul et militaris calamitate squaleret. His Lotharius rex per multos cognitis, filium inde revocare cogitabat, non ignorans in peius eum lapsurum, cum illic nullum dignitatis regiae haberet honorem. Equitatum itaque parat filium repetiturus. Aquitaniam ingressus, Briddam petiit. Filium repetit et reducit. Regina sese viduatam dolens, et verita maioris incommodi iniuriam, Wilelmum Arelatensem adiit eique nupsit. Et sic ex divortio adulterium publicum perpetratum[67] est.

96

Obitus Ottonis

Hac tempestate Otto cum barbaris congressus, miserabili fortunae succubuit. Nam et exercitum fusum amisit, et ipse captus ab hostibus, divina vero gratia reversus fuit. Post cum ex indigestione Romae laboraret et intestini squibalas ex melancolico humore pateretur, aloen ad pondus dragmarum quatuor sanitatis avidus sumpsit. Conturbatisque visceribus, diarria iugis prosecuta est. Cuius continuus fluxus emorróides tumentes procreavit. Quae etiam sanguinem

the troops at his command, now languished in poverty and despair, having squandered his personal property and his military forces.[105] When Lothar learned of this from many different sources, he decided to recall his son from Aquitaine. He was not unaware that Louis might sink into deeper difficulties, since he maintained none of the respect due to the royal title there. So he assembled a troop of knights to go and get his son. He advanced into Aquitaine and traveled to Brioude. There he found Louis and brought him back home. The queen grieved to find herself bereft of her husband, and fearing that she might come to some greater harm, she fled to William of Arles[106] and married him. And so what had begun in divorce ended in public adultery.

982

96

The Death of Otto

At this time Otto suffered a crushing defeat in battle against the barbarians.[107] He lost his army in a rout and was taken captive by his enemies, but by the grace of God he was able to return home. Later, when he was back at Rome, he was troubled by indigestion and began to suffer from constipation caused by black bile. Desperate for a remedy, he took four drams of aloe, which upset his bowels and induced continuous diarrhea. The constant flux gave rise to swollen

983

immoderatum effundentes, mortem post dies non plures operatae sunt.

97

Cui defuncto filius quinquennis Otto superstes erat. Quem patri succedere in regnum cum aliquot primates voluissent, id ab aliquibus contradictum est. Ingenti tamen virtute variaque fortuna ei regnum postea paraverunt. Nam Hezilo, regis paulo ante defuncti patruelis, qui adhuc in carcere vinctus ab eo tenebatur, eo quod adversus eum regnum appeteret, pravorum dolis in pernitiem rei publicae elapsus et quorundam munitionibus receptus est, vir aeque ut Otto nobilis, corpore eleganti ac valido, honoris cupidus ac factiosus, animo vasto, sed fallaci. Hic regnandi avidus, omnes sacrilegos aut iuditiis convictos, sive etiam pro factis iuditium timentes, postremo omnes flagitiosos quos conscius animus exagitabat, sibi proximos ac familiares fecit. Talium dolis regis defuncti superstitem filium Ottonem parvum rapuit, eius loco sese regnaturum ratus. Regnum ergo sic in suum ius refundi arbitrans, sceptrum et coronam sibi paravit. Quod dum a Lothario expetendum cogitaret eumque

hemorrhoids, from which copious quantities of blood flowed forth, leading to his death several days later.[108]

97

At his death the king was survived by his five-year-old son, Otto.[109] While a number of the magnates wanted Otto to succeed his father upon the throne, others were opposed to this. Yet through tremendous perseverance, and after various turns of fortune, they later secured the throne for him. Hezilo,[110] the cousin of the recently deceased king, who was still chained up in prison and being held captive by him because he had tried to usurp the throne, escaped through the schemes of wicked men and took refuge in the strongholds of certain people, which proved disastrous for the realm. He was a man equal to Otto in nobility, handsome and powerful, covetous of distinction and quarrelsome, insatiable yet deceitful. Eager to win the throne for himself, he made friends and companions out of all those who had committed sacrilege or had been convicted of a crime, those who merely feared judgment for what they had done, and eventually every criminal who was hounded by a guilty conscience.[111] Through the devices of such men he kidnapped the boy Otto, the son of the deceased king, planning to rule in his stead. Thinking that in this way he would transfer the kingdom to his own authority, he acquired a scepter and a crown for himself. And because he believed that Lothar had aspirations toward the throne, he sought to make him a friend and

984

concessa Belgica sibi sotium et amicum facere moliretur, legatos premisit, apud quos sacramento commune negocium firmaretur; quo etiam sacramento utrique reges sibi pollicerentur sese super Rhenum loco constituto sibi occursuros.

98

Quibus per legatos iuratis, Lotharius tempore statuto cum exercitu per Belgicam transiens, ne teneretur sacramenti obnoxius, ad locum Rheni condictum devenit. Hezilo sese metuens in suspitionem principum venire si Lothario occurreret, acsi eum in regnum recipere vellet, periurii reus occurrere distulit. Lotharius se illusum advertens, rediit, non tamen sine difficilis laboris incommodo. Nam Belgae per quorum medium cum equitatu transierat, indignati transisse, vias transpositis arboribus impediunt, aut fossis inmersis revertentes prohibent; non ut aperto campo comminus dimicent, sed ut his impedimentis cunctantes a tergo urgeant, aut montium iugis securi per inferiora transeuntes missilibus figant. Et quia aperta fronte stare animo non fuit, sagittarii cum arcubus et balistis per montana dispositi sunt. Dum ergo exercitus subiret, illi a superioribus alios sagittis figebant, alios diversis missilibus saucia-

ally by ceding Belgica to him, and he sent envoys ahead to confirm their mutual agreement with an oath. In this same oath both kings also promised to come to meet one another at a specified location on the Rhine.

98

After his envoys had sworn to these terms, Lothar crossed through Belgica with his army and went to the agreed-upon place on the Rhine[112] at the appointed time, so as not to be found guilty of violating his oath. Hezilo, however, fearing that he would arouse suspicion among the leading men if he went to meet Lothar (as if he were eager to welcome him into his kingdom), put off going to meet him, making himself guilty of perjury. When Lothar realized that he had been duped, he returned home, but not without inconvenience and considerable difficulty. For the men of Belgica were outraged that he and his knights had crossed through the middle of their territory, and they put trees across the roads to block them and used concealed ditches to obstruct their passage. They had no intention of engaging them at close quarters on an open battlefield, but instead planned to attack them from behind as they struggled against these obstacles or to strike them with missiles as they passed below from the security of the mountain ridges. Because they wanted to avoid facing them directly, they positioned archers with bows and ballistas on the hillsides, and as Lothar's army passed beneath them, they struck some of

bant. At tirones, sicubi ascensui pervium locum videbant, in huiusmodi hostes vertebantur, armisque efferati, quosdam vulnerabant, quosdam vero morte afficiebant. Tantum in eis ter debacchati, ut caesorum cadaveribus aggerata moles collibus assimilaretur. Alii vero aut[68] vibratis gladiis frondium oppositarum densitatem metebant, aut trudibus adactis transpositam arborum molem amovebant sibique iter aperiebant. Tandem multo conatu de medio hostium educti sunt.

99

Hac tempestate[69] Germania nullo regis imperio tenebatur, quippe cum et Ottonem infantem aetatis infirmitas regnare prohiberet, et Heziloni regnandi cupido a potioribus regnum contradiceretur. Unde Lotharius occasionem nactus, de Belgicae pervasione iterum cogitabat, ut videlicet ad

his men with arrows and wounded others with various types of projectiles.[113] But wherever the new recruits could find a path up into the hills, they set upon their attackers with savage fury, wounding some and killing others. Three times they rampaged among them with such violence that the bodies of the slain were heaped up in a mound as high as the surrounding hills.[114] Others hacked away with their swords to clear away the dense foliage that stood in their way or used poles to remove the masses of trees that lay piled up before them, clearing a path for themselves. And at last, by dint of a tremendous effort, they managed to escape from the midst of their enemies.

99

At that time Germany was not subject to the authority of a king, since Otto was still a child, and his tender age prevented him from ruling, while Hezilo, although eager to assume the throne, was opposed by the more powerful magnates. Lothar thus seized upon this opportunity to plan another invasion of Belgica, hoping to subject it to his do-

suae dominationis ius eam retorqueret, cum Otto[70] non esset, et principes dissiderent, regnique dignitas nullo regis administraretur imperio.

100

Itaque Odonem atque Herbertum, viros illustres et potentia claros, advocans, eis sui voti secretum aperit. Et quia paulo ante eorum patrui absque liberis defuncti terra optima cum oppidis munitissimis illos liberaliter donaverat, ipsi mox domi militiaeque esse paratissimos responderunt. Quibus faventibus, cum rex sibi in animo esse diceret ut Belgicam repeteret eamque militaribus copiis expugnaret, ipsi huius rei initium Virduni faciendum dicunt, eo quod ipsa propinquior civitas esset; et sese multa obsidione eam aggressuros, nec umquam ab ea nisi capta recessuros. Qua capta, et sacramento atque obside regi annexa, ulterius processuros. Tandiu etiam moraturos in Belgica, donec aut armis expugnetur, aut victi Belgae in deditionem omnes trans-

minion now that Otto was dead, the leading men were at odds with one another, and there was no king to exercise authority over the realm.

Ａnd so he summoned Odo[115] and Heribert,[116] illustrious men who were renowned for their power, and he revealed to them the secret of his intentions. Because a short time earlier he had generously bestowed upon them the rich lands and heavily fortified strongholds of their uncle,[117] who had died without children, they replied that they were ready to serve him at a moment's notice, at home or on campaign. After receiving their assurances of support, the king told them that he planned to march on Belgica again and conquer it through military force. In response they told him that his first objective should be Verdun, since it was the closest city. They themselves would assault it with a major siege operation, nor would they ever withdraw from the city until it had fallen. After Verdun had been captured and bound over to the king through hostages and oaths, they would press on with the campaign. In fact, they would remain in Belgica until it was conquered by force of arms, or else all the men of Belgica admitted defeat and surrendered

eant. Quorum sponsione suscepta, rex cum ipsis exercitum mox Virdunum admovit.

101

Virduni expugnatio

Quae civitas eo situ posita est, ut a fronte planitie pervia meantibus accessum prebeat, a tergo inaccessibilis sit. Ibi enim a summo in posteriora profundo hiatu circumquaque distenditur. Ab inferioribus vero ad summum rupibus preruptis artatur. Quae non solum scatens fontibus puteisque incolis accommoda, sed et fluvio Mosa eam a prerupta parte abluente nemorosa. Ubi ergo a fronte planitien prefert, pugnaturi machinas bellicas generis diversi aptavere. Nec minus qui in urbe erant ad resistendum sese expediebant. Pugnatum est tandem VIII ferme continuis diebus. At cives cum viderent nulla a suis extrinsecus suffragia mitti, nec iugis prelii pondus se tolerare posse,[71] consilio inito, indempnes

to them. The king took them up on their promises and led his army to Verdun with them.

101

The Capture of Verdun

Verdun is situated such that there is a flat plain in front of the city that provides access to those approaching it. From behind, however, it is inaccessible. For there a deep chasm extends around it on all sides from the top of the city down to the back, while from bottom to the top it is hemmed in by sheer cliffs.[118] Not only does the city abound in springs and wells that serve the needs of the inhabitants, but because the steep part of the city is washed by the River Meuse, it is heavily wooded.[119] On the level ground in front of the city the invaders set about building siege engines of various types, while the townsmen were busy making preparations to hold out. In the end the fighting between them continued virtually uninterrupted for eight days. When the townsmen realized that their allies outside the city were not going to send help, and they themselves could not endure the strain of a continuous siege, they decided to yield to the

et intacti hostibus cessere. Urbem aperuerunt et sese Lothario victi obtulerunt.

102

Quibus peractis, rex ad urbem tuendam reginam Emmam in ea reliquit. Ipse cum exercitu Laudunum rediit, suos etiam ad sua redire permisit, tantae benivolentiae favore apud eos usus, ut repetito itinere se ulterius ituros, si iuberet, pollicerentur, et neglectis pro tempore domibus et natis, cum hoste comminus dimicaturos. Lotharius interea apud suos deliberabat utrum potius foret sese ulterius ire, armisque et viribus totam Belgicam sibi subiugare, an residendo Virduni, per legatos habitis suasionibus, mores hostium ad suum animum informare. Si enim eos ferro vinceret, cum id sine multo sanguine fieri non posset, cogitabat in posterum minus eis credendum, eo quod amicorum labem eis intulerit. Si vero per benivolentiam reversuros expectaret, cavendum putabat ne in tanto otio hostes insolentiores redderentur.

enemy while they were still unharmed and intact. They opened up the city and offered themselves in surrender to Lothar.

102

When the siege was over, the king left Queen Emma behind to guard the city, while he went back to Laon with his army and allowed his troops to return home. He treated them with such favor and goodwill that they promised to resume the campaign and march even further if he should command it, temporarily leaving behind their homes and their children in order to fight the enemy in open battle. Meanwhile Lothar discussed with his men whether it would be better to continue the campaign and subjugate all of Belgica by force of arms, or to remain at Verdun and send envoys to persuade his enemies to come around to his way of thinking. It would require a great deal of bloodshed to conquer them by the sword, and he thought that it would make them less reliable in the future, because he would have visited destruction upon their friends. If, on the other hand, out of goodwill he waited for them to submit to him of their own accord, he would have to take care that his enemies did not grow more insolent because they had been left in peace for so long.

103

Virduni invasio a Belgis

Dum haec multa consultatione ventilaret, Belgicae dux Teodericus, necnon et vir nobilis ac strenuus Godefridus, Sigefridus quoque vir illustris, Bardo etiam et Gozilo fratres clarissimi et nominatissimi, aliique principes nonnulli, latenter pertemptant Virdunum irrumpere eamque a Gallis[72] evacuare. Factisque insidiis, negotiatorum claustrum, muro instar oppidi extructum, ab urbe quidem Mosa interfluente seiunctum, sed pontibus duobus interstratis ei annexum, cum electis militum copiis ingressi sunt. Annonam omnem circumquaque milites palantes advectare fecerunt. Negotiatorum quoque victus in usum bellicum acceperunt. Lignorum trabes ex Argonna aggregari iusserunt, ut si ab hostibus extra machinae muris applicarentur, ipsi quoque interius obnitentibus machinis obstare molirentur. Crates quoque viminibus et arborum frondibus validas intexuerunt, machinis erectis, si res exposceret, supersternendos. Sudes ferro acuminatos et igne subustos ad hostes transfodiendos quamplures aptaverunt. Missilia varii generis per fabros expediere. Funium millena[73] volumina ad usus diversos con-

103

An Attack on Verdun by the Men of Belgica

While he was subjecting this matter to careful delibera-tion, Duke Thierry of Belgica,[120] the noble and energetic Godfrey,[121] the illustrious Siegfried,[122] the eminent and fa-mous brothers Bardo and Gozelo,[123] and several other lead-ing men[124] made a clandestine attempt to break into Verdun and drive the Gauls out of the city. They employed a ruse to infiltrate the merchants' quarter with a picked body of fight-ing men. This area was protected by a wall like a stronghold and separated from the rest of the city by the Meuse River, although it was linked to it by two bridges. Their soldiers went around requisitioning all the grain in the area and ap-propriating provisions from the merchants to use in the war effort. They gave orders for timber to be brought in from the Argonne Forest so that if siege engines were brought up to the walls from outside by the enemy, they could deploy their own engines to resist them from inside the city. They also wove strong lattices out of twigs and tree branches, which could be spread on top of the engines if the situation called for it. They fashioned a large number of stakes, which were fire-hardened and sharpened with iron, to impale their enemies on, and they had artisans make various types of projectiles. They brought in a thousand coils of rope to

vexerunt. Clipeos quoque habendae testudini ordinandos instituerunt. Preterea centena mortis tormenta non defuere.

104

Repetito[74] Virduno a Lothario

Nuntiantur haec Lothario. Qui tantum facinus accidisse acerrime indignatus, exercitum dimissum revocavit. Et sic cum $\overline{X}$ pugnatorum Virdunum petiit atque adversarios repentinus aggressus est. Primo impetu sagittarii contra hostes ordinati sunt. Missaeque sagittae et arcobalistae cum aliis missilibus tam densae in aere discurrebant, ut a nubibus dilabi terraque exsurgere viderentur. Horum contra impetum testudinem ante se et super capita hostes muro aptavere. In quam relisa missilia ictu frustrato decidebant. Hoc impetu facto, Galli circumquaque obsidionem disposuere

be put to various uses, and they procured shields that could be deployed to form a tortoise.[125] Nor in addition, did they want for a hundred deadly engines of war.

104

Lothar's Second Assault on Verdun

When the news was reported to Lothar, he responded   985
with furious indignation to the perpetration of such a terrible crime and recalled the army that he had disbanded. He advanced to Verdun with ten thousand fighting men and fell upon his enemies without warning. During the initial assault he deployed archers against his foes, and they filled the air with so many arrows, crossbow bolts, and other projectiles flying around in all different directions that they seemed to be falling from the clouds and coming up out of the ground. To defend themselves from this onslaught, the enemy formed a tortoise adjoining the wall, protecting the area in front of themselves and above their heads, so that when the projectiles collided with their shields, they fell harmlessly to the ground. When this assault was over, the Gauls invested the city on all sides and fortified their camp

fossisque preruptis obfirmaverunt castra, ne si ad incautos adversarii prosilirent, accessum facilem invenirent.

105

Compositio cuiusdam machinae bellicae

Quercus proceras radicitus succisas ad machinam bellicam extruendam advexerunt. Ex quibus quatuor trabes tricenorum pedum straverunt solo, ita ut duae in longum proiectae et decem pedum intervallo distinctae, duabus aliis per transversum eodem intervallo superiacentibus cohererent. Longitudinis et latitudinis spatium quod intra commissuras earum tenebatur decem pedum erat. Quicquid etiam a commissuris extra proiectum erat, simili modo decem pedibus distendebatur. In harum trabium commissuris quatuor sublicas quadragenorum pedum, quadrato quidem scemate sed procero, aequo spatio a se distantes, adhibitis trocleis erexerunt. Transposueruntque bis per quatuor latera festucas decem pedum, in medio scilicet, et in summo, quae traductae sublicas sibi fortiter annecterent. A capitibus vero trabium quibus sublicae nitebantur quatuor trabes eductae et pene usque ad festucas superiores obliquatae sublicis iun-

with steep ditches, so that if their enemies made a sortie against them when they were not expecting it, they would not find an easy means of approach.

105

The Construction of a Siege Tower

They also cut down some large oak trees at the roots and brought them in to be used in the construction of a siege tower. From the trees they cut four beams thirty feet in length, which they placed on the ground so that two of them were positioned lengthwise with a distance of ten feet between them; the two other beams were laid atop them horizontally with the same spacing and joined to the beams below. The distance between the joints measured ten feet in both length and width, and the beams extended beyond the joints for ten feet in either direction. At the joints of the beams they used pulleys to erect four forty-foot-long wooden piles with an equal distance between them so that they were in the shape of a large rectangle. Then they put rods ten feet in length through each of the four sides at the middle and at the top to bind the piles together firmly. From the ends of the beams on which the piles were resting four more beams were extended upward, reaching diagonally almost as far as the rods on the upper story. These diagonal

gebantur, ut sic ex eis machina extrinsecus firmata non titu-
baret. Super festucas quoque quae in medio et in summo
machinam conectebant, tigna straverunt. Quae etiam cra-
tibus contexerunt, super quas dimicaturi stantes et emi-
nentiores facti, adversarios deorsum iaculis et lapidibus ob-
ruerent. Hanc molem extructam, ad stationem hostium
deducere cogitabant. Sed quia sagittarios suspectos habebant, rationem querebant qua hostibus sine suorum lesione
appropinquaret. Tandem ratione subtilius perscrutante, re-
pertum est eam ad hostes optima arte detrudi posse.

106

Deductio ad hostes
superioris machinae

Dictabant enim quatuor stipites multae grossitudinis
terrae solidae mandandos, decem pedibus in terra defossis,
VIII vero a terra eiectis; qui etiam transpositis per IIII latera repagulis vehementissimis solidarentur; repagulis quoque transmissis, funes inserendos. Sed funium capita ab hos-

beams were attached to the vertical piles so that the siege engine would be supported from the exterior and would not wobble. On top of the horizontal rods that connected the engine at the middle and at the top they laid planks and bound them together with latticework so that men could stand and fight atop them and attack their enemies down below with javelins and stones from their elevated position. When this huge engine was finished, they intended to take it down to the enemy position. But because they were worried about the enemy archers, they wanted to find a way to get it close to the city without risking injury to their own men. At last, after scrutinizing the matter carefully, they hit upon an ingenious method to propel the tower toward the enemy.

106

The Siege Tower Is Moved
Toward the Enemy

They gave instructions for four stout logs to be planted firmly in the earth, ten feet deep in the ground with eight feet sticking up. On all four sides the logs were to be reinforced horizontally with solid bars, and ropes would be passed around the bars. Both ends of the ropes would lead away from the enemy: the upper ends would be attached to

tibus abducta,[75] superiora quidem machinae, interiora vero bobus annecterentur. At interiora longius superioribus protenderentur. Superiora vero breviore ductu machinam implicitam haberent, ita ut inter hostes et boves machina staret. Unde et fieret ut quanto boves ab hostibus trahendo discederent, tanto machina hostibus attracta propinquaret. Quo commento, chilindris suppositis quibus facilius motum acciperet, machina hostibus nullo laeso appulsa est.

107

Victoria Lotharii

Adversarii quoque similem quidem machinam extruunt, sed altitudine et robore inferiorem. Utraque ergo exstructa,[76] a parte utraque ascensum est. Conflictumque ab utrisque promtissime, nec tamen ullo modo cedunt. Rex cum propior muris adesset, fundae iaculo in labro superiore sauciatus est. Cuius iniuria sui accensi, vehementius bello incubuere. Et quia hostes machina et armis fortes nullatenus cedebant, rex uncinos ferreos adhiberi precepit. Qui fu-

the siege tower, and the lower ends would be attached to a team of oxen. The lower ropes would extend over a much greater distance than the upper ropes, which would be tied around the siege tower so that it would stand between the enemy and the oxen. In this way however far the oxen pulled away from the enemy, the siege tower would be drawn that same distance toward the walls. Through this contrivance the tower, which was put on top of rollers so that it could move more easily, was propelled toward the enemy without any casualties.

107

Lothar's Victory

The enemy constructed a similar device for themselves, although it was neither as tall nor as strong. When both towers were complete, men from the opposing armies climbed up into them. Both sides fought resolutely, and neither gave any ground. When the king drew nearer to the walls, he was wounded in the upper lip by a stone cast from a sling. His men were enraged by his injury and threw themselves into battle with even more ferocity.[126] And because the enemy remained steadfast behind their siege engine and their arms and were not giving any ground, the king instructed his men to employ iron grappling hooks. These

nibus alligati, cum hostium machinae iniecti essent lignisque
transversis admorsi, funes alii demittebant, alii demissos excipiebant. Quibus adversariorum machina inclinata atque
pene demersa est. Unde alii delabentes per lignorum commissuras descendebant; alii vero saltu sese ad terram demittebant; nonnulli quoque turpi formidine tacti, latibulis
vitam sibi defendebant. Hostes mortis periculum urgere vi-
dentes, adversariis cedunt vitamque supplices petunt. Iussi
quoque arma deponunt et reddunt. Statimque[77] a rege decretum exivit, hostes sine aliqua ultionis iniuria comprehen-
dendos ac illesos sibi adducendos. Comprehensi itaque,
inermes et indempnes preter ictus quos in militari tumultu
acceperant, ante regem admissi sunt. Qui regis pedibus ad-
voluti, vitam petebant. Nam regiae maiestatis rei atque con-
victi, de vita diffidebant.

108

Rex victoria potitus, Belgicae principes captos suis cus-
todiendos, sed et congruo tempore reddendos mandavit.
Reliquam manum redire permisit. Ipse Laudunum cum exercitu rediit ibique procinctum solvit. Urbem Virdunum us-

were attached to ropes and hurled at the enemy tower. Once the hooks had caught onto the crossbeams, some men released the ropes, while others picked them up and used them to tilt the tower until it almost fell over. As a result, some of the men on the tower slipped and fell through the joints in the beams, while others leapt off and plunged to the ground; a number of men were also stricken with fear and hid in order to save themselves. The enemy, seeing that they were in imminent danger of death, surrendered to their foes and pleaded for their lives. Thereupon they were ordered to lay down their arms and relinquish them. A decree immediately went forth from the king that there were to be no reprisals against the enemy, but that they were to be seized and brought before him uninjured. And so they were taken and brought before the king unharmed and without injury, save for those blows that they had received during the battle. They threw themselves at the feet of the king and begged him for mercy. For they were guilty men who had been convicted of treason, and they feared for their lives.

108

Having obtained the victory, the king gave orders that the captured magnates of Belgica were to be held in custody by his men,[127] but that they would be released when the time was right. The rest of the group were allowed to return home. He himself went back to Laon with his troops, and there he lay down his arms. Lothar held the city of Verdun

que in diem vitae eius supremum absque ulla refragatione obtinuit. Disponebat preterea quomodo ulterius procedendo regnum suum dilataret, cum res suae successum optimum haberent, regnique fortuna per captos[78] primates id persuaderet. Sed divinitas res mundanas determinans, et Belgis requiem, et huic regnandi finem dedit.

109

Obitus Lotharii

Nam cum vernalis clementia eodem anno rebus bruma afflictis rediret, pro rerum natura inmutato aere, Lauduni egrotare coepit. Unde vexatus ea passione quae colica a phisicis dicitur, in lectum decidit. Cui dolor intolerabilis in parte dextra super verenda erat. Ab umbilico quoque usque ad splenem, et inde usque ad inguen sinistrum, et sic ad anum infestis doloribus pulsabatur. Ilium quoque ac renium iniuria nonnulla erat; thenasmus assiduus; egestio sanguinea; vox aliquoties intercludebatur. Interdum frigore fe-

without any opposition for the rest of his life. He even considered trying to expand his kingdom with a new campaign, since his affairs were in such a prosperous state, and the good fortune that had befallen the realm in the form of his prominent captives recommended this course of action to him. But God, who assigns limits to all earthly things, brought peace to the men of Belgica and an end to Lothar's reign.

109

The Death of Lothar

For that same year,[128] when the mild spring weather returned after the harsh winter, there was a seasonal change in the air, and Lothar fell ill while he was at Laon. He began to suffer from the sickness physicians call colic and took to his bed. He had intolerable pain on his right side above his private parts, and he was plagued with recurring pains from his navel to his spleen, from there to the left side of his groin, and from there to his anus. His bowels and his kidneys were also affected, and he had continuous difficulty in voiding, as well as bloody stool. His voice was occasionally stifled in his throat and he periodically went numb with chills from fever.

986

brium rigebat. Rugitus intestinorum, fastidium iuge, ructus conationes sine effectu, ventris extensio, stomachi ardor non deerant. Ingenti itaque luctu tota personat[79] domus. Fit sonitus diversus, clamor varius. Nemini enim eorum qui aderant inlacrimabilis erat ea calamitas. Decem igitur annis Ottoni superstes, tricesimo et septimo anno ex quo patre defuncto regno potitus est, quadragesimo vero et octavo quo a patre regnante coronam et sceptrum regnaturus accepit, a natu autem sexagesimo VIII, deficiens naturae concessit.

110

Interea magnifice funus regium multo divitiarum regalium ambitu accuratur. Fit ei lectus regalibus insignibus adornatus. Corpus bissina[80] veste induitur ac, desuper palla purpurea gemmis ornata auroque intexta operitur. Lectum regnorum primates deferebant. Preibant episcopi et clerus cum evangeliis et crucibus. Penes quos etiam qui eius coronam ferebat, multo auro gemmisque pretiosis nitentem, cum aliis multis insignibus, eiulando incedebat. Funebre melos lacrimis impedientibus vix proferebatur. Milites etiam mesto vultu suo ordine prosequebantur. Reliqua quoque manus

He had a rumbling in the bowels and continual nausea. He tried to belch, but without success; his abdomen swelled up, and he had heartburn. His whole household resounded with loud mourning, and there were various cries and sounds of grief. For there was no one who did not look upon this as a tragedy to be lamented.[129] And so, having outlived Otto by ten years, in the thirty-seventh year after he had succeeded to the throne upon his father's death,[130] in the forty-eighth year after he had taken up the crown and scepter of rule from his father the king, and in the sixty-eighth year of his life,[131] he died and yielded to nature.

110

In the meantime, a splendid funeral was prepared with all the trappings of royal wealth. The body was dressed in a linen shroud and covered with purple cloth adorned with gems and interwoven with gold.[132] His bier was decorated with royal insignia and carried by the chief men of the realm. The bishops and the clergy went before them, carrying gospel books and crosses. Amid the procession there walked a man[133] bearing Lothar's crown, resplendent with gold and precious gems, along with many other insignia, wailing as he came forward. The funeral dirge could scarcely be sung because it was continuously interrupted by weeping. His knights came next, arrayed in rank, with mournful countenances, and the rest of the procession followed after them

cum lamentis succedebat. Sepultus est Remis in coenobio monachorum sancti Remigii, cum patre et matre, sicut ante iusserat suis. Quod etiam abest CCXL stadiis ab eo loco in quo finem vitae accepit; multo obsequio universorum parique affectu per tantum spatii deductus.

in tears. Lothar was buried in the monastery of Saint-Rémi at Reims alongside his mother and father, in accordance with his prior instructions. This was 240 stades[134] from where he had died, and all along the route his funeral cortège was met by everyone with profound devotion and an equal degree of affection.[135]

BOOK FOUR

I

Sepulto Lothario, Ludovicus filius a duce aliisque principibus in regnum subrogatur. Circumvallatur ergo ambitu
universorum. Promittunt benivolentiam, spondent fidem.
Stipatores etiam vario motu[1] facienda dictabant. Alii enim
in palatiis[2] ei residendum censebant, ut principes ad se con-
fluentes eius imperio deservirent, ne regia dignitas vilesceret si alias utpote inops alieni suffragii peteret opes. In omni
etiam dignitate id esse cavendum, ne in primordio suscepti
honoris segnities et ignavia virtutem habendam superent.
Nam si id fit, totam etiam rem in contemptum et vilitatem
pernitiosissime deventuram. Alii quoque cum duce ei com-
morandum[3] asserebant, eo quod adolescens tanti principis
prudentia simul et virtute informari indigeret. Sibi quoque
utillimum fieri si potentis dispositioni ad tempus cederet,
cum sine eo nec regnandi potentiam habere ex integro posset, et per eum strenue atque utiliter omnia administrari

I

After Lothar's burial, his son Louis was installed on the 986 throne by the duke and the other leading men.[1] Consequently everyone closed ranks around him, promising him their goodwill and pledging fealty to him.[2] The members of his court also gave him conflicting advice about what he should do. Some advised him to remain in his palaces so that the leading men would have to come to him and obey his command; in this way the royal dignity would not grow contemptible, as it would if he were to go around like a beggar asking other people for help. In every position of importance one had to exercise care after assuming office, lest sloth and laziness should get the better of the virtue that was required. If this happened, then his rule would proceed along a ruinous course until he became an object of contempt and scorn. Others advised him to stay close by the duke, since as a young man he needed to mold himself according to the wisdom and virtue of so great a prince. It would also be greatly to his advantage to yield temporarily to the authority of this powerful figure, since without him he could not exercise complete control over his kingdom, but through his agency everything could be managed capa-

199

valerent. Rex, partibus auditis, sententiam distulit. Collato vero cum duce consilio, ei abinde tota mente addictus favit.

2

Oratio Ludovici apud ducem ceterosque primates in Adalberonem metropolitanum

Apud quem aliosque quam paucos, preteritorum non immemor, sic conquestus est: 'Pater meus in egritudinem qua et periit decidens, mihi precepit ut vestro consilio, vestra dispositione regni procurationem haberem; vos etiam loco affinium, loco amicorum[4] ducerem, nihilque precipui preter vestram scientiam adorirer. Si vestra fide potirer, sine dubio divitias, exercitus, munimenta regni asserebat me habiturum. Quae mens in me maxime valet.[5] Placeat itaque consilium profuturum dare, cum a vobis proposui me non discessurum. In vobis enim meum consilium, animum, fortunas sitas esse volui. Adalbero Remorum metropolitanus episcopus, homo omnium quos terra sustinet sceleratissimus, con-

bly and successfully. The king listened to the competing arguments but put off making a decision. After taking counsel with the duke, however, he became completely devoted to him and favored him from that time forward.

2

Louis's Speech Against Archbishop Adalbero to the Duke and the Other Magnates

Not unmindful of what had happened in the past, Louis delivered a complaint of the following sort to the duke and a very few other men: "When my father was stricken with the illness from which he eventually died, he instructed me to employ your counsel and direction in administering the kingdom, to regard you as my kinsmen and my friends, and to undertake nothing of importance without your knowledge. If I had your loyalty, he told me, then I would surely come to possess the riches, armies, and fortifications of the realm.[3] His advice carries great weight with me, and I hope that you will be willing to furnish me with useful counsel, since I am determined not to become estranged from you. For it was my desire to place my plans, my intentions, and my fortunes in your hands. Adalbero, the archbishop of Reims, the most debased of all men who walk the face of the earth,[4] scorning

tempto patris mei imperio, Ottoni Francorum hosti in omnibus favit. Eo cooperante, Otto exercitum nobis induxit. Eius subtilitate Gallias depopulatus est. Eo itineris duces prestante, indempnis cum exercitu rediit. Qui ut poenas pro tanto commisso solvat, aequum et utile videtur,[6] quatinus pestilente compresso, metus adoriendi talia quibusque pravis inferatur.'

3

Cuius oratio vim suadendi non habuit, eo quod suggestionibus malorum in summum pontificem efferatus, preter iustum aliqua indigna dixisse videretur. Pro parte tamen ei fautum est, pro parte vero suppressum, ita tamen, ut et regi iniuria non fieret, et operi nefario dux non consentiens pareret. Rex tanto animo preceps, in metropolitanum assumpto duce cum exercitu fertur. Ipsam urbem appetit atque irrumpere contendit. Primatum tamen consilio usus, legatos premisit per quos quaereret an episcopus resisteret regi an ex obiectis purgari statuto tempore paratus esset. Si contra staret, sese mox obsidionem urbi adhibiturum dice-

the authority of my father, supported Otto, the enemy of the Franks, in all that he did. It was with Adalbero's cooperation that Otto led his army against us; it was through Adalbero's cunning that Otto was able to ravage Gaul; and it was because of guides supplied by Adalbero that Otto and his army were able to return home unscathed. I think that it would be both just and useful for him to pay a penalty for his misdeeds, for by wiping out this contagion we shall make wicked men fear to do anything like this in the future."

3

Louis's speech failed to persuade them because he had been worked up into a fury against the archbishop by the insinuations of wicked men, and he was thought to have made a number of unseemly allegations without any justification. They supported him to some degree, while in part they restrained him, but only to the extent that no harm would be done to the king, and the duke would not willingly cooperate in this criminal endeavor. Driven by his single-minded animosity, the king summoned the duke and marched against the archbishop with his army. He advanced on the city of Reims and tried to force his way inside. On the advice of the magnates, however, he sent messengers to ask if the archbishop was planning to resist the king, or if he was instead prepared to answer to the charges against him at a specified date. If he continued to hold out, they said,

987

rent, captamque urbem cum ipso hoste compressurum. Si vero obiectis respondere non dubitaret, obsides ab eo sese accepturum ducturumque.

4

Ad haec metropolitanus: 'Cum constet,' inquit, 'bonos quosque pravorum calumniis assidue dilacerari, non miror huic iniuriae locum accidisse. Multo amplius vero miror egregios principes tam facile posse illici, ut certissime esse credant quod nec sub iudice sit discussum, et si in discutiendo conferatur, nullis rationibus probabile fiat. Quod si credita discutere placuit, cur armis et exercitu id exigitur? Nonne ergo alia pro aliis nos cogitare faciunt? Si de preteritis agitur, regum salutem hactenus optavi. Eorum[7] genus colui. Principum quoque commoda pro ratione amavi. Si de presentibus, regis iussa exsequi non moror, obsides quos vult trado, rationem contra obiecta intendere non differo.'

then the king would lay siege to Reims, and when it fell, he would exact revenge against both the city and his foe. If, however, he was willing to respond to the charges, then the king would accept hostages from him and lead them away.

4

In response the archbishop declared: "Since good men never cease to be torn to shreds by the false accusations of the wicked, I am not surprised that an occasion has arisen for this attack upon me. What surprises me much more is the fact that noble princes could be misled so easily as to put complete faith in an accusation that has not been laid before a judge, and which could not be made credible by any arguments if it were submitted to judicial scrutiny. If they are willing to undertake an examination of the allegations, then why are demands being made using weapons and armed men? Are they not implying that I have changed my views? If the issue under consideration is my conduct in the past, then up until now I have prayed for the salvation of the kings and devoted myself to their family, and I have cherished the interests of the leading men insofar as it was reasonable to do so. If the issue is my present conduct, then I have not been slow to carry out the orders of the king, I shall hand over the hostages that he wants, and shall not hesitate to answer to the charges against me." After negotiations between the two parties, Adalbero handed over hostages, in-

Factis ergo utrimque rationibus, obsides dedit, Ragenerum virum militarem, nobilitate et divitiis clarum, pluresque alios dum regi sufficeret.

5

Obitus Ludovici

Rex itaque exercitum amovit Silvanectimque devenit. Ubi dum aestivam venationem exerceret, pedestri lapsu decidens, multo epatis dolore vexatus est. Nam quia in epate sanguinis sedem phisici perhibent, ea sede concussa, sanguis in emathoicam redundavit. Cui sanguis copiosus[8] per nares et gulam diffluebat. Mamillae doloribus assiduis pulsabantur. Fervor totius corporis intolerabilis non deerat. Unde uno tantum anno patri superstes, XI Kal. Iun. defitiens, naturae debitum solvit. Cuius discessus eo tempore accidit quo et metropolitani purgatio de obiectis habenda erat. Aderat igitur purgandus et regiae maiestati satisfacturus. Sed regii funeris calamitate hac lite suppressa, nec controversia partes habuit, nec ex ea iuditium promulgatum fuit. Plurima vero commiseratione ipse episcopus de morte regis conquestus est. Postquam autem regium funus curassent,[9]

cluding Rainier,[5] a man of the knightly order who was distinguished for his nobility and wealth, and many others, until the king was satisfied.

5

The Death of Louis

Louis subsequently took his army away and went to Senlis. While he was hunting there during the summer, his foot slipped and he fell, and he began to suffer from a tremendous pain in his liver. Now because the liver is the seat of the blood, as the physicians tell us, when he received this injury, he began to hemorrhage violently. A torrent of blood poured out of his nostrils and his throat. His nipples throbbed with constant pain, and an unbearable fever pervaded his whole body. On the twenty-second of May he succumbed and paid his debt to nature, having outlived his father by just one year. His death occurred at the time when the archbishop was supposed to answer to the charges against him. For this reason Adalbero had come to Senlis to exonerate himself and give satisfaction to his royal majesty. The dispute was set aside because of the funeral, however, and no arguments took place; nor was any verdict issued in the matter. And with great compassion Adalbero bewailed the death of the king. After they had attended to the king's

principum decreto Compendii tumulatus est, cum ipse vivens secus patrem tumulari petierit. Id autem consulto factum est, ne dum itineris longitudinem eorum quamplures vitarent et a se divisi discederent, rei publicae utillimum differretur consultum. Placuit itaque ante discessum convenire et ex regni commodis consulere.

6

Purgatio Adalberonis de obiectis a Ludovico

Quibus dispositis, dux sic orsus coepit: 'Huc ex locis diversis regio iussu vocati, ad discutiendum ea quae summo pontifici Adalberoni obiecta sunt, multa fide, ut puto, convenistis. Sed dignae[10] memoriae rex qui intendebat, quoniam hac vita privatus est, controversiae statum nobis discutiendum reliquit. Si ergo preter eum est qui intendere audeat, eoque animo valet ut exsequendae litis partem arripiat, adsit

funeral, the leading men decided to have Louis buried at
Compiègne, although while he was alive he had asked to be
buried next to his father.[6] This was done intentionally, to
forestall the possibility that a large number of the magnates
would refuse to attend the funeral because of the length of
the journey and would leave without reaching a decision on
what was best for the kingdom. For this reason they agreed
to meet prior to departing and to deliberate over the interests of the realm.

6

Adalbero Defends Himself Against the Charges Brought by Louis

After this had been settled, the duke proceeded to address them as follows: "You were all summoned here from
different places by the order of the king to investigate the
charges brought against Archbishop Adalbero, and you have
come, I believe, as loyal subjects. But because King Louis of
worthy memory, who brought these accusations, has departed from this life, it has been left to us to decide the issue
under dispute. Therefore, if there is anyone else who would
presume to make an accusation, and who has the courage to
assume the role of the prosecution, let him come forward,
say what he thinks, and state his case against the accused

coram, quid sentiat edicat, nihil metuens criminato intendat. Si vera proferat, eius verborum approbatores nos sine
dubio habebit. Quod si calumniator falsa confinxit, vocem
supprimat, ne tanti facinoris argutus, poenas solvat.' Ter ac-
clamatum est ut delator procederet; ter ab omnibus nega-
tum est.

7

Dux itaque iterum locutus ait: 'Si lis iam decidit, quia qui
intendat non est, metropolitano utpote viro nobili et multa
sapientia inclito cedendum est. Ab hac ergo suspitione penitus discedite, summumque presulem multo honore excolite.
Reveremini hunc talem virum, et quantae virtutis, sapien-
tiae, nobilitatis sit, hactenus predicate. Quid enim prodest
suspitionem[11] habere, cui in iuditio non fuere vires quicquam
dicere?'

8

Ergo[12] summo pontifici dux, reliquorum primatum consensu, exsequendae rationis honorem de utilitate regni at-
tribuit, eo quod ipse divinarum et humanarum rerum scien-

without fear. If he speaks the truth, then he can be certain that we will accept the validity of what he says. But if he is a slanderer who has fabricated lies, then let him keep quiet, lest he be found guilty of this crime and compelled to pay the penalty." Three times they cried out for an accuser to come forward, and three times the opportunity was refused by everyone.

7

The duke then addressed them for a second time. "If this case is now at an end because there is no one who is willing to bring a charge, then we must defer to the archbishop, inasmuch as he is a noble man who is famed for his great wisdom. Abandon therefore any suspicions that you have and honor him with all due reverence. Venerate this man for his qualities, and proclaim the great virtue, wisdom, and nobility that he has shown up to now. What point is there for anyone to continue to harbor suspicions against him if he lacks the courage to say anything in court?"

8

Subsequently the duke, with the consent of the rest of the magnates, granted the archbishop the honor of expressing his opinion about what was best for the realm, since he was

tia excelleret, atque facundiae efficacitate plurimum valeret. Factus itaque cum duce omnium medius, ait: 'Rege nostro piissimo inter intellectibilia translato, magni ducis ceterorumque principum benivolentia ab obiectis purgatus, rei publicae consulturus consedi. Nec sedet animo ut quicquam nisi ad profectum rei publicae edicam. Commune consilium quaero, quia omnibus prodesse cupio. Cum videam non omnes principes adesse quorum quoque prudentia et diligentia res regni administrari valeant, ratio querendi regis, ut mihi videtur, ad tempus differenda est, ut statuto tempore et omnes in unum confluant, et uniuscuiusque ratio, elimata et in medium prolata, suam utilitatem accommodet. Unde et vobis qui hic consulturi adestis placeat vos mecum magno duci sacramento alligari, et coram spondere de principe statuendo vos nihil quesituros, nihil molituros, donec in unum redeamus et sic de habendo principe agitemus. Plurimum enim valet deliberationi dari spatium temporis, in quo quamcumque rem quisque discutiat, et discussam multa diligentia poliat.' Haec sententia ab omnibus suscepta laudatur. Sacramento itaque duci alligantur. Tempus redeundi et conveniendi constituitur. Sic quoque a se soluti sunt.

preeminent in the knowledge of divine and human affairs and a speaker of powerful eloquence. Taking his place in their midst alongside the duke, the archbishop spoke as follows: "After our most pious king was taken up into the realm of the intellectible,[7] and I was cleared of the charges against me through the goodwill of the duke and the other leading men, I took my seat here in order to deliberate upon the interests of the realm; nor is it my intention to say anything unless it contributes to the advancement of the common weal. I seek everyone's counsel, because it is my desire to act for the good of all. Because I can see that not all of the leading men whose wisdom and devotion are required for the effective governance of the realm are present here, I think that we should temporarily postpone our discussions concerning the choice of a king, so that at a designated time we can all assemble in one body, and each person can usefully contribute by publicly presenting his considered opinion. May it please those of you who are present for these deliberations to join me in binding yourselves to the great duke with an oath, and to swear publicly to make no efforts or attempts to establish a new king until we can assemble once more and take up the question of the succession again. It is a sound principle that plenty of time should be accorded to all deliberations, so that each person may come to a decision on whatever subject is under discussion and refine that decision through careful reflection." This advice was received with praise by everyone, and they all bound themselves to the duke with an oath. A time was appointed when they would return to meet again, and with that they parted from one another.

9

Conquestio Karoli apud metropolitanum de regno

Interea Karolus, qui fuerat Lotharii frater, Ludovici patruus, Remis metropolitanum adiit atque sic de regno eum convenit: 'Omnibus notum est, pater venerande, iure hereditario debere fratri et nepoti me succedere. Licet enim a fratre de regno pulsus sim, tamen natura nihil humanitatis mihi derogavit; cum omnibus membris natus sum, sine quibus quivis ad dignitatem quamlibet promoveri non potuit. His etiam non careo, quae in regnaturis quibuslibet plurimum queri solent, genere, et ut audeam virtute. Cur ergo a finibus eiectus sum, quos a maioribus meis possessos nemo dubitat, cum frater non sit, neposque obierit, prolemque nullam reliquerint? Pater nos duos fratres superstites reliquit. Frater regnorum dominium totum possedit nihilque mihi concessit. Ego fratri subditus, fideliter non minus aliis militavi. A quo tempore fateor nihil mihi carius fuisse salute fratris. Abiectus ergo et infelix, quo me potius vertam, cum etiam omnia generis mei presidia extincta sint? Quos preter vos, omnium honestarum rerum egens, appellem? Per quos

9

Charles's Lament to the Archbishop Concerning the Kingdom

In the meantime Charles, the brother of Lothar and the uncle of Louis, approached the archbishop of Reims and spoke to him on the subject of the succession: "Everyone knows, venerable father, that by hereditary right I ought to succeed my brother and my nephew. For although I was driven out of the kingdom by my brother, nature has taken none of my humanity away from me. I was born with all of my limbs, without which no one can be elevated to any position of rank. Nor do I lack the qualities that are customarily much sought after in a future ruler, namely noble birth and the courage to act boldly. Why, then, have I been expelled from this land, which no one denies that my ancestors ruled, when my brother is no more, and my nephew is deceased, and neither one has left behind an heir? When my father died, he left behind two sons. My brother took control of the entire realm and granted me nothing, but I submitted to his authority and served him no less faithfully than anyone else. From that time forward I contend that nothing was of greater concern to me than my brother's well-being. Where am I to turn now, luckless castoff that I am, when all the bulwarks of my family line have disappeared? Whom can I call upon but you, lacking as I am in all that is worthy of respect? Who else but you can help restore the lands and titles

nisi per vos paternis honoribus restituar? Utinam mihi for-
tunisque meis honestus exitus accidisset. Quid enim abiectus spectantibus nisi spectaculum esse potero? Tangat vos
aliqua humanitatis miseratio. Compatimini tantis iniuriis
fatigato.'

10

Postquam Karolus finem querimoniae fecit, metropolitanus animo immobili[13] persistens, pauca admodum ei respondit, 'Cum,' inquiens, 'periuris et sacrilegis aliisque nefariis
hominibus ipse semper deditus fueris, nec ab eis adhuc discedere velis, quomodo per tales et cum talibus ad principa-
tum venire moliris?' Ad haec Karolo respondente non opor-
tere sese suos deserere, sed potius alios adquirere, episcopus
intra se recogitabat, 'Cum,' inquiens, 'omnium dignitatum
nunc egens, pravis quibusque annexus est quorum sotietate
nullomodo carere vult, in quantam pernitiem bonorum esset, si electus procederet in fasces?' Tandem sine principum
consensu se super hoc nihil facturum respondens, ab eo dimotus est.

of my forefathers to me? Would that an honorable death had put an end to me and my misfortunes. For what else can I do in my current lowly position but serve as a spectacle for onlookers? May some measure of human compassion touch you. Have pity on one who has been driven to exhaustion by his great sufferings."[8]

10

When Charles had finished his complaint, the archbishop, remaining fixed in his resolve, offered only a brief response. "You have always been devoted to perjurers, blasphemers, and other wicked men, and you are still unwilling to detach yourself from them. How can it be that you are striving to reach the throne, when you continue to associate with and employ the services of these sorts of people?" When Charles replied that it was incumbent upon him not to abandon his men, but to win over new followers instead, the archbishop reflected to himself: "This man, who is now without any claim to power, is bound to all sorts of wicked people whose company he is completely unwilling to forsake. How much harm would he do to good men if he were elected and ascended to the throne?" He concluded by saying that he could do nothing in this matter without the consent of the leading men, and he took his leave of Charles.

II

Oratio metropolitani
pro duce

Karolus spe regni decidens, animo turbato in Belgicam iter dimovit. Preterea tempore constituto Galliarum principes iurati Silvanecti collecti sunt. Quibus in curia residentibus, duce annuente metropolitanus sic locutus est: 'Dignae[14] memoriae Ludovico sine liberis orbi[15] subtracto, querendum multa deliberatione fuit qui eius vices in regno suppleret, ne res publica absque gubernatore neglecta labefactaretur. Unde et huiusmodi negotium nuper differri utile duximus, ut unusquisque quod singularis a deo datum haberet hic coram consulens post effunderet, ut collectis singulorum sententiis, summa totius consilii ex multitudinis massa deformaretur. Reductis ergo iam nunc nobis in unum, multa prudentia, multa fide videndum est ne aut odium rationem dissipet, aut amor veritatem enervet. Non ignoramus Karolum fautores suos habere, qui eum dignum regno ex parentum collatione contendant. Sed si de hoc agitur, nec regnum iure hereditario adquiritur, nec in regnum promovendus est, nisi quem non solum corporis nobilitas, sed et animi sapientia illustrat, fides munit, magnanimitas firmat. Legimus in

II

The Archbishop's Speech on Behalf of the Duke

His hopes of winning the throne dashed, Charles left for Belgica in dismay. At the appointed time the magnates of Gaul who had sworn to do so assembled at Senlis. They took their seats in the palace, and at the duke's behest the archbishop addressed them: "When Louis of worthy memory was taken from this world without an heir, it became necessary to give careful thought to who would take his place on the throne, lest the realm should be neglected and come to grief in the absence of a ruler to govern it. Hence I thought it prudent that this task should be delayed recently, so that each one of us could come before the council and impart what had been revealed to him by God. In that way, after everyone's opinion had been heard, the consensus of the council as a whole could take shape from the general mass of ideas. Therefore, now that we have assembled here, we must exercise great prudence and faith to see to it that enmity does not undermine our judgment, nor partisanship weaken the truth. I am not unaware that Charles has supporters who contend that he deserves the crown by virtue of his birth. But if this is the point at issue, a kingdom cannot be acquired by hereditary right, nor should anyone be elevated to the throne unless he is distinguished not only by nobility of body, but also by wisdom of mind, and unless he is forti-

annalibus clarissimi generis imperatoribus ignavia ab dignitate precipitatis,[16] alios modo pares, modo impares successisse. Sed quid dignum Karolo conferri potest, quem fides
non regit, torpor enervat, postremo qui tanta capitis immi-
nutione hebuit, ut externo regi servire non horruerit, et uxorem de militari ordine sibi imparem duxerit?[17] Quomodo
ergo magnus dux patietur de suis militibus feminam sump-
tam reginam fieri sibique dominari? Quomodo capiti suo
preponet, cuius pares et etiam maiores sibi genua flectunt,
pedibusque manus supponunt? Considerate rem diligenter,
et Karolum sua magis culpa precipitatum quam aliena vi-
dete. Rei publicae beatitudinem magis quam calamitatem
optate. Si eam infelicem fieri vultis, Karolum promovete; si
fortunatam, egregium ducem Hugonem in regnum coro-
nate. Ne ergo Karoli amor quemque illiciat, nec odium ducis
ab utilitate communi quemlibet amoveat. Nam si bonum vi-
tuperetis, quomodo malum laudabitis? Si malum laudetis,
quomodo bonum contempnetis? Sed talibus quid intermi-
natur ipsa divinitas? "Vae," inquit, "qui dicitis malum bonum, bonum malum, ponentes lucem tenebras, et tenebras
lucem." Promovete igitur vobis ducem, actu, nobilitate, copiis clarissimum, quem non solum rei publicae, sed et priva-
tarum rerum tutorem invenietis. Ipsa eius benivolentia fa-

fied by faith and strengthened by greatness of spirit. I have read in the annals that when emperors of the most distinguished lineage fell from office through weakness of character, they were sometimes succeeded by equals, and sometimes by those who were inferior. But what honor can be granted to Charles, who is not governed by faith, but enervated by lethargy, who has ultimately become so weak-witted that he has not scrupled to serve a foreign king[9] and to take from the ranks of the warrior class a wife who is beneath his station? How can a great duke allow a woman taken from among his knights to become queen and rule over him? How can he set over himself a person whose equals and even whose betters bend their knees to him and place their hands under his feet?[10] Consider this matter carefully, and be aware that it is Charles himself, and no one else, who is responsible for his downfall. Choose prosperity rather than disaster for the realm. If you wish misfortune upon it, then elevate Charles to the throne; if you wish it to be blessed, then crown the distinguished Duke Hugh as king. Let no one's affection for Charles lead him astray, nor his hostility toward the duke distract him from the common advantage. For if you curse the good, how will you praise the bad? If you praise the bad, how will you scorn the good? What does God himself threaten such people with? 'Woe to you' he says, 'that call evil good, and good evil; that put darkness for light, and light for darkness.'[11] In conclusion, set the duke over yourselves, a man famed for his deeds, his nobility, and his wealth, whom you will find a guardian not only of the common weal but also of your private property. In favoring you

vente, eum pro patre habebitis. Quis enim ad eum confugit
et patrocinium non invenit? Quis suorum auxiliis destitutus,
per eum suis non restitutus fuit?'

12

Promotio Hugonis in regnum

Hac sententia promulgata, et ab omnibus laudata, dux
omnium consensu in regnum promovetur, et per metropolitanum aliosque episcopos Noviomi coronatus, Gallis, Brittannis, Dahis, Aquitanis, Gothis, Hispanis, Wasconibus rex[18]
Kal. Iun. prerogatur. Stipatus itaque regnorum principibus,
more regio decreta fecit[19] legesque condidit, felici successu
omnia ordinans atque distribuens. Et ut beatitudini suae
responderet, multo successu rerum secundarum levatus, ad
multam pietatem intendit. Utque post sui discessum a vita
heredem certum in regno relinqueret, sese consultum cum
principibus contulit. Et collato cum eis consilio, Remorum
metropolitanum Aurelianis de promotione filii sui Rotberti
in regnum prius per legatos, post per sese convenit. Cui cum

with his kindness he shall be like a father to you. For who has fled to him and not found protection? Who has been deprived of the aid of his men and not been restored to them through his agency?"

12

The Elevation of Hugh to the Throne

When the archbishop had delivered this speech, and his sentiments had met with universal praise, the duke was elevated to the throne by unanimous consent. On the first of June he was crowned at Noyon by the archbishop and other bishops and established as king over the Gauls, the Bretons, the Normans, the Aquitainians, the Goths, the Spanish, and the Gascons. Surrounded by the leading men of the realm, he issued decrees and established laws in royal fashion, organizing and arranging everything with auspicious success. Since he been raised to the throne amid such favorable circumstances, he gave himself over to pious devotion in order to give thanks for his good fortune.[12] And so that he might leave behind an undisputed heir to the throne after his death, he took counsel with the leading men. After conferring with them, he discussed the elevation of his son Robert to the throne with the archbishop of Reims at Orléans, first via envoys, and later in person. When the archbishop replied that

metropolitanus non recte posse creari[20] duos reges in eodem anno responderet, ille mox epistolam a duce citerioris[21] Hispaniae Borrello missam protulit, quae ducem petentem suffragia contra barbaros indicabat. Iam etiam Hispaniae partem hostibus pene expugnatam asserebat, et nisi intra menses X copias a Gallis accipiat, barbaris totam in deditionem transituram. Petebat itaque iterum[22] regem creari, ut si bellico tumultu[23] duorum alter decideret, de principe non diffideret exercitus. Fieri quoque asserebat posse, rege interempto, et patria desolata, primatum discordiam, pravorum contra bonos tirannidem, et inde totius gentis captivitatem.

13

Promotio Rotberti in regnum

Metropolitanus sic posse fieri intelligens, dictis regiis cessit. Et quia tunc in nativitate domini regnorum principes convenerant ad celebrandum regiae coronationis honorem, in basilica sanctae Crucis eius filium Rotbertum, Francis laudantibus, accepta purpura sollempniter coronavit et a

two men could not lawfully be made king in the same year, Hugh produced a letter that he had received from Duke Borrell of Catalonia in which the duke asked him for aid against the barbarians.[13] Already, he said, the enemy had all but overrun part of Spain, and if he did not receive troops from Gaul within the next ten months, then the whole country would fall into the hands of the barbarians. And so Hugh asked that another king be crowned, so that if one of them fell in battle, the army would not be left in a state of uncertainty about their leader. He added that if the king were killed and the fatherland left abandoned, then the end result could be discord among the magnates, the tyranny of the wicked against the good, and the subsequent enslavement of the whole populace.

13

The Elevation of Robert to the Throne

Realizing that this could very well happen, the archbishop acceded to the king's request. Because the leading men of the realm had assembled at Christmas to celebrate the honor of the king's coronation in the basilica of Sainte-Croix,[14] the archbishop solemnly crowned his son Robert, who had been dressed in purple, to the acclamation of the Franks, establishing and ordaining him as king over the men

Mosa fluvio usque Oceanum occidentalibus regem prefecit et ordinavit; tanta industria atque sollertia clarum, ut et in rebus militaribus precelleret, et divinis ac canonicis institutis clarissimus haberetur, liberalibus studiis incomberet,[24] episcoporum etiam sinodis interesset, et cum eis causas aecclesiasticas discuteret ac determinaret.

14

Conquestio Karoli apud amicos de regno

Interea Karolus apud amicos et cognatos motu gravissimo movebat querelam atque in sui suffragium querimoniis excitabat. Qui lacrimis suffusus, 'Video,' inquit, 'aetatem meam procedere et me ipsum in dies patrimonii rebus exui. Unde nec sine lacrimis parvulos meos aspicere valeo, infelicis germina patris. Quibus potius auctor sum futuri doloris quam honoris. Satis infelix pater fui, qui natis adesse vix aliquando potui. Sed saltem vos, amici,[25] consulite dolenti patri, subvenite destituto parenti. Adestote natis in aetate tenerrima erumnas iam scientibus. Providete abiectis in casus, an irre-

of the West from the River Meuse all the way to the ocean. Robert was remarkable for his great industry and cleverness, so much so that he not only excelled in military affairs, but was also renowned for his knowledge of scripture and canon law. In addition, he devoted himself to the study of the liberal arts and participated in episcopal synods, deliberating and passing judgment in ecclesiastical cases alongside the bishops.

14

Charles's Complaint to His Friends Concerning the Succession

In the meantime Charles aired his grievances to his friends and kinsmen with passionate intensity, rousing them to come to his aid with his complaints. With tears in his eyes he addressed them: "I see myself growing older, and with every passing day I am deprived of more and more of my patrimony. I cannot look upon my little ones, the offspring of an unfortunate father, without tears; for to them I am the source of griefs to come rather than future honors. I have been a most ill-fated father, who was scarcely ever able to be at the side of my children.[15] You at least, my friends, should show sympathy for a grieving father and come to the aid of a destitute parent. Provide support for children who even at a

vocabiles nescio, exituris. Suadeat vobis saltem sanguinis communis affinitas;[26] suadeat et nobilitas non neglegenda; suadeat et recompensatio, quae sit non sine multiplici fructu reditura.'

15

Mox omnes commoti[27] auxilium spondent et sese ad auxiliandum promptissime parant. Quorum consilio usus, exploratores Karolus mittere cepit qui sagaciter perpenderent si qua oportunitas pateret qua Laudunum ingredi valeret. Directi investigaverunt deprehenderuntque nullum aditum patere. Cum quibusdam tamen civibus secretum contulere, qui[28] effectum negotio quererent. Quo tempore Adalbero, eiusdem urbis[29] episcopus, suis civibus plus iusto iniurias de lege agraria irrogabat. Unde quidam ab eo latenter animo discedentes benivolentiamque simulantes, exploratoribus Karolum sese in urbem recepturos promittunt.

very young age have come to know suffering. Make provision for those who have been reduced to humble circumstances and who are destined to meet with misfortunes that may prove to be irreversible. Let yourself be swayed, at the very least, by the common tie of blood that you share, by their nobility, which should not be disregarded, and by the recompense that will be returned to you with profit many times over."

15

Moved by what they had heard, they all promised him their assistance and set about helping him in any way that they could. On their advice Charles sent spies to Laon to examine in detail if there was any way for him to get into the city. After looking into the matter, however, those who had been sent could not discover any obvious means of entry. They did, however, share their information with some of the townsmen who were eager to bring their plans to fruition. At that time Adalbero, the bishop of Laon, was imposing unfair tax burdens on the lands of the citizens. As a result, some of them had developed a secret hostility toward the bishop, and while feigning goodwill toward him, they promised Charles's spies that they would welcome him into the city.

16

Qualiter Karolus Laudunum ingressus sit

Mox etiam urbis proditionem si Karolus veniat pollicentur, et si eis[30] sua dimittat et insuper augeat. Exploratores, pacto sacramentis firmato, haec Karolo reportant. Ille
mox suis quos superiore conquestione excitaverat hoc man-
datum aperuit. Qui unanimes, oportuno tempore collecti,
ei sese obtulere. Ille, copiis assumptis, Laudunum dum sol
occideret tempestivus advenit[31] misitque[32] exploratores ad
transfugas, ut quid esset agendum referrent. Latebant itaque inter vinearum dumeta et sepes, parati urbem ingredi si
fortuna admitteret, et armis obniti si eventus id afferret. Qui
missi fuerant ad insidias per loca constituta et nota prodito-
ribus occurrunt et Karolum cum multo equitatu advenisse[33]
nuntiant. Proditores gavisi, exploratores remittunt et Karolo[34] cito adesse mandant. Quibus cognitis, Karolus cum
suis per montis devexa[35] urbis portam aggressus est. Sed vigiles,[36] cum ex fremitu equorum et aliqua collisione armorum
aliquos adesse persentirent, et quinam essent a muro incla-
marent lapidibusque[37] iactis urgerent, proditores mox ali-

16

How Charles Entered Laon

In addition, they also promised that they would betray the city to Charles if he came, and if he would renounce his claims to their property and enrich them on top of that. After sealing an agreement with oaths, Charles's spies brought the news back to him, whereupon he revealed his plans to those of his men whom he had stirred up with his earlier complaint. At a suitable time they assembled, united in purpose, and presented themselves to him. Charles took his forces and made a timely arrival at Laon just as the sun was going down. He sent his spies to find the traitors and report back to him what he was supposed to do. And so they hid among the bushes and hedges of the vineyards, ready to enter the city if fortune gave them an opportunity to do so, or to take up arms if it came to that. The men whom Charles had sent to carry out the secret plan met with the traitors in previously designated locations and informed them that Charles had arrived with a large force of knights. The traitors rejoiced and sent the spies back with instructions for Charles to come quickly. When Charles was apprised of this, he and his men advanced up the slope of the hill toward the gate of the city. The watchmen, however, perceived from the neighing of horses and the clanging of arms that someone was there. They shouted down from the wall to ask who it was, and when they began to hurl down stones at them to

quos esse de civibus responderunt. Quo commento corrup-
tis vigilibus, introrsum portam aperuerunt atque exercitum
ipso crepusculo exceperunt. Mox exercitus urbem implevit.
Portae etiam, ne quis aufugeret, custodibus adhibitis perva-
sae sunt. Alii itaque personabant[38] bucinis, alii vocibus fre-
mebant, alii armorum sonitu tumultuabantur. Unde cives
territi, utpote qui ignorabant quid esset, et de domibus ebul-
lientes, profugio se eripere conabantur. Quorum alii aeccle-
siarum secretis se occultabant, alii diversis latibulis se clau-
debant, alii vero saltu se de muris precipitabant. Quorum
unus[39] episcopus, cum per declivia montis iam elapsus et in
vineis ab observatoribus[40] repertus esset, Karolo deductus
est et ab eo carcere detrusus. Emmam quoque reginam,
cuius instinctu sese repulsum a fratre arbitrabatur, ibi comprehendit eique custodes adhibuit. Reliquam etiam urbis
nobilitatem pene totam pervasit.

17

Postquam sedatis tumultibus civitas tranquilla reddita est,
Karolus de urbis munitione et militum victu deliberare atque ordinare coepit. Deputavit ergo vigiles quingentenos,[41]
qui noctibus singulis armati excubias per urbem et moenia

press the issue, the traitors replied that they were just some of the townsmen. Taken in by this ruse, the guards opened the gate and let them in as dusk was falling that very evening. Charles's army soon spread throughout the city. They took over the gates and posted detachments of guards to prevent anyone from leaving. Some of them sounded horns, some raised a clamor with their voices, and others caused a great commotion with the din of their arms. The townsmen were terrified because they had no idea what was going on, and they poured out of their houses and tried to flee to safety. Some concealed themselves in the hidden corners of churches, while others shut themselves away in various hiding places. Some even jumped and threw themselves down from the walls. Among them was the bishop, who had already slipped down the slope of the hill and was discovered in the vineyards by lookouts, whereupon he was brought before Charles, who had him thrown in prison. Charles also captured Queen Emma, whom he blamed for his estrangement from his brother, and put her under guard. In addition, he seized almost all of the city's remaining nobility.

17

After the violence had been quelled and order restored, Charles began to consider how to make arrangements for the defense of the city and the provisioning of the garrison. He assigned 500 armed guards to keep watch inside the city and on walls every night, and he ordered grain to be

exercerent. Annonam etiam ex toto pago Veromandensi advehi iussit. Et sic urbem ad resistendum munivit. Nam turrim, quae adhuc muris humilibus perstabat, pinnis eminentibus exstruxit, fossisque patentibus circumquaque vallavit. Machinas etiam hostibus effecit, necnon et ligna[42] advectantur machinis educendis idonea. Valli quoque exacuuntur, cratesque contexuntur. Nec minus fabri accersiuntur qui missilia fabricent ac quaeque necessaria ferro instaurent. Nec defuere qui tanta subtilitatis arte balistas emittant, ut apothecam in recta diametro duplici foramine patentem certo iactu traiciant, aves quoque in aere volantes indubitato ictu impeterent, transfixasque de sublimi praecipitarent.

18

Impetus Hugonis in Karolum

Quae dum aguntur, regum auribus delata sunt. Qui vehementissime moti, non tamen precipiti impetu, sed ut in omnibus solebant, super hoc diligentissime consultaverunt; utcumque etiam cordis dolorem dissimulabant. Legatos quaquaversum dirigunt. Gallos quos hinc Matrona, inde abluit Garunna contra tirannum invitant. Quibus in unum

brought in from all over the county of Vermandois. He also strengthened the city's defenses by fortifying the keep, which up until now had been enclosed behind low walls, with lofty battlements and surrounding it on all sides with open ditches. He had siege engines constructed for use against the enemy and brought in timbers to use in building them. Stakes were sharpened and wicker frames woven together, and craftsmen were called in who could fashion projectiles and make whatever was needed out of iron. There were also men there who could fire bolts[16] with such precision that with one cast they could send a shot straight through both ends of an open storehouse and hit birds dead-on in midflight, causing them to drop straight out of the sky.

18

Hugh's Attack on Charles

In the meantime, news of what was happening was brought to the kings. They were sorely aggrieved, but rather than acting on impulse, they deliberated carefully, as was their custom in all situations, concealing the anguish in their hearts as best they could. They sent envoys in all directions, summoning the Gauls washed by the Marne on one side and the Garonne on the other against the tyrant. When these men had assembled and the kings had mustered

coactis, cum exercitum collegissent, deliberabant an urbem
aggressi expugnarent antequam ab hostibus amplioribus copiis muniretur et expugnata tirannum confoderent, eo quod
si is solummodo captus aut occisus foret, mox sese regnum
quiete habituros, an cum benivolentia susciperent supplicem, si forte is se supplicem conferret et dono regum se
posse tenere res pervasas exposceret. At qui acrioris animi
et constantioris fuere censebant fore obsidioni incomben-
dum,[43] hostes urgendos, regionem etiam quam pervaserant
igne penitus consumendam. Collectis itaque $\overline{\text{VI}}$ equitum, in
hostem vadunt. Tempore statuto urbem appetunt. Obsidio-
nem disponunt. Castrisque loca metati, fossis et aggeribus
vallant.

19

Ubi cum diebus multis resederint, nihil virium, nihil dam-
nationis in hostes exerere valuerunt. Tanta eminentia[44] et
laterum obiectione urbs inexpugnabilis erat. Dies etiam au-
tumnales breviore circulo ducti, his exercitiis non sufficie-
bant. Noctes quoque prolixae multo sui tempore vigiles affi-

their army, they considered how they should proceed. On the one hand, they could move to assault Laon before the enemy could fortify it with reinforcements and then put the tyrant to the sword after the city fell, since all it would take was for him to be captured or killed, and the kingdom would be pacified in short order. On the other hand, they could receive him with kindness as a suppliant, if by chance he should humbly submit himself to their authority and ask to retain control over the territory he had usurped by virtue of a royal grant. Those who were of a more aggressive and determined frame of mind advised them to move ahead with the siege, hem their enemies in, and put all of the territory that Charles had captured to the torch. In the end they assembled a force of six thousand knights and moved against their foes. At a fixed time they advanced to Laon. They invested the city, and after establishing a camp, they fortified their position with mounds and ditches.

19

They remained encamped there for many days, but they were unable to exert any pressure or inflict any damage on the enemy, because the great height and sheer slopes of the city rendered it virtually impregnable. Moreover, as the autumn days grew shorter, there was no longer enough daylight for them to carry out the necessary operations, and the extended nights were tiring out the watchmen through their

ciebant. Unde cum primatibus consilio habito, redeunt, post vernali tempore redituri. Quibus abductis, Karolus urbem circumquaque perambulat. Sicubi etiam hostibus facilis locus patet, explorat. Obstruit itaque portas hostium ingressui faciles. Obturat postica post domos latentia. Restaurat muros vetustate lapsos. Turrim quoque potioribus edificiis intra et extra dilatat ac firmat.

20

Profugium episcopi

In quam episcopus detrusus, cum in conclavi teneretur, funibus per fenestram demissus, tempore nocturno equo vectus aufugit. Et ut se Karolo non favisse monstraret, ad regem[45] sese contulit et a tanta suspitione purgavit. Arbitrabatur enim quasdam coniecturas posse a calumniatoribus confingi, acsi ipse capiendi oportunitatem parasset. Qui susceptus a rege, utpote fidelitatis exsecutor, non minore gratia habitus est.

long duration. And so, after taking counsel with their chief men, the kings decided to withdraw and return later, during the springtime. When they had departed, Charles walked all around the city looking for any place that might provide an easy point of access for the enemy. He barricaded the gates that were vulnerable to enemy attacks and blocked up the smaller postern gates that lay exposed behind houses. He rebuilt walls that had collapsed from old age and expanded and strengthened the keep inside and out with improved structures.

20

The Bishop's Escape

It was here that Adalbero had been imprisoned. Although he was being held under lock and key, he managed to let himself down from the window with ropes and flee on horseback during the night. To prove that he was not in league with Charles, he went before the king and defended himself against this very serious suspicion. For he was concerned that slanderers might have fabricated false allegations against him, to the effect that he himself had arranged for the capture of the city. But he was received by the king as a loyal follower and treated with no less favor than before.

21

Interea rigore hiemali elapso, cum aere mitiori[46] ver rebus arrideret et prata atque campos virescere faceret, reges exercitu collecto urbem predictam cum $\overline{VIII}$ aggressi sunt. Castra inprimis aggere et fossa muniunt.

22

Compositio arietis

Inde exstruitur aries, muris frangendis obnisurus. Cuius machinam ex quatuor mirae grossitudinis et longitudinis trabibus longilatero scemate erexerunt, in cacumine et basi per quatuor latera repagulis transverse annexis. In medio vero solummodo levum latus et dextrum ligna transmissa habuere. At super trabium erectarum superiores commissuras longurios duos straverunt inmotosque effecerunt, partem tertiam superioris spatii trabium in medio obtinentes. A quibus longuriis funes implicitos deposuerunt. Funibus quoque trabem cum ferrato capite multae grossitudinis suspenderunt. Cui etiam trabi in medio et extremo funes alli-

21

In the meantime, when the winter frost had melted and spring with its milder weather was smiling upon the world and bringing life back to the meadows and fields, the kings assembled their army and mounted an attack on Laon with eight thousand men. Their first order of business was to fortify their camp with a mound and a ditch. 988

22

The Construction of a Battering Ram

After this a battering ram was built to try to break down the walls. The frame was constructed out of four beams of great thickness and length, laid out in the shape of a rectangle, joined together at both the bottom and the top with crossbeams on all four sides. In the middle they only extended horizontal beams through the right and left sides. On top of the upper joints that connected the vertical beams they laid down and firmly secured two long poles, which were each positioned a third of the way toward the middle. They fastened ropes to the top of the poles, which hung down and supported a beam with a very thick iron-plated head. They also tied ropes around the middle and the ends

gatos adhibuerunt,[47] qui a multitudine tracti et remissi, ferratae moli motum darent. Unde et huiusmodi machina, quia more arietis retro tracta[48] ante cum impetu ruit, aries appellatur, cuiuscumque soliditatis muris frangendis aptissimus. Quam etiam machinam super tres rotas triangulo scemate positam aptaverunt, quo facilius obliquata, quocumque oporteret verti valeret. At quia urbis situs accedere prohibuit, eo quod ipsa urbs in eminenti montis cacumine eminet,[49] aries fabricatus cessit.

23

Digressio Hugonis cum exercitu a Lauduno

Post haec cum per dies plurimos in obsidione urbis vigiliis et curis pugnisque frequentibus laboravissent, die quadam,[50] custodibus castrorum vino somnoque aggravatis,[51] urbani vino exhilarati cum armis ad castra pedestres venerunt. Equites vero consequenter armati subsecuti sunt, rei eventum prestolantes, ut si pugnae locus adesset prosperaque fortuna felicem annueret[52] eventum, cum hoste comminus

of this beam, which a large number of men could haul back and then release, setting the iron-plated weight in motion. Because it rears back and springs forward rapidly with considerable force, this type of siege engine is called a ram, and it is ideally suited for breaking down walls, no matter how strong they are. They fitted it out on three wheels arranged in a triangular shape so that it could be more easily turned to face in any direction. But the position of the city, which sits atop the summit of a lofty hill, made it impossible for them to get close to the walls, and for this reason the ram that they had built had to be withdrawn.

23

The Departure of Hugh and His Army from Laon

The siege continued for many days after this, and Hugh's army suffered under the strain of sleepless nights, burdensome duties, and frequent skirmishes. One day, when the camp guards were weighed down with wine and sleep,[17] some of the townsmen, emboldened by drink, armed themselves and made their way to the camp on foot. Armed knights subsequently followed after them, waiting to see what happened and intending to engage the enemy if the opportunity for battle presented itself and good fortune

confligerent. Cum ergo pedites iam castris propinquassent custodesque consopitos intellexissent, faces castris immisere. Quorum incendii fumo aer densatus, non solum intuentium visibus tetra nigredine obstabat, at gravi vapore narium et faucium meatus intercludebat. Pedites mox vociferari, clangere milites cepere. Rex et qui cum eo erant, elementorum confusione multoque virorum clamore et tubarum clangore turbati, ab urbe sedes mutavere. Nam castra cum cibis et rebus omnibus absumpta videbat.[53] Unde et[54] exercitum ad tempus reducere disposuit, ut reditum amplioribus copiis post appararet. Quae omnia Augusti tempore patrata sunt.

24

Obitus Adalberonis metropolitani

His ita gestis, non multo post metropolitanus in egritudinem decidens quae a Grecis causon, a Latinis incendium dicitur, per legatos regi tunc Parisii commoranti indicavit sese in gravem valitudinem decidisse; unde et ei maturandum, ne Karolus qui cetera[55] Remos etiam pervaderet. Rex, accitis qui aderant, mox ire disposuit. Quo in itinere aliquantisper tardante, cum metropolitanus insomnietate si-

granted a successful outcome. When the foot soldiers came closer and saw that the guards were fast asleep, they threw torches into the camp. Smoke from the resulting fire filled the air, not only obstructing the vision of those who tried to see through the foul blackness, but choking their nostrils and throats with its thick fumes. Thereupon the foot soldiers began to cry out and the knights to sound horns. Thrown into confusion by the intermingling of the elements, the frequent cries of men, and the noise of horns, the king and his retinue abandoned their position and left the city. For he could see that their camp had been ransacked along with their food and all their other supplies. For this reason he decided to withdraw temporarily so that he could make preparations to return later with more troops. All of this took place in the month of August.[18]

24

The Death of Archbishop Adalbero

Not long after this the archbishop fell ill with the sickness that the Greeks call *causos* and the Latins *incendium*.[19] He sent envoys to the king, who was then at Paris, informing him that he was gravely ill and urging him to move quickly to prevent Charles from capturing Reims, as he had other places. The king summoned such men as were with him and made arrangements to leave immediately. While he

989

mulque et mentis alienatione nimium vexaretur, nullaque crisi omnes dies creticos huic egritudini commodos preteriret, dissolutis elementis debitum humanitatis X Kal. Febr. exsolvit. Qua die rex tempestivus adveniens,[56] urbe receptus est. In exsequiis etiam pontificis plurima[57] commiseratione condoluit, nec vero sine lacrimis aliquot de eo querimonias habuit. Corpus quoque multo honore sepulturae dedit. Cives domino destitutos mira benivolentia solatus est. Qui de fidelitate regi servanda et urbe tuenda interrogati, fidem iurant, urbis tuitionem pollicentur. Quibus sacramento astrictis, eisque libertate eligendi domini quem vellent ab rege concessa, rex ab eis dimotus Parisium devenit.

25

Quomodo Arnulfus episcopatum[58] petiit

Ubi cum de liberalitate et fide civium Remensium laetus moraretur, Arnulfus Lotharii filius per quosdam[59] regis stipatores ab rege episcopatum expetebat, Karolum quoque

was briefly delayed en route, the archbishop began to suffer
from both insomnia and dementia, and after he had gone
through all of the critical days common to this illness without any break in the fever, he died and paid the debt of his
humanity on the twenty-third of January. The king arrived
just in time that very same day and was welcomed into the
city. During the archbishop's funeral he grieved sorrowfully
and gave way to tearful lamentations. He saw to it that the
body was buried with great ceremony, and he consoled the
townsmen, who were now bereft of their lord, with remarkable sympathy. When they were asked about preserving
their loyalty to the king and protecting the city, they swore
fealty to him and promised that they would keep the city secure. After they had bound themselves to him with an oath,
the king granted them the right to elect their lord freely,
whereupon he departed and returned to Paris.

25

How Arnulf Sought the Bishopric
for Himself

While he was staying there, heartened by the generosity
and loyalty of the townsmen of Reims, Arnulf,[20] the son
of Lothar, approached several members of the king's court
to petition for the bishopric of Reims. He gave notice that
he would abandon his uncle Charles, and he pledged fe-

patruum sese deserturum mandat, fidem spondet; regisque iniuriam ulturum, contra hostes etiam regis plurima nisurum; urbem Laudunum ab hostibus pervasam in brevi redditurum. Regii stipatores letati, episcopatum petenti quam cito dari suadent, regi nil perditurum asserentes, si sibi militaturo et fidem servaturo quod petit largiatur. Multo etiam sibi profuturum, si id faciat, quod cum factum sit, omnium salutem affectet. Rex eorum suasionibus adquiescens, Remos devenit, civibus hanc petitionem ostensurus, ne malefidae sponsionis teneretur obnoxius.

26

Oratio regis[60] ad cives Remenses

Et omnibus accersitis, sic locutus ait: 'Quoniam fidei exsecutores vos probavi, nec me a fide alienum experiemini. Cum enim sit fides cum quod dicitur fit, quia vos id fecisse perspitio, et me penitus observasse idem fateor. Arnulfus, dignae[61] memoriae Lotharii ex concubina filius, huius sedis

alty to the king, declaring that he would requite the injury done to him, exert himself to the utmost against his foes, and quickly restore to him the city of Laon, which had fallen into the hands of his enemies. The king's counselors were delighted, and they urged the king to grant the bishopric to Arnulf as soon as possible. They declared that he would lose nothing by granting the request of a man who would serve him as a loyal vassal. On the contrary, this decision would be very much to his advantage, since it promised to bring safety and security to everyone. The king yielded to their efforts to persuade him and went to Reims to present this request to the townsmen, so as not to be judged guilty of breaking his promise to them.

26

The King's Speech to the Townsmen of Reims

After summoning all of the townsmen, he addressed them as follows: "Since I have found you to be faithful to your word, you will not find me a stranger to mine. Trust is established when words are matched by deeds, and because I can see that you have acted in accordance with this principle, I declare to you that I have done exactly the same. Arnulf, the son of Lothar of worthy memory by a concubine,

dignitatem per aliquos[62] qui mihi assistunt expetiit, quicquid nobis nuper derogatum est se restituturum pollicitus,
necnon et contra hostes multa moliturum. Cuius promissio-
nes et fidem ad vestrum contuli examinanda iuditium, ut aut
vestro approbetur examine aut improbetur. Ille petitionibus
instat. Potestatis vestrae sit utrum quod petit accipiat. Nec
vero in quoquam ei a me fautum est. Nihil etiam deliberatum. Quicquid id foret, utile duxi ad vestram deferri debere
censuram, ut si honestum fiat, vobis utilitatem et mihi gloriam comparet; si autem pernitiosum, ego quidem nullius
perfidiae, nullius doli, nullius fallatiae penitus arguar. Vos
vero aut suffecti[63] doli falsam opinionem cum doloso subibitis, aut si non, in desertorem manus assidue exseretis.'

has approached some of my advisers to ask me for the episcopal see of Reims, promising to restore whatever was recently removed from my possession, and to take forceful action against my enemies. I have decided to submit his promises and his profession of loyalty to your judgment, so that you may determine whether they ought to be believed or not. He is insistent in his requests, but it is in your power to decide whether he should be granted that which he asks for. He has not yet received my support in any way, nor has anything been decided. However it turns out, I thought it best for the decision to be entrusted to you, so that if your choice turns out to be an honorable one, it may bring advantages to you and glory to me, whereas if it proves disastrous, then at least there is no way that I can be accused of faithlessness, treachery, or deception. You, on the other hand, will either have to endure with the deceiver the unwarranted reputation of being complicit in the treachery that has been perpetrated, or else you will be constantly up in arms against the traitor."

27

Responsio civium ad regem

Ad haec cives: 'Cum,' inquiunt, 'vestrae maiestatis dono eligendi domini optio nobis data sit, multa fide, multo ingenio enitendum est[64] ut et regiae dignitatis derogatio nulla fiat, et nos falsae criminationis notam casumque futuri incommodi vitemus. Arnulfus, quem paulo ante memoratum audivimus, a nobis nuper idem expoposcit, plurima fide, si hoc fiat, regis commoda sese exsecuturum pollicens, erga cives non modicam benivolentiam habiturum. Sed quia eius utpote adolescentis mores affectusque incertos habemus, nostras solummodo rationes non sufficere ad haec arbitramur. Adsint ergo qui vobis id suadent. Conferamus[65] utrimque rationes. Dicat quid quisque potius cogitet; quid potissimum ne abscondat, ut et ex honesto gloria sit communis, et ex pernitie incommodum aeque patiamur.'

27

The Response of the Townsmen to the King

This was the response of the townsmen: "Because your majesty has given us the freedom to choose our lord, we must strive faithfully and conscientiously to make sure that nothing detracts from the royal dignity, and to avoid both the opprobrium of a false accusation and the possibility of future misfortunes. Arnulf, whom you just mentioned, recently came to ask the same thing of us, assuring us that if his request were granted, he would faithfully pursue the interests of the king and show great generosity toward the townsmen. But because he is a young man and we cannot be certain of his character and intentions, our own judgment does not seem sufficient to us. Hence, it is our opinion that those who are urging Arnulf's candidacy upon you should come here so that we may compare the arguments on both sides. Let each person say what he thinks best, and let no one keep his opinion hidden. In that way we will all partake of the glory of an honorable decision, and we will share the misfortune equally if the end result proves to be disastrous."

28

Promotio Arnulfi

Rex civium sententiam approbat; ut coram deliberent iubet. Rationes coram dispositae sunt. Arnulfum itaque, si quod spondet faciat, dignum summo sacerdotio asserunt. Itaque vocatus et ante regem admissus est. Qui de fide habenda erga regem sciscitatus, ad omnium vota modestissime respondit. Ad coenobium ergo monachorum[66] sancti Remigii, quod ab urbe uno miliario situm est, ubi ordinatio episcoporum ex antiquo habenda est, a rege et primatibus deductus est. Ubi rex cum suorum medius resideret, post consilia apud suos secessim habita, liberali eloquio sic affatus est: 'Dignae[67] memoriae Ludovico, Lotharii filio, orbi subtracto, si proles superfuisset, eam sibi successisse dignum foret. Quia vero regiae generationi successio nulla est, idque omnibus ita fore patet, vestri caeterorumque principum, eorum etiam qui in militari ordine potiores erant, optione assumptus premineo. Nunc vero quoniam ex linea regali hic unde sermo est solus superfuit, ne tanti patris nomen adhuc oblivione fuscetur, hunc superstitem alicuius dignitatis honore expoposcistis donari. Si ergo fidei servandae ius

28

The Ordination of Arnulf

The king approved of the townsmen's proposal and ordered that the issue be debated publicly. After arguments had been presented on both sides, they declared Arnulf worthy of the office of archbishop so long as he remained true to his promises. He was then summoned and brought before the king. When he was asked whether he would remain loyal to the king, he responded very humbly and to the satisfaction of everyone there. He was then escorted by the king and the magnates to the monastery of Saint-Rémi, which is located a mile from the city of Reims, where since ancient times the ordination of the archbishop has been meant to take place. The king took his seat in the midst of his men, and after conferring with them in private for a short time, he spoke with noble eloquence: "If Louis of divine memory, the son of Lothar, had left behind a son when he died, then it would have been proper for him to succeed his father as king. But because there is no successor to the royal line, and it is obvious to everyone that this is the case, I was elevated to the throne by you and the other magnates, and by the most important members of the knightly order. Because this man who is the subject of our discussions is the sole surviving member of the royal line, you have asked that he be granted some title of honor so that the name of his distinguished father might not be blackened by

polliceatur, urbis tuitionem spondeat, hostibus etiam in nullo sese communicaturum, immo illos impetiturum promittat, vestri iuditii censura concedere ei episcopatum non pigebit, ita tamen ut secundum prudentium ordinationem sacramenti auctoritate mihi conexus sit.'

29

Cirographi scriptum

'Et ut penitus mentis conceptum aperiam, post iurationis sacramentum, cirographum ab eo scribendum puto. In quo maledictionis anathema habeatur huiusmodi, quod ei imprecetur pro felicibus contumeliosa, pro salutaribus pernitiosa, pro honestis turpia, pro diuturnitate punctum, pro honore contemptum, et ut totum concludatur, pro omnibus bonis omnia mala. Quod etiam bipertitum fieri placet; alterum mihi, sibi alterum concedatur. Quandoque etiam hoc illi calumnias ingeret, si turpiter a fide declinet.' Hac promulgata sententia, id ita faciendum ab omnibus laudatum est. Procedit itaque Arnulfus coram. Si id inventum laudet

oblivion. If, then, he swears an oath to preserve his loyalty, if he pledges to protect the city, if he promises to have no communication with my enemies, but rather to take up arms against them, then I will not hesitate to yield to your judgment and grant him the bishopric, provided that, according to the practice of wise men, he is bound to me by the sanction of an oath."

29

A Chirograph[21] Is Drawn Up

"To clarify more fully what I have in mind, I think that after swearing this oath he should draw up a chirograph containing an anathema of malediction that calls down upon him humiliation instead of happiness, ruin instead of prosperity, disgrace instead of good repute, a short span of life instead of longevity, contempt instead of honor, and to sum up, every type of misfortune in place of every good thing. It should be divided into two parts, one of which will be given to him, and the other to me, so that this document will heap up opprobrium against him should he ever prove so dishonorable as to deviate from his word." When he had stated his opinion, everyone agreed that they should proceed as he had suggested. Arnulf then came forward. He was asked if he approved of this idea and if he would accept the office

consulitur. An sic suscipiat quod petit sciscitatur. Ille honoris cupidus, inventum laudat. Sese sic posse suscipere asse-
verat. Iussus itaque cirographum bipertitum notavit. Regi
alterum, alterum sibi servavit.

30

Eukaristia causa
perditionis data

Quod cum regi penitus sufficeret, episcopis tamen, ut
fertur, non satis id visum est nisi illud etiam adderetur, ut
in missarum celebratione eukaristiam a sacerdote sumeret,
eamque perditionis causam sibi imprecando coram optaret
si fidem violando umquam desertor fieret. Quod et factum
fuit. Nam sacerdos inter celebrandum eukaristiam optulit,
et ille consequenter sumpsit atque ad iuditium sibi fieri op-
tavit, si ullo modo fidei violator existeret. Quod tandem regi
et primatibus fidem fecit.

that he sought on these terms. In his desire for the bishopric, he agreed to the proposal and declared that he could accept it on these terms. He was then required to sign a chirograph that was divided into two parts. The king kept one half and he kept the other for himself.

30

The Eucharist Is Administered to Confirm the Threat of Damnation

While this was sufficient for the king, the bishops reportedly would not be satisfied unless an additional provision was made that during the celebration of the mass Arnulf would receive the Eucharist from a priest and publicly pronounce a curse against himself, asking that he suffer damnation if he ever violated his oath and proved a traitor to his word. And this, too, was done. The priest offered him the Eucharist during the mass, and Arnulf took it from him, asking that it be used as a judgment against him if he ever violated his oath in any way. This finally won him the trust of both the king and the magnates.

31

Reprehensio de eadem[68]

Nonnullis tamen quorum mens purgatior erat nefarium et contra fidei ius id creditum est. Eiusmodi enim naturae hominem esse aiebant, ut facile per sese corrumpatur in se, amplius vero impulsionibus ad flagitium extrinsecus posse pertrahi. Asserebant quoque ex decretis patrum et canonum scriptis neque invitum ad eucaristiam impellendum, neque eucaristiam perditionis causa cuiquam offerendam, cum redemptionis gratia et petentibus offerendam et invitis negandam credendum sit. Indignum etiam videri[69] panem angelorum et hominum temere indignis dari, cum ipsa divinitas et immundos abhorreat et puros mira parcitate foveat, iuxta quod scriptum est: 'Spiritus sanctus disciplinae effugiet fictum, et auferet se a cogitationibus quae sunt sine intellectu, et corripietur a superveniente iniquitate.'

31

Criticism of the Aforementioned Procedure

Nonetheless, there were some men of purer intention who considered this procedure wicked and contrary to the tenets of the faith.[22] Man, they said, was naturally inclined to be corrupted within if left to his own devices; he was even more likely to be drawn to sin when incited by others. They also declared that according to the decrees of the fathers and the text of the canons no one should be compelled to receive the Eucharist against his will. Nor could the Eucharist be administered to anyone for the purpose of damnation, for it was an article of faith that the Eucharist was to be given for the sake of redemption to those who asked for it, and that it was to be denied to those who were unwilling to receive it. It seemed improper for the bread of men and angels rashly to be given to the unworthy, since God himself abhors the unclean and cherishes the pure with marvelous discrimination, according to the scripture: "The Holy Spirit of discipline will flee from the deceitful, and will withdraw himself from thoughts that are without understanding, and he shall not abide when iniquity cometh in."[23]

32

Quod amplius iusto Karolum
Arnulfus dilexerit

Ab episcopis ergo Remorum dioceseos ordinatus Arnulfus et sacerdotalibus infulis decenter insignitus est. Nec multopost a papa Romano missum apostolicae auctoritatis pallium sumpsit. Qui cum ex tanta[70] dignitate procederet insignis, illud tamen infortunii genus arbitrabatur, quod ipse superstes de patrio genere nullum preter Karolum[71] habebat. Miserrimum quoque sibi videri, si is[72] honore frustraretur, in quo solo spes restituendi genus paternum sita foret. Patruo itaque miserescebat, illum cogitabat, illum colebat, illum pro parentibus carissimum habebat. Apud quem collato consilio, querebat quonam modo in culmen honoris illum provehere posset, sic tamen ut ipse regis desertor non appareret.

32

How Arnulf Loved Charles
More Than Was Proper

Arnulf was thus ordained by the bishops of the province of Reims and duly adorned with the insignia of episcopal office. Not long after this he took up the pallium of apostolic authority that had been sent from Rome by the pope.[24] Although he had now advanced to a position of prominence by virtue of the prestigious office that he occupied, he nonetheless regarded it as a stroke of misfortune that he had no one left to him out of his father's family except for Charles. He thought it deplorable that Charles should be deprived of honor, when he remained the only hope for the restoration of his father's line. Arnulf pitied his uncle, thought about him, treated him with affection, and cherished him as his dearest relative in place of his own parents. And after entering into deliberations with Charles, he sought to find a way to advance him to the height of power without seeming to be a traitor to the king.

33

Remorum captio

Cuius rei rationem sic fieri arbitrabatur, ut statueretur tempus quo primates quot posset in urbe, acsi aliquid magnum ordinaturus, ipse colligeret. Tunc etiam Karolus per noctis silentia cum exercitu ad portas urbis adventaret.[73] Nec tunc deesset qui exercitui irruenti[74] portas panderet, iuratus secreti fidem.[75] Exercitus intromissus urbem invaderet atque sese cum primatibus collectis comprehenderet, vim inferret, ac ergastulo[76] detruderet. Itaque factum foret ut et regia potestas infirmaretur, et patruo virtus dominandi augesceret, nec ipse desertor videretur. Quod et effectum habuit.

34

G. et V. comites atque alios viros claros[77] invitat. Quiddam magnum sese ordinaturum mandat, unde et multum eis maturandum. Illi sine dilatione advenere, in obsequio do-

33

The Capture of Reims

He decided that the way to accomplish this was to set a
time when he would bring as many of the magnates as possible into the city, under the pretext that he was planning
something important. Meanwhile, Charles and his troops
would come to the gates of the city in the dead of night, at
which time an accomplice sworn to secrecy would open the
gates to the invading army. Once Charles's men were inside
the walls, they would seize control of the city, take Arnulf
and the rest of the magnates captive by main force, and put
them in prison. In this way the king's power would be weak-
ened and his uncle's authority increased, while he himself
would not be revealed as a traitor. And this is indeed what
came to pass.

34

Arnulf summoned Counts Gislebert and Wido[25] and several other men of rank, sending word to them that they
should come quickly because he was planning something of
importance. They came to him without delay and showed
themselves ready to serve their lord in any way that they

mini paratissimos se demonstrantes. Arnulfus alia pro aliis dans, quod vere molitur penitus dissimulat. Ad quid potius intendat, omnes ignorant. Uni tantum, de cuius taciturnitate et fide non diffidebat, id totum credulus commisit. Qua nocte Karolus[78] intromittendus[79] esset aperuit, et ut tunc portarum claves a suo cervicali tolleret urbemque armatis aperiret iussit. Nec multopost nox cui hoc debebatur flagitium affuit. Karolus cum exercitu tempore deputato ad portas urbis nocturnus affuit. Algerus presbiter (sic enim vocabatur) introrsum cum clavibus se presentem habuit. A quo mox portae patefactae sunt, exercitusque intromissus. Urbs quoque a predonibus direpta et spoliata.

35

Arnulfi suorumque captio

Unde cum clamor per urbem fieret, tumultusque discurrentium cives incautos excitaret, Arnulfus aeque turbatum clamore sese simulat. Et fingens metum, turrim petiit atque conscendit. Quem comites[80] secuti, post se ostia observavere. Karolus Arnulfum perquirens nec reperiens, ubinam lateret

could. Arnulf completely deceived them about the nature of their mission, keeping his true intentions hidden, so that no one had any idea what he was actually planning. He put the entire plan in the hands of a single individual whose discretion and loyalty he trusted, revealing to him the night on which Charles was to be admitted into the city, and instructing him to take the keys from his pillow at that time and open the gates of the city to Charles's troops. Not long after came the night on which this shameful act was due to take place. Charles arrived at the gates of the city with his army at the appointed hour of night. The priest Alger[26] (for that was his name) was waiting inside with the keys. He immediately opened the gates to Charles's army, whereupon the city was plundered and despoiled by those robbers.

35

The Capture of Arnulf and His Men

As noise spread throughout the city and the commotion of men running to and fro awoke the unsuspecting townsmen, Arnulf pretended to be just as disturbed as they were by the uproar. Acting as though he were afraid, he hurried to the tower and climbed to the top. The counts followed after him and barred the doors behind them. Charles, meanwhile, was looking for Arnulf everywhere, but could not find him,

scrutabatur. Cui cum proderetur in turris cacumine latere, ostio mox custodes adhibuit. Et quoniam nec cibum nec arma ante congesserant, Karolo cedunt atque a turri egressi sunt.

36

Comprehensique et Laudunum ducti, custodibus deputati sunt. Karolo redeunte et fidem ab eis querente, unanimiter[81] refragantur. Odium ergo utrimque simulant; pium affectum nullomodo produnt. Ab utroque querimonia nonnulla simulabatur, eo quod alter desertor, alter invasor alterius ab utroque enuntiaretur.[82] Tandem Arnulfus[83] sacramento fidem faciens, libertate potitus est et ad sua reversus. Karolo exinde in omnibus favit. Ius quoque fidei regi servandum penitus abrupit. G. et V. per dies aliquot carcere detrusi, non multopost sacramento astricti, redire permissi sunt. Karolus ergo, felici successu insignis, Remorum metro-

and he was investigating where he could possibly be hiding. When someone told him that Arnulf was holed up at the top of the tower, he immediately sent guards to bar the door. Since the men who had taken refuge there had stockpiled neither food nor arms, they surrendered to Charles and came down out of the tower.

36

They were subsequently taken prisoner and brought to Laon, where they were put under guard. When Charles returned from Reims, he asked them to swear an oath of fealty to him, but they all refused to do so. Charles and Arnulf both feigned animosity toward one another, keeping their true feelings of mutual devotion completely hidden. Each made a show of complaining about the other, calling his opponent a traitor or a usurper. Eventually, after swearing an 990 oath of fealty to Charles, Arnulf was set free and returned home. Thereafter he supported Charles in all that he did and completely violated the oath of fealty that he had sworn to the king. Gislebert and Wido were thrown into prison for a few days, but after being bound by an oath, they were permitted to leave. Charles had now distinguished himself with

polim cum Lauduno ac Suesionis earumque oppidis optinuit.

37

Impetus Hugonis

Nec defuit qui id ad regis[84] aures perferrent.[85] Qua rex
contumelia perstrictus, quid inde agendum foret sciscitabatur. Comperitque non precibus, non donis, sed viribus et armis, invocata divinitate, hoc esse labefactandum. In tirannum ire disponens, $\overline{VI}$ itaque militum collegit,[86] obsidionem
ei adhibere cupiens, si copiae sibi sufficiant; et si ei felix adsit fortuna, tandiu id committere volens, donec aut armis
aut inedia hostem precipitet. Proficiscitur ergo magnanimis.
Et per terram[87] unde annonam hostes asportabant exercitum duxit. Quam etiam penitus depopulatus combussit, sic
efferatus ut nec tugurium saltem deliranti anui relinqueret.
Post animo precipiti exercitum in hostem retorquens, obsidionem adhibere nitebatur. Karolus cum ante sibi copias

remarkable success, having captured the metropolitan see of Reims, as well as Laon and Soissons, and the strongholds that belonged to them.

37

Hugh's Assault on the City

There was no dearth of informers to bring the news to the king. Stung by this humiliation, he asked what he should do in response. He was told that the enemy would not be brought to heel with entreaties and gifts, but through men and force of arms, after first invoking God's aid. The king resolved to move against the tyrant, and assembled a force of six thousand fighting men, intending to lay siege to Laon if his troops proved sufficient. If he met with good fortune, he would continue the siege until he had vanquished his foe through force of arms or starved him into submission. The king departed in high spirits and led his army through the lands that were supplying his enemies with grain. He devastated and burned the entire area with such fury that not even a humble cottage was left standing for a demented old woman. Then without warning he wheeled back upon his enemy and tried to lay siege to Laon. Charles had prepared

parasset, venienti resistere viriliter conabatur. $\overline{\text{IIII}}$ etenim pugnatorum Lauduni collegerat animoque firmaverat, ut si non impeteretur, quiesceret, et resisteret, si urgeretur.

38

Exercitus tripertito ordinatur[88]

Rex interea exercitum inducens, Karoli legionem ordinatam pugnatum videt. Exercitum ergo tripertito dividit, ne multus exercitus, mole sui gravatus, propriis viribus frustraretur. Tres itaque acies constituit, primam belli primos impetus[89] inituram; secundam quae labenti succurreret viresque referret; tertiam vero spoliis eripiendis ordinavit. Quibus sic divisis et ordinatis, prima acies signis erectis congressura cum rege incedebat. Reliquae duae locis constitutis paratae succurrere opperiebantur.

his forces well in advance and strove manfully to repulse the attackers. He had assembled four thousand fighting men at Laon, having resolved to take no action if he was not attacked, but to fight back if he was threatened.

38

The Division of Hugh's Army into Three Parts

As the king brought his army forward, he saw Charles's troops drawn up in formation for battle. He therefore decided to divide his own army into three sections, so that his substantial force would not be encumbered by its own size and deprived of its full strength. He drew the army up into three lines of battle. The first was responsible for bearing the brunt of the initial attack, the second was tasked with coming to its assistance and reinforcing it when it faltered, and the third was given orders to seize spoils from the enemy. After the troops had been divided up and drawn up in rank, the first line raised its standards and marched forward with the king into battle. The other two lines waited in their assigned positions, ready to come to their aid.

39

Karolus cum $\overline{IIII}$ obvius procedit, summam divinitatem invocans ut ab innumeris paucos protegat, multitudini non fidendum et paucitati non diffidendum demonstret. Quem incedentem Arnulfus comitabatur, suos adhortans ut animo forti starent, ordinati et indivisi procederent, de victoria a deo nullo modo diffiderent; si viriliter invocato deo starent, cum multa gloria et fama victoriam in brevi adepturos. Processit exercitus uterque donec alter alterum in prospectu haberet, et sic uterque fixus herebat. Utrimque non mediocriter dubitatum est, cum Karolus rei militaris inopiam haberet, regem vero animus sui facinoris conscius contra ius agere[90] argueret, cum Karolum paterno honore spoliaverit, atque regni iura[91] in sese transfuderit. His uterque herens persistebat. Tandem ratione congrua a primatibus regi suggestum est aliquantisper cum exercitu standum. Si hostis adventaret, comminus congrediendum; si nullus lacessiret, cum exercitu redeundum. Nec minus a Karolo idem deliberatum fuit. Unde quia uterque constitit, uterque sibi cessit. Rex exercitum reduxit, Karolus vero Lauduni sese recepit.

39

Charles came out to meet him with four thousand men, calling upon almighty God to protect his small band of troops against their innumerable adversaries and demonstrate that no one should put his faith in numerical advantage or despair at being overmatched. Arnulf accompanied him into battle, urging his men to hold their ground courageously and advance forward without breaking rank. They should have no doubt, he told them, that they would prevail by God's hand; if they stood their ground manfully and invoked the name of God, then glory, fame, and victory would soon be theirs. The two armies advanced until they could see one another, whereupon both sides came to a halt. There was considerable hesitation on both sides, since Charles lacked a sufficient number of troops, while the king's conscience accused him of having acted unlawfully in despoiling Charles of his father's throne and seizing control of the realm. Both men were preoccupied by these thoughts and remained fixed in place. At last some of the magnates made the reasonable suggestion to the king that he should keep the army in place for a little while. If the enemy marched toward them, then they should give battle, but if they made no hostile gestures, then he should take his troops and withdraw. Charles had in fact come to the same conclusion. And so, because neither of them was willing to advance, each yielded in the face of the other. The king led his army away, while Charles withdrew to Laon.

40

Odo interea Drocarum cupidus, de Lauduni captione sese plurimum diffidere apud regem simulate quaerebatur, cum aries cesserit, militesque viribus diffiderent,[92] immo etiam urbs ipsa inaccessibili situ obnitentes contempnat. Rex merore confectus, ab Odone subsidia petit; sese vicem recompensaturum, si copias suppeditet et ad integrum urbem expugnet. Quod si inpresentiarum aliquid quod largiendum sit petat, sine dubio sese liberaliter exhibiturum. Odo Lauduni inpugnationem simulque et captionem in proximo pollicetur, si tantum a rege Drocas accipiat. Rex vincendi gloriam cupiens, petenti castrum accommodat. Palam omnibus cedit, promissionum de Lauduno credulus. Odo quoque urbem amissam in brevi sese redditurum palam omnibus spondet. Castrum ergo a rege concessum absque mora petit, castrenses sibi sacramenti iure annectens, eisque alios aliquot quorum fidei vigorem sciebat assotians; regia negotia exinde utiliter satagens. Cuius tamen voluntatis effectus nullus fuit, eo quod tempestiva[93] urbis proditio vetaret, et casus repentini[94] aliter fieri arguerent.

40

Meanwhile Count Odo, who coveted the castle of
Dreux, went before the king with feigned regret and expressed grave doubts that Laon could be captured, since the
battering ram had given way, the soldiers lacked confidence
in their strength, and the city itself defied anyone who attempted to take it by virtue of its inaccessible position. The
king was greatly disheartened and asked Odo for help,
promising to repay him if he could raise an army and recapture the city. He added that if there was anything that Odo
wanted to ask for at the present time, he could be assured
that it would be freely granted to him. Odo promised that
he would assault and capture Laon in short order if the king
would only give him Dreux in return. Eager for the glory
of the conquest, the king complied with his request and
granted him the castle, and he made the concession publicly
because he believed Odo's promises. Odo likewise pledged
before everyone there that in a short time he would restore
the captured city to the king. He then went immediately to
the castle that had been granted to him and bound the garrison to himself with an oath, adding to their number several other men whose loyalty he knew he could trust. Thereafter he busied himself productively to advance the king's
interests. His intentions came to naught, however, because
the timely betrayal of the city thwarted his efforts, and an
unforeseen turn of events produced an outcome that no one
had anticipated.

41

Subtilis machinatio Adalberonis in Karolum et Arnulfum

Ab hoc tempore Adalbero Laudunensium episcopus, qui ante a Karolo captus aufugerat, omni ingenio oportunitatem quaerebat qua versa vice et Laudunum caperet et Karolum comprehenderet. Legatos itaque huiusmodi negotii officiosissimos Arnulfo dirigens, amicitiam, fidem, suppetiarum subsidia mandat. Ei quoque utpote suo metropolitano sese velle reconciliari. Sibi etiam iniuriae esse quod transfuga et desertor diceretur, eo quod Karolo post fidem factam non obsecutus sit. Et si vacuum sibi esset, a se id dedecoris velle abicere. Ad eius celsitudinem redire velle et Karoli amicitiam utpote domini sese optare. Unde et sibi quocumque libitum foret occurrendum mandaret. Arnulfus simulatam fidem nesciens, legatos fallentes excipit et utpote boni alicuius nuntios humanissime honorat. Per hos itaque locum quo occursuri et sibi collocuturi forent letabundus designat. Illi se decepisse letati, haec domino referunt. Qui fallatiae seminarium utiliter positum considerans, alcioris machina-

41

The Subtle Machinations of Adalbero Against Charles and Arnulf

From that time forward Adalbero, the bishop of Laon, who had escaped from captivity at the hands of Charles, used all of his cunning to try to find an opportunity to get even by capturing Laon and taking Charles prisoner. To that end, he dispatched envoys ideally suited for this sort of task to Arnulf to assure him of his friendship, loyalty, and support. He also expressed the desire to be reconciled with him, inasmuch as he was his archbishop. Moreover, he said that he was aggrieved that people were calling him a traitor and a deserter because he had failed to render service to Charles after pledging fealty to him, and he wanted to rid himself of this dishonor if there was an opportunity to do so. He wished to be reconciled with his highness and to be friends with Charles, who was, after all, his lord. Accordingly, he sent word that Arnulf should come to meet him wherever it was convenient. Unaware that Adalbero's profession of loyalty was insincere, Arnulf welcomed the deceitful envoys and honored them with every courtesy, as though they were the messengers of some good man. He happily sent word of a place where he and Adalbero could meet and talk with one another. Delighted that they had succeeded in deceiving him, the envoys brought his reply back to their lord. Adalbero saw that he had effectively sowed the seeds

menti dolos prodire posse advertit. Post haec in locum statutum sibi occurrunt, amplexibus pluribus atque osculis sibi congratulantes, tantos ibi demonstrantes affectus animi ut nulla simulatio, nullus dolus videretur.

42

Adalberonis dolosa oratio[95]

At postquam satis amplexationum, osculorum satis factum est, Adalbero, penes quem simulationis color et doli onus erat, incautum sic prior alloquitur: 'Idem casus eademque fortuna ambos nos male perstringit. Unde et idem consilium eademque ratio nobis captanda videtur. Nuper enim ambo lapsi, vos ab gratia regis, ego a Karoli amicitia decidi. Unde et nunc vos Karolo, ego regi faveo. Ille vobis, iste mihi promptissime credit. Si itaque per vos Karoli amor mihi restituatur, regis gratia vobis non aberit. Quod et facto difficile non erit. Karolum igitur convenite et, pro me, si forte concesserit, orate. De fide erga eum habenda multa dicere

of deception and realized that a more loftily conceived scheme might bear fruit. They subsequently met at the appointed location, greeting one another joyfully with numerous embraces and kisses, and demonstrating such affection that there was no sign of pretense or deceit.

42

Adalbero's Deceptive Speech

When they had finished embracing and kissing one another, Adalbero, adopting a duplicitous facade and taking upon himself the task of deceit, addressed the unwary Arnulf: "The same unfortunate circumstances and the same bad luck have unfortunately affected both of us. Hence it seems to me that we should both employ the same strategy and the same plan of action. Of late we have both suffered a fall—you from the favor of the king, and I from Charles's friendship, whence it is that you are now a supporter of Charles, and I of the king. The former is quick to place his confidence in you, the latter in me. If, then, you can help me to regain Charles's affection, you shall not lack the favor of the king. This will not prove difficult to do. Go to Charles and speak to him on my behalf, if he will allow it. It will be helpful if you go on at some length about how I can be

non inutile erit. De quibus si quid ei dubium visum fuerit, post dicite probandum sacramentis. Si his episcopatus reddiderit sedem, adsint sanctorum reliquiae, paratus sum fidem facere. Si hoc satis erit et reddiderit, de regis gratia plurimum confidite. In hac lingua et manu pax sita est et dissidentia. Regem adibo. Commodum quoddam spondebo, quod non solum sibi, sed et posteris sit profuturum. Dolos Karoli proferam. Incauto nimis metropolitano preiuditium factum asseram. Et quod penitus hoc metropolitanum peniteat, nonnullis amplificationibus asseverabo. Rex suapte mihi credulus, hoc gratissimum accipiet. Et quia haec ratio utrimque agitabitur, duo commoda gignentur. Ex quibus duobus tertium elucebit. Nam cum et vobis gratia regum, et mihi Karoli reddetur, per nos consequenter aliorum utilitas comparabitur. Sed hic iam verborum finis; iam nunc dicta factis probentur.' Datisque strictim osculis, promissa polliciti ab se digressi sunt.[96]

trusted to remain loyal to him. If he appears to doubt anything that you say, tell him that at a future date he may confirm my fidelity through oaths. Tell him that if he will restore the bishopric to me on these terms, then I am ready to swear fealty to him before the relics of the saints. If this suffices and he agrees to make restitution of my see, then you can be assured of winning the king's favor. Peace and discord alike depend upon my words and my deeds. I will go to the king and promise him something advantageous that will not only benefit him, but also his descendants. I will tell him of Charles's machinations and of how he took advantage of you, his utterly unsuspecting metropolitan. I will also declare emphatically and at length that you, the archbishop, thoroughly repent of what you have done. The king trusts me implicitly and will be very glad to hear what I have to say. Because this plan involves both of us, we shall both benefit from it, and from our mutual advantage a third benefit will be clear. For when you have acquired the favor of the king, and I have won the favor of Charles, others will benefit in turn from what we have done. But this is enough talk.[27] Let words now be matched by deeds." After they had kissed one another closely and engaged to carry through with their promises, they parted from one another.

43

Arnulfus per ignorantiam Karolum patruum seducit

Arnulfus Karolum petens, Adalberonem magnificat, deceptorem nesciens; valde etiam profuturum asserit, fidemque servaturum testatur. Tandem in eo nil dubitandum seductus persuadet. Karolus nepoti favens, sese id facturum spondet, episcopatum sic redditurum non abnuit. Dum haec apud Karolum fideliter ordinabantur, Adalbero apud regem de Karolo et Arnulfo urbisque captione quaerebat. Et cum tecnas supperiores effunderet,[97] gratulatio inde spesque urbis repetendae non modica erat. Nec multopost Arnulfus Adalberoni legatos dirigit, Karoli gratiam sibi indultam liberaliter indicat atque[98] cum multa ambitione excipiendum in urbem; honorem quoque absque mora recepturum. Unde nec moras faceret, sed quantotius adveniret largitatem[99] pollicitam experturus.

43

Arnulf Unwittingly Misleads His Uncle Charles

Arnulf went to see Charles. Unaware that he had been duped by Adalbero, he heaped praise upon him, assuring Charles that he would be very useful to them and vouching for his future loyalty. And in the end, having himself been deceived, he convinced Charles that there was no reason to distrust Adalbero. Yielding to his nephew's wishes, Charles promised that he would do as he asked and restore the bishopric to Adalbero on the terms agreed. Now while Arnulf was attending to these matters with Charles as he had promised, Adalbero was busy plotting with the king about Charles and Arnulf and the capture of Laon. And when he explained the machinations described above, there was rejoicing and high hopes that the city would be retaken. Not long after this Arnulf sent messengers to Adalbero to tell him that Charles had generously bestowed his favor upon him, and that he was to be welcomed into the city with a great show of honor, after which he would immediately be restored to office. Hence, Adalbero should not delay, but come as quickly as possible to avail himself of the largesse that had been promised him.

44

Adalbero Karolum et Arnulfum
sacramento decipit

Adalbero sine dilatione in loco constituto Karolo et Arnulfo accitus occurrit. A quibus benigniter exceptus, non
mediocrem letitiam repperit. Si quid discordiae precessit,
levi et raro sermone tactum preteriere. Ius amicitiae inter
sese exinde amplius colendum diversis rationibus extulere.
Quanta etiam commoditas sit profutura si amicitia bene usi
sint, sepenumero retulere; quanta quoque gloria, quantus
honor, quantum presidium. Necnon et illud libatum est, in
brevi fieri posse et suae partis provectionem, et hostium pre-
cipitationem. Nihilque his[100] obstare posse, si sola divinitas
non impediat. Si vota sua effectus consequatur, quandoque
futurum ut per sese res publica multo honore, multa gloria
cumuletur et floreat. His dictis, sacramento sibi annexi sunt
atque a se digressi. Adalbero regi se contulit,[101] quae aegerat
explicans.[102] Quibus rex auditis, negotium approbat. Arnulfum sese recepturum si veniat pollicetur, eius purgationem
de obiectis se sponte auditurum. Et si recte purgetur, non

44

Adalbero Deceives Charles and Arnulf with an Oath

Adalbero responded to this summons by going at once to meet Charles and Arnulf in the location that they had designated. He received a warm reception and found them in high spirits. Whatever discord had previously existed between them was touched on briefly and fleetingly and then set aside. They articulated the various reasons why they should devote themselves to the mutual obligations of their friendship from that time forward, and they made frequent mention of the benefits that they would enjoy if they properly exploited their friendship, as well as the glory, honor, and mutual protection that would be afforded to them. They also touched on the potential for the swift triumph of their own party and the downfall of their enemies. Nothing could oppose them as long as God did not stand in their way. If their wishes came to fruition, then one day they would see the realm prosper, exalted with honor and glory, thanks to their efforts. When their discussions were over, they bound themselves to one another with oaths and departed. Adalbero went before the king to explain what he had done. After listening to his account, the king approved of his actions. He promised to receive Arnulf if he came to see him, to listen willingly to his attempt to vindicate himself, and to treat him with no less favor than before if he were lawfully exon-

minori gratia quam ante habendum. Adalbero haec Arnulfo refert; regem benivolum, clementem sibi asserit; eum etiam eius purgationem sponte audire velle suique gratiam sine mora reddere. Unde et ei esse maturandum et quantotius id petendum. Otius ergo regem adeundum, ne aliquorum dolus consilium abrumpat.

45

Arnulfus ad regem se contulit et gratiam ab eo accepit

Ad regem itaque ambo profecti sunt. Arnulfus admissus regi, ab eo osculum accepit. Et cum de obiectis aliquam purgationi operam dare vellet, rex sibi sufficere dixit ut a preteritis quiesceret et exinde sibi fidem inviolabiliter servaret. Sese penitus non ignorare Karolum ei vim intulisse, et summa id necessitudine factum, ut ad tempus a se discederet et Karolo etiam nolens faveret. Sed quia id factum erat quod labefactari non poterat, multa ratione ei esse videndum ut amissae urbis dampnum aliquo modo suppleret. Si

erated. Adalbero brought this news back to Arnulf. He declared that the king was benevolent and merciful, and that he was willing to listen to his defense and restore him to favor at once. Hence, he should hurry to make his appeal as soon as possible. It was important that he go to the king soon, lest anyone's schemes alter his resolve.

45

Arnulf Goes before the King and Is Received Back into His Favor

And so both men went before the king. When Arnulf was admitted into his presence, he was received with a kiss. Although he wanted to make an effort to clear himself of the charges against him, the king declared that it would be sufficient for him to refrain from his previous activities and preserve his fidelity toward him inviolate from that day forward. He was well aware, he said, that Charles had used force against him, and that it was only through the most urgent necessity that he had been compelled even against his will to abandon him temporarily and support Charles. But because what had been done could not be undone, it was now incumbent upon him to find some way to make restitution for the loss of Laon. If it were not possible for the king to hold the city as he had previously, then Arnulf should at

urbem habere ut ante non posset, saltem Karolum ad se transire faceret, ut se consentiente quod pervaserat teneret. Haec et ampliora Arnulfus sese facturum pollicetur, tantum ut regis gratia sibi reddatur et ipse apud eum ut metropolitanus honoretur. Rex gratiam indulsit et ut plurimum coram se honorem haberet concessit. Unde et factum est ut in prandio die eadem regi dexter, Adalbero reginae levus resideret. His ita sese habentibus, Arnulfus ab rege dimotus est. Miram regis benivolentiam Karolo indicavit; quanto quoque honore apud eum habitus sit explicans, de eius gratia plurimum gloriabatur. A quo tempore regis et Karoli reconciliationem atque favorem quaerebat.

46

Exceptio Adalberonis a Karolo

Quae dum sic sese haberent, Adalbero a rege digressus est, Karolumque petens, Lauduni multa ambitione exceptus est. Ad se sui redeunt, qui ante ab urbe exulaverant. Rem familiarem ut ante disponunt, in nullo dubitantes, et pacem postmodum sperantes. Clerum quem amiserat revisit, eique

least convince Charles to be reconciled with him, so that he would hold what he had usurped with the agreement of the king. Arnulf promised that he would do this and more, if only he were restored to the king's favor and accorded the honor due to him as archbishop. The king in turn granted him his favor and allowed that he would possess full honors before him. Thus it happened that on that very same day Arnulf took his seat at the right hand of the king during the midday meal, while Adalbero sat to the queen's[28] left. Afterward the archbishop took leave of the king and brought word to Charles of the king's remarkable goodwill, describing the honor with which he had been treated at his court and boasting of the favor that he enjoyed. From that time forward Arnulf sought to reconcile Charles and the king and to remain in their good graces.

46

Adalbero Is Received by Charles

Meanwhile Adalbero left the king and went to see Charles. He was received at Laon with great fanfare. His followers, who had previously been exiled from the city, returned to him and took charge of their personal property as before, without any misgivings, hopeful that there would now be peace. He also visited the clergy whom he had left

compatitur; benivolentiam spondet, ut a se non deficiant hortatur. Postquam satis colloquii cum suis habuit, de securitate fidei et urbis a Karolo convenitur. Qui sic orsus coepit: 'Quoniam divinitas, in omnibus misericors, etiam dum punit misericorditer operatur, iusto eius iuditio me et abiectum et receptum cognosco. Eius aequitate hac urbe me exceptum arbitror, eius benignitate quod superest prestolor. Ipsum etiam vos et hanc urbem mihi reddidisse opinor. A deo itaque redditum mihi adiungi quaero. Adsunt sancta; superponite dexteram, fidem contra omnes spondete. Exceptio nulla erit, si vultis mihi comes fieri.' Ille sui voti avidus, quicquid expetitur spondet.[103] Super sancta dextram extendit, non veritus iurare quodcumque propositum fuit. Unde et cunctis credulus, nulli suspectus fuit. In nullo negotio a quoque vitatur. De urbe munienda ipse querit et deliberat; omnium causam sciscitatur; pro omnibus consultat. Quare ignotus cunctos[104] latuit.

behind, expressing his sympathy, promising them his good-will, and urging them not to abandon him. When he had finished speaking with his men, he was approached by Charles, who sought guarantees of his loyalty and the security of the city, and spoke to him as follows: "Because God, who is merciful in all things, shows mercy even as he metes out punishment, I know that it was through his just judgment that I was cast out and then received again. It was through his fairness that I was welcomed back into this city, and it is through his benevolence that I await what remains. He himself, I believe, has restored both you and this city to me. Now I ask that what has been returned to me by God should be joined to me. Behold the holy relics. Place your right hand upon them and swear fealty to me over and against all men. There can be no exceptions, if you wish to be my companion." Eager to get what he desired, Adalbero promised everything that was asked of him. He extended his right hand over the holy relics and swore whatever was put to him without fear. As a result, everyone believed him, and no one regarded him with suspicion or avoided dealing with him. He inquired into and gave his opinion about the city's defenses; he asked after each person's affairs; he considered everyone's interests. And for this reason, his true character remained hidden to everyone.

47

Comprehensio Karoli ab Adalberone

Interea cum Karoli suorumque habitum penitus pervidisset, sese etiam nulli esse suspectum, dolos multifariam pretendebat, ut et urbem sibi redderet et Karolum regi captum traderet. Karoli itaque colloquio utitur saepius, benivolentiam profert amplius. Sese quoque si oporteat sacramentis magis stringendum offert, tanta cautela calliditatis usus ut omnino dolum simulationis colore obvelaret. Unde cum nocte quadam inter cenandum hilaris resideret, Karolus craterem aureum in quo panem infregerat vinoque temperaverat tenens, post multum cogitatum ei obtulit: 'Quoniam,' inquiens, 'ex patrum decretis palmas et frondes hodie sanctificastis, atque plebem[105] sacris benedictionibus consecrastis, nobisque eukaristiam porrexistis, aliquorum susurronum calumnias qui vobis fidendum negant vilipendens, cum instet dies passionis domini et salvatoris nostri Iesu Christi, hoc vasculum vestrae dignitati aptum cum vino et pane infracto vobis porrigo. Hoc poculum in signo habendae et servandae fidei ebibite. Si vero fidem servare animo non stat,

47

Charles Is Taken Prisoner by Adalbero

After Adalbero had carefully observed the behavior of 991 Charles and his own followers and satisfied himself that no one harbored any suspicions toward him, he began to spread plots in many directions in order to regain possession of the city and hand Charles over to the king as a prisoner. To that end, he had frequent conversations with Charles and made further declarations of his goodwill toward him. He even offered to bind himself with additional oaths if that were necessary, making such careful use of his cunning that he kept his treacherous intentions completely hidden behind a deceitful facade. One night as Adalbero sat at dinner in high spirits, Charles took a golden cup, into which he had crumbled bread mixed with wine, and after careful reflection he offered it to him, saying, "Since today, in accordance with the decrees of the fathers, you have consecrated the palm branches, blessed the people with your holy benedictions, and offered the Eucharist to us, and because this is the day of the passion of Our Lord and Savior Jesus Christ, setting at naught the slanders of those who whisper that you are not to be trusted, I extend to you this vessel, suitable for a man of your stature, which contains wine and broken bread. Drink up this cup as a sign of the fealty that you owe me and which you will preserve toward me. If, however, you do not intend to remain faithful to me, then abstain from drinking

poculo parcite, ne horrendam Iudae proditoris speciem re-
feratis.' Quo respondente, 'Craterem recipiam et potum li-
bere ebibam,' Karolus mox prosecutus addendum dixit, 'et
fidem faciam.' Ille ebibens prosecutus est, 'et fidem faciam;
alioquin cum Iuda interearn.' Et multa his similia anathematis verba cenantibus dedit. Nox futuri luctus et proditionis
conscia instabat. Quietum ire constitutum est, dormitum-
que in mane. Adalbero sui doli conscius, dormientibus Karolo et Arnulfo, gladios et arma a capitibus eorum amovit
latibulisque mandavit. Hostiarium huius doli ignarum ac-
cersiens, cursum accelerari[106] et quendam suorum accersire
iubet, ostium sese servaturum interim pollicens. Quo di-
gresso, Adalbero in ipso ostio sese medium fixit, gladium
sub veste tenens. Cui mox sui assistentes, utpote huius facinoris conscii, ab Adalberone omnes intromissi sunt. Karolus
et Arnulfus matutino somno oppressi quiescebant. Coram
quibus cum hostes facto agmine adessent, et illi expergefacti
adversarios advertissent, a lectis prosilientes et arma capes-
sere nitentes, nec reperientes, querunt quidnam matutinus
eorum afferat eventus. Adalbero vero, 'Quoniam,' inquit,
'arcem hanc mihi nuper surripuistis et ab ea exulem abire
coegistis, et vos hinc dissimili tamen fortuna pellemini. Ego
enim proprii iuris remansi; vos alieno subibitis.' Ad hec Karolus, 'An,' inquit, 'o episcope, hesternae cenae memor sis
nimium miror. Non ergo ipsa divinitatis reverentia inhi-

lest you recall the terrible image of the traitor Judas." In response Adalbero said, "I will take the cup and drink the draft freely." Charles then told him to say in addition, "I will pledge fealty," and so, drinking from the cup, Adalbero added, "I will pledge fealty. Otherwise let me perish with Judas!" And he spoke many other words of anathema similar to these to his dinner companions. As night was now upon them—a night that was soon to know both grief and betrayal—they decided to retire for the evening and rest until morning. As Charles and Arnulf slept, Adalbero, plotting treachery, took their swords and weapons from beside their heads and hid them away. Then he summoned a doorkeeper who knew nothing of his plot and ordered him to hurry and call one of his men, assuring him that he would guard the door in the meantime. When the doorkeeper had left, Adalbero positioned himself in the middle of the doorway, holding his sword beneath his cloak. A short time later his men were before him, all accomplices in his criminal plot, and Adalbero let them inside. Charles and Arnulf lay still, sunk in early-morning slumber. As their enemies stood over them in a group, they awoke to the sight of their foes. They leapt from their beds, desperate to get their hands on weapons, but finding none, they asked what this early morning visit portended for them. In reply Adalbero said, "Because you recently took this citadel from me by stealth and forced me to go into exile, you too shall be driven from here, but under different circumstances. For I have remained under my own authority, but you will have to submit to another." Charles replied, "I wonder to myself, O bishop, if you recall yesterday's evening's dinner. Does your reverence for the Lord not restrain you? Does the oath that you swore mean nothing,

bebit? Nihilne ius sacramenti? Nihil hesternae cenae im-
precatio?' Et hec dicens, preceps in hostem fertur. Quem
furentem armati circumdant atque in lectum repulsum com-
primunt. Nec minus Arnulfum pervadunt. Quos comprehensos in eadem turri includunt. Turrim quoque clavibus et
seris repagulisque custodibus adhibitis muniunt. Unde cum
clamor feminarum puerorumque simul et famulorum ulula-
tus in caelum ferretur, cives per urbem turbati et expergefacti sunt. Quicumque Karoli partibus favebant mox profugio sese liberaverunt. Quod etiam vix factum fuit. Nam
cum pene adhuc[107] fugerent, statim tota civitas obfirmari ab
Adalberone iussa est, ut omnes quos sibi adversos putabat
comprehenderet. Quaesiti fuere, nec reperti. Subductus est
et Karoli filius biennis, patris vocabulum habens, et a capti-
vitate liberatus. Adalbero regi Silvanectim legatos otius mit-
tit; quondam amissam urbem iam receptam, Karolum cum
uxore et natis captum, atque Arnulfum inter hostes inventum et comprehensum mandat. Unde et sine mora cum
quotcumque possit veniat. Exercitui colligendo moram nul-

or the curses that were called down upon you at yesterday's dinner?" And as he said this, he hurled himself headlong at his foe, but armed men surrounded him in his fury, drove him back onto the bed, and held him down. At the same time they seized Arnulf. When they had them both under control, they shut them up inside the tower. They fortified it with locks, bolts, and bars, and set guards over them. As the cries of women and children and the wailing of servants were carried toward the heavens, townsmen throughout the city were disturbed and awoke. Those who supported Charles's party quickly took flight and escaped. They only just managed to do so, however, because at almost that same moment Adalbero ordered the whole city to be sealed off immediately so that he could seize all those whom he suspected of being his enemies. But although he searched for these men, he could not find them. Charles's two-year-old son, who shared the same name as his father, was also spirited away and delivered from captivity. Adalbero quickly sent messengers to the king at Senlis to report that the city that had once been lost to him had now been recaptured, that Charles had been seized along with his wife and children, and that Arnulf had been found among the enemies and taken prisoner. Thus he told the king to come at once with as many men as possible, to assemble his army without delay, and to send messengers to all of his trusted neighbors,

lam intendat. Vicinis quibuscumque confidit, ut post se veniant, legatos mittat. Moxque etsi cum paucis veniat.

48

Rex captis Karolo et Arnulfo Laudunum ingreditur

Rex quotcumque potest assumit et sine dilatione Laudunum petit. Nactusque urbem et regia dignitate exceptus, de salute fidelium urbisque ereptione et hostium comprehensione quesivit et addidicit. Die altera civibus accitis, de fide sibi habenda pertractat. Illi acsi qui capti erant, et qui iam in ius alterius cesserant, fidem faciunt et regi sacramento asciscuntur. Urbisque securitate facta, rex Silvanectim post cum captis hostibus rediit. Suos deinde sciscitans, deliberandi rationem querebat.

asking them to follow after him. He urged him to come right away, even if he had only a few men with him.

48

The King Enters Laon After the Capture of Charles and Arnulf

The king took as many men as he could and set out for Laon without delay. After arriving in the city and receiving a welcome befitting his royal status, he asked after and was informed about the safety of his faithful men, the liberation of the city, and the capture of his foes. On the next day he summoned the townsmen to discuss the fidelity that they owed him. They, like prisoners who had now passed under another's authority, swore fealty to the king and bound themselves to him with an oath. After he had secured the city, the king returned to Senlis with the enemy prisoners. There he questioned his men and sought their counsel.

49

Deliberatio quorumdam apud regem de[108] Karolo

Q ua de re aliorum sententia erat a Karolo viro claro[109] et regio genere inclito eius natos omnes cum natabus obsides accipiendos. Petendum etiam ab eo sacramentum quo[110] regi fidem faciat regnum Franciae numquam sese repetiturum, contra natos quoque testamentum inde facturum. Quo facto, Karolum dimittendum censebant. Aliorum vero sententia[111] huiusmodi erat: tam clarum et antiqui generis virum non mox reddendum, sed apud regem tam diu habendum donec qui eius captionem indignaturi sint[112] appareant. Si eo numero et nomine atque duce premineant ut indigni non sint qui hostes regis Francorum dicantur, sive inferiores sint attendendum. Si ergo pauci et inferiores indignentur, tenendum censebant; si vero maiores et quamplures, reddendum superiori ratione suadebant. Karolum ergo cum uxore Adelaide et filio Ludovico et filiabus duabus, quarum altera Gerberga, altera Adelaidis dicebatur, necnon et Arnulfo nepote carceri dedit.

49

Deliberations Before the King Regarding the Fate of Charles

Some expressed the opinion that because he was an illustrious personage distinguished by royal blood, Charles should hand over all of his sons and daughters as hostages. He should also be asked to swear an oath of fealty to the king in which he would promise to renounce any future claims upon the kingdom of Francia and make a will disinheriting his children. After he had done this, they said, the king could release him. Others, however, were of the opinion that a man of such distinction and from such a venerable family should not be released immediately, but should instead be kept at the king's court until unfavorable reaction to his capture made itself felt. The king should then carefully scrutinize whether Charles's partisans had the numbers, the prestige, and the leadership to be considered worthy adversaries of the king of the Franks, or whether they were men of lesser status. If they were few and of no account, then they advised the king to hold on to him. If, on the other hand, they were greater in number and of nobler status, then they urged him to hand Charles over in accordance with the plan outlined above. In the end, the king put Charles in prison, along with his wife Adelaide, his son Louis, his two daughters (one named Gerberga and the other Adelaide), and his nephew Arnulf.

50

De difficultate sui itineris ab urbe
Remorum ad[113] Carnotum

Ante horum captionem diebus ferme XIIII, cum aviditate discendi logicam Yppocratis Choi[114] de studiis liberalibus saepe et multum cogitarem, quadam die equitem
Carnotinum in urbe Remorum positus offendi. Qui a me interrogatus quis et cuius esset, cur et unde venisset, Heri-
brandi clerici Carnotensis legatum sese et Richero sancti
Remigii monacho se velle loqui respondit. Ego mox amici
nomen et legationis causam advertens, me quem querebat
indicavi, datoque osculo secreti[115] secessimus. Ille mox epistolam protulit hortatoriam ad aphorismorum lectionem.
Unde et ego admodum laetatus, assumpto quodam puero,
cum Carnotino equite iter Carnotum arripere disposui.
Digressus autem ab abbate meo unius tantum parvaredi so-
latium accepi. Nummis etiam, mutatoriis, ceterisque necessariis vacuus, Orbatium perveni, locum multa caritate incli-
tum. Ibique domni abbatis D. colloquio recreatus, simulque
et munificentia sustentatus, in crastino iter usque Meldim
peragendum arripui. Ingressus vero cum duobus comitibus

50

On the Difficulty of the Author's Journey from Reims to Chartres

One day, about fourteen days before the capture of Charles and Arnulf, when I was thinking often and at length[29] about the liberal arts out of a desire to learn the *logica* of Hippocrates of Cos,[30] I encountered a knight from Chartres while I was in the city of Reims. When I asked him who he was and who had sent him, and why and whence he had come, he said that he was a messenger sent from Heribrand, a cleric of Chartres, and that he wished to speak with Richer, a monk of Saint-Rémi. Recognizing right away the name of my friend and the reason for which he had been sent, I told him that I was the one he was looking for, and after bestowing a kiss upon him, we withdrew in private. He immediately produced a letter urging me to come read the *Aphorisms*.[31] I was delighted at this, and taking a boy along with me, I arranged to make the journey to Chartres with the knight. Upon setting out, however, the only help I received from my abbot[32] was a single horse. Lacking in money, a change of clothes, and other necessities, I arrived at Orbais, a place known for its great hospitality. There I was refreshed by the conversation of the lord abbot D[33] and sustained by his generosity, and on the next day I undertook to travel as far as Meaux. But when my two companions and I entered the winding paths of the woods, we were not

lucorum anfractus, non defuere infortunii casus. Nam fal-
lentibus biviis, sex leugarum superfluitate exorbitavimus.
Transmisso vero Teodorici castello, parvaredus ante visus
bucephalus fieri coepit asello tardiusculus. Iam sol a me-
sembrino discesserat, totoque aere in pluvias dissoluto, in
occasum vergebat, cum fortis ille bucefalus supremo labore
victus, inter femora insidentis pueri deficiens corruit, et
velut fulgure traiectus, VI^{to}[116] miliario ab urbe exspiravit.
Quanta tunc fuit perturbatio, quanta anxietas, illi perpendere valent qui casus similes aliquando perpessi sunt, et
ex similibus similia colligant. Puer inexpertus tanti itineris
difficultatem, fessus toto corpore equo amisso iacebat. Im-
pedimenta sine vectore aderant. Imbres nimia infusione
ruebant. Caelum nubila pretendebat. Sol iam in occasu mi-
nabatur tenebras. Inter haec omnia dubitanti consilium a
deo non defuit. Puerum namque cum impedimentis ibi reliqui. Dictatoque ei quid interrogatus a transeuntibus responderet, et ut sommo imminenti resisteret, solo equite Carnotino comitatus Meldim perveni. Pontem quoque vix de luce
videns ingredior. Et dum diligentius contemplarer, novis iterum infortuniis angebar. Tantis enim et tot hiatibus patebat
ut vix civium necessarii die eadem per eum transierint. Car-
notinus inpiger, et in peragendo itinere satis providus, navi-

spared the vicissitudes of ill fortune. For we chose the wrong
path at a crossroads and wandered six leagues out of our way.
Then, after we had passed Château-Thierry, the horse that
up to now had seemed like Bucephalus became slower than
a reluctant little donkey. The sun had already passed midday
and was edging into dusk when the whole sky dissolved into
a downpour, and that hardy Bucephalus, done in by his final
exertions, succumbed and collapsed beneath the legs of the
boy who was riding him, dropping dead at the sixth mile-
stone from the city as if he had been struck by lightning.
Those who have ever suffered similar misfortunes can judge
from their own experiences how great my agitation and anx-
iety were at that moment. After the loss of his horse, the boy,
who was not accustomed to the rigors of such a long journey, lay down, completely exhausted. The baggage sat there
without anyone to carry it. Rain was coming down in a tremendous downpour. Clouds filled the sky. The sun was already setting and casting threatening shadows. Yet amid all
of this, God's counsel was not lacking to one in doubt. And
so I left the boy there with the baggage. After telling him
what to say if he was questioned by passersby, and urging
him not to fall asleep, I arrived at Meaux accompanied only
by the knight of Chartres. I started out across the bridge,
which I could scarcely make out in the dim light, and as I
inspected it carefully I was tormented once more by new
misfortunes. For it was riddled with so many and such large
gaps that it was scarcely possible that those connected with
the townsmen could have crossed over it on the same day.
The intrepid Chartrian, who showed considerable foresight
during the course of the journey, looked around everywhere
for a boat, but finding none, he returned to the perils of

culam circumquaque inquirens et nullam inveniens, ad pontis pericula rediit et ut equi incolumes transmitterentur e
caelo emeruit. Nam in locis hiantibus equorum pedibus aliquando clipeum subdens, aliquando tabulas abiectas adiungens, modo incurvatus, modo erectus, modo accedens,
modo recurrens, efficaciter cum equis me comitante pertransiit. Nox inhorruerat mundumque tetra caligine obdux-
erat, cum basilicam sancti Pharonis introii, fratribus adhuc
parantibus potum caritatis. Qua die sollempniter pranse-
rant, recitato capitulo de cellarario monasterii, quod fuit
causa tam serae potationis. A quibus ut frater exceptus, dul-
cibus alloquiis cibisque sufficientibus recreatus sum. Carnotinum equitem cum equis vitata pontis pericula iterum at-
temptaturum puero relicto remisi. Arte premissa pertransiit
et ad puerum secunda noctis vigilia errabundus pervenit.
Vixque eum saepius inclamatum repperit. Quo assumpto,
cum ad urbem devenisset, suspectus pontis pericula, quae
pernitiosa experimento didicerat, cum puero et equis in
cuiusdam tugurium declinavit. Ibique per totam diem inci-
bati, nocte illa ad quiescendum, non ad cenandum, collecti
sunt. Quam noctem ut insomnem duxerim, et quanto in ea
cruciatu tortus[117] sim, perpendere possunt qui cura carorum
aliquando vigilasse coacti sunt. Post vero optata luce red-

the bridge, and with God's help saw to it that the horses crossed safely. Sometimes putting a shield down under the horses' feet in the gaping holes and sometimes joining together discarded planks, sometimes bending down and sometimes standing up straight, sometimes coming forward and sometimes running back, he successfully made it all the way across the bridge with the horses, while I accompanied him. Gloomy night had fallen and covered the world in foul darkness when I arrived at the church of Saint-Faro, where the brothers were still preparing the fraternal libation. On that day they had celebrated a solemn feast, and the chapter of the rule concerning the cellarer[34] of the monastery had been read aloud, which was the reason that they were taking their drink so late. I was received by them as a brother and refreshed with pleasing conversation and ample food. I sent the knight of Chartres back with some horses to try the perils of the bridge (which we had escaped) once more and find the boy. He crossed the bridge in the manner previously described, and in the course of his wandering he came across the boy during the second watch of the night.[35] Despite calling out to him many times, he was barely able to find him. He took the boy along with him, and when he arrived at the city and considered the perils of the bridge (which he knew from experience to be exceedingly dangerous), he turned aside and took the boy and the horses to someone's cottage instead. Although they had eaten nothing the whole day, they stopped there that night only to rest and not to eat. Those who have ever been compelled to stay awake at night because they are worried about those dear to them can imagine how sleeplessly I passed that night, and with what great torments I was afflicted. Shortly after the longed-

dita, nimia esurie confecti, maturius affuerunt. Eis etiam cibi illati; annona quoque cum paleis equis anteposita est. Dimittensque abbati Aug. puerum peditem, solo Carnotino comitatus, Carnotum raptim deveni. Unde mox equis remissis, ab urbe Meldensi puerum revocavi. Quo reducto, et omni sollicitudine amota, in aphorismis Yppocratis vigilanter studui apud domnum Herbrandum, magnae liberalitatis atque scientiae virum. In quibus cum tantum prognostica morborum accepissem, et simplex egritudinum cognitio cupienti non sufficeret, petii etiam ab eo lectionem eius libri qui inscribitur de concordia Yppocratis, Galieni, et Surani. Quod et obtinui, cum eum in arte peritissimum dinamidia farmaceutica, butanica, atque cirurgica non laterent.

51

Quod ex querela reprehendentium captionem Arnulfi regio iussu sinodus habita est

Sed ut iam superioris negotii seriem repetamus, cum de episcopi captione aliqui amicorum[118] indignarentur, nonnulli etiam scolasticorum in eius defensionem alia scriberent, alia scripta de canonibus proferrent, idque ad aures regum rela-

for light of day had returned, they arrived, weak from their great hunger. Food was brought to them, and fodder and straw were set before the horses. After sending the boy away on foot to the abbot, I hastened to Chartres accompanied only by the knight. Then, after sending back the horses, I recalled the boy from Meaux. After he had returned and all my worries had been put to rest, I applied myself diligently to the *Aphorisms* of Hippocrates with master Heribrand, a man of great generosity and learning. But since I only learned about the prognosis of disease in this work and a basic understanding of illnesses would not satisfy my desire, I also asked to read one of his books entitled *On the Concordance of Hippocrates, Galen, and Soranus.* This I obtained, since the powers of pharmacology, botany, and surgery were not hidden from one so skilled in medicine.

51

How the Kings Ordered a Synod to Be Held Because of the Complaints of Those Who Criticized Arnulf's Capture

But to return once more to the series of events detailed above, some of Arnulf's friends expressed outrage over his capture, and a number of scholars either wrote in his defense or produced excerpts from the canons to that end.

tum esset, edicto[119] regio decretum est ut episcopi[120] Galliae omnes qui valent, et maxime qui comprovinciales sunt, in unum conveniant. Qui autem adesse non possent, suam absentiam per legatos idoneos a suspitione purgarent. Ibique certis ac firmis decretorum rationibus aut convictum[121] dampnarent aut pristinae sedis dignitati purgatum restituerent. Collecti sunt ergo in coenobio monachorum sancti Basoli confessoris Remorum diocesanei, Remensis quidem metropolitani comprovinciales[122] Guido Suesorum episcopus, Adalbero Laudunensis episcopus, Heriveus Belvacensis episcopus, Godesmannus Ambianensis episcopus, Ratbodus Noviomensis episcopus, Odo Silvanectensis episcopus; Daibertus Bituricensium metropolitanus; Lugdunensis metropolitani comprovinciales[123] Gualterus Augustudunensis episcopus, Bruno Lingonensis episcopus, Milo Matisconensis episcopus, Siguinus Senonensium metropolitanus cum suis, Arnulfo Aurelianensi episcopo, Herberto Autisiodorensi episcopo. Qui in unum considentes, diversorum[124] locorum abbates qui aderant post solitariam sui disputationem secum consedere iusserunt.

When news of this reached the kings, they issued a royal edict declaring that all the bishops of Gaul who could attend, and particularly those who were suffragans of the ecclesiastical province of Reims, were to assemble in one body. Those who were unable to come were to send suitable envoys to clear themselves of suspicion. There, based on the authoritative and indisputable arguments of the canons, they would either condemn Arnulf if he were found guilty, or restore him to his former see if he were proven innocent. And so, at the abbey of Saint Basil the Confessor[36] in the diocese of Reims, there assembled Bishops Wido of Soissons,[37] Adalbero of Laon, Hervey of Beauvais, Godesmann of Amiens, Ratbod of Noyon, and Odo of Senlis, who were suffragans of the archbishop of Reims; Archbishop Daibert of Bourges; Bishops Walter of Autun, Bruno of Langres, and Milo of Mâcon, who were suffragans of the archbishop of Lyons; and Archbishop Siguin of Sens, along with his suffragans Arnulf of Orléans and Herbert of Auxerre. They all took their seats together, and after a private discussion among themselves, they bid the abbots who had come there from various places to be seated with them.[38]

52

Deliberatio de dignitate habendi iuditii et prelatura[125]

De habenda igitur sinodo ratione facta, ordinandum putabant cui potestas iudicandi de singulis conferretur, quem etiam habendarum rationum[126] custodem atque interpretem accommodarent. Iudicandi itaque dignitas Siguino Senonensium metropolitano commissa est, eo quod aetatis reverentia et vitae merito plurimum commendaretur. Ordinandi vero facultas ac magisterium interpretandi Arnulfo Aurelianensi episcopo credita est, eo quod ipse inter Galliarum episcopos eloquii virtute et efficatia dicendi florebat. His ergo sic habitis, post cleri ingressum, sententiis ad negotium facientibus recitatis, Arnulfus sic praefatus ait:

52

Deliberations Concerning the Authority to Render Judgment and the Presidency of the Synod

After they had come to a decision on how the synod should be conducted, they thought it best to determine who should be given the power of ruling on particular issues, and who should be appointed to oversee and interpret the proceedings. The office of president was entrusted to Archbishop Siguin of Sens, because his venerable age and meritorious way of life strongly recommended him. The power of administering the synod and the task of interpreting was given to Bishop Arnulf of Orléans, because he was preeminent among the bishops of Gaul for the power of his eloquence and the effectiveness of his speaking. After these matters had been settled, and following the entrance of the clergy and the recitation of opinions relevant to the proceedings, Arnulf addressed them as follows:[39]

53

Prelocutio[127] Arnulfi in sinodo

'Quoniam, patres reverendi, serenissimorum regum iussu necnon et sacrae religionis causa huc convenimus, multa fide, multo etiam studio cavendum videtur, ne nos qui gratia sancti spiritus hic collecti sumus aut odium alicuius aut amor a rectitudinis norma exorbitare faciat. Et quia hic in nomine domini collecti sumus, ante conspectum summae divinitatis veridicis sententiis debemus omnia agitare; nulli loquendi locum surripere; veritati operam dare; pro veritate vivaciter[128] stare; contra obiecta simplicibus ac puris sententiis et intendere et respondere. Unicuique debitus honor servetur; dicendi potestas omnibus sit. Intendendi etiam et refellendi libertas omnibus concessa sit. Nunc deinde, quoniam me ante omnes fari voluistis, causam huius sinodi coram edicendam arbitror, quatinus bene digesta, omnibus ut est videatur. Clarissima illa Remorum metropolis proditione nuper pervasa ab hostibus fuit. Sancta sanctorum hostium impetu contaminata sunt, sanctuarium dei nefariis quibusque violatum, cives quoque a predonibus direpti. Quorum malorum ille auctor esse criminatur,[129] qui ab hostibus tutari

53

Arnulf's Address to the Synod

"Reverend fathers, because we have come here at the behest of our most serene kings in the service of our holy faith, we must exercise good faith and determination to see to it that none of us who have gathered here by the grace of the Holy Spirit are moved by love or hatred for any person to deviate from the standard of rectitude. And because we have assembled here in the name of the Lord, it is incumbent upon us that in the sight of the most high Divinity we conduct all of the proceedings by employing truthful and valid statements; that we deprive no one of the opportunity to speak; that we strive for the truth and be quick to defend what is true; that we challenge and respond to objections with plain and simple arguments; that we respect the honor owed to each person; that the power to speak be available to everyone, and the freedom to make and refute accusations be granted to all. Now then, because you have expressed the desire that I should speak before anyone else, I think that the occasion for this synod should be stated publicly, so that through clear expression its truth may be made plain to all. That most illustrious metropolitan see of Reims was recently betrayed and sacked by its enemies. Its holy of holies was defiled by enemy incursions, the sanctuary of God was violated by every sort of outrage, and the townsmen were despoiled by robbers. The man who is accused of

debuit, Arnulfus, eiusdem urbis episcopus. Hoc ei intenditur. Ad hoc discutiendum regalis dignitas hic nos collegit. Elaborate igitur, patres reverendi, ne unius perfidia dignitas sacerdotalis vilescat.' Contra haec cum quidam residentium responderent huiusmodi hominem quantotius[130] convincendum et sic iusto iuditio puniendum, Siguinus episcopus non id sese permissurum respondit ut is qui maiestatis reus accusatur sub discutiendi censura ponatur, nisi ante ex iureiurando promissionem indulgentiae ab regibus et episcopis accipiat. Idque faciendum asserebat ex concilii Toletani capitulo[131] XXXI. Quod quia brevitati studemus, omisimus ponere.

54

Ratiocinatio[132] Daiberti de[133] iuditio dando

Daibertus Bituricensium archiepiscopus[134] dixit: 'Cum constet factum, et de nomine facti dubitatio nulla sit, quantum quoque facinus perpendatur, quomodo ex necessitate reo sit indulgendum penitus non adverto. Hic enim incur-

being responsible for these evils is the very person who ought to have defended the city against its enemies, namely Arnulf, the archbishop of Reims. This is the charge against him, and their royal majesties have brought us here to rule upon it. Therefore, reverend fathers, strive to ensure that the office of the priesthood does not become contemptible because of the perfidy of this one man." In response to this, some of those in attendance said that a man of this sort ought to be convicted at once and given a fitting punishment. Archbishop Siguin, however, replied that he would not allow someone accused of treason to be placed under the censure of judgment unless he first received a sworn assurance from the kings and the bishops that the punishment would be remitted. As justification, he cited the thirty-first chapter of the Council of Toledo,[40] which I will forgo including here because I am striving to be concise.[41]

54

Daibert's Argument Concerning the Rendering of Judgment

Daibert, the archbishop of Bourges, now spoke: "Since it is evident that a crime has been committed, and there is no argument about what to call it or how serious it is, I cannot understand why it should be thought necessary that the de-

rere necessitas videtur, cum iuditium promulgandum non sit, nisi prius supplicii indulgentia convincendo concessa fuerit. At si ad secularia iura respiciatur, quodcumque scelus quisque commiserit, secundum sceleris modum poenitentiae severitati subiacebit.'

55

Heriveus Belvacensis episcopus dixit: 'Cavendum summopere est ne leges divinas forensibus comparemus. Plurimum enim a se differunt, cum divinarum sit de aecclesiasticis negotiis tractare, et secularium secularibus adhiberi. Quarum primae tanto secundas superant, quanto secundae primis inferiores sunt. Unde et divinis per omnia suus honor servandus est. Si ergo frater et coepiscopus noster Arnulfus maiestatis reus convictus fuerit, pro sacerdotali reverentia et sanguinis affinitate a serenissimis regibus indulgendum aliquatenus non abnuo. Iuditii tamen sententiam[135] omnino non effugiet, si sua confessione indignus sacerdotali dignitate manifestabitur.'

fendant receive a pardon. And yet necessity is thought to apply here, since judgment is not to be rendered unless the defendant is first granted remission from punishment in the event that he is found guilty. But if we look to secular law, whatever crime anyone has committed is subject to a punishment the severity of which is based upon on the gravity of the act."[42]

55

Bishop Hervey of Beauvais responded: "We should be very careful not to compare divine laws to the laws of the courtroom. There is a great difference between them, because divine laws apply to matters concerning the church, whereas secular laws apply to worldly affairs. The former are superior to the latter to the same degree as the latter are inferior to the former. Wherefore the honor accorded to divine laws must be preserved in every instance. If, then, our brother and fellow bishop Arnulf is found guilty of treason, I do not deny that he ought to receive some degree of leniency from our most serene kings out of respect for his priestly status and because of his blood relations.[43] Nonetheless, if he is shown by his own confession to be unworthy of the priestly office, then there is no way that he will escape the judgment of this court."[44]

56

Indignatio Brunonis in Arnulfum

Bruno Lingonensis episcopus dixit: 'Hunc unde hic sermo habetur in has miserias precipitasse videor, cum contra multorum bonorum vota ad honoris culmen provexi. Et hoc non solum propter carnis affinitatem effeci, sed etiam ut ad melioris vitae statum illum attraherem, cum non ignorarem ipsum Laudunensis urbis pervasorem atque nefariae factionis temerarium principem sub iure cirographi regibus fidem spopondisse pro nullo preterito aut futuro sacramento fidem promissam sese umquam violaturum, regum hostes pro ingenio et viribus impetiturum illisque in nullo communicaturum. Sed quia Karolus avunculus meus regum adversarius patet, cum ei is de quo loquimur communicavit fidemque sacramento dedit, ius fidei promissae penitus abrupit. An Manasse et Rotgerus regum adversarii dicendi non sunt, qui cum Karolo urbis Remorum pervasores fuere, et sanctae dei genitricis Mariae basilicam cum armata manu ingressi sunt sanctuariumque nefario ingressu violaverunt? Hos etiam iste sui consilii custodes et amicorum precipuos habebat. Quod quia evidentissimum est, dicat nunc ipse cuius[136] im-

56

Bruno's Indignation Against Arnulf

Bruno, the bishop of Langres, now spoke: "It appears that
I am responsible for the downfall of the man who is the subject of our current discussions, since it was I who elevated
him to the summit of office against the wishes of many good
men.[45] I did this not only because of the kinship tie that ex-
ists between us,[46] but also so that I might bring him to a better station in life, although I was not unaware that he had
invaded the city of Laon[47] and become the reckless leader
of a wicked faction. He subsequently pledged fealty to the
kings in a chirograph, promising that he would never violate
his trust for the sake of any past or future oath, and swearing
that he would pursue the king's enemies to the utmost of his
ability and hold no communication with them. But because
Charles my uncle is revealed to be an enemy of the kings,
and the man we are speaking of here communicated with
him and swore fealty to him, he has completely violated the
oath of fealty that he took. And are Manasses[48] and Roger[49]
not to be declared enemies of the kings, men who took part
in the sack of Reims with Charles and marched into the
church of Mary, the holy mother of God, with an armed
band, violating the sanctuary with their sacrilegious intru-
sion? These are the very men whom Arnulf took into his
confidence and regarded as his dearest friends! Because the
evidence of his guilt is so clear, let him tell us who it was who

pulsione aut suasione istud[137] aggressus sit. Aut certe alii intendet aut convictus testimoniis labascet. Nullus consanguinitatis amor, nulla habitae familiaritatis gratia a recti iudicii forma me aliquo modo seducent.'

57

Laus Godesmanni de magnanimitate[138] Brunonis et[139] ut ab eo iuditium quaeratur[140] postulatio

Godesmannus Ambianensis episcopus dixit: 'Novimus venerabilis Brunonis magnanimitatem, quem nullus affinitatis[141] amor, nulla familiaritas a veritate sequestrat, at rigor animi et morum probitas veridicum et cui credendum sit promtissime indicant. Ergo[142] quia de examinatione reatus fratris et coepiscopi nostri Arnulfi mentio superius facta est, ab eo quaerendum videtur quale ex hac re habendum sit iuditium, eo quod ipsum oporteat iuditii temperare censuram, cum ipse sic inter utrumque sit constitutus, ut et regi fidem et Arnulfo ex consanguinitate dilectionem debeat. Unde et

impelled or persuaded him to do what he did. Surely he will either accuse someone else, or be convicted by the testimony presented here and admit his guilt. No affection for my blood relatives, nor any partiality born of personal acquaintance, will cause me to deviate in the slightest from the standard of correct judgment."[50]

57

Godesmann's Praise of Bruno's High-Mindedness and a Request That He Should Render a Verdict

Godesmann, the bishop of Amiens, said, "We are familiar with the high-mindedness of the venerable Bruno, whom neither love of kin nor the bond of friendship can separate from the truth, but whose mental resolve and probity of conduct instead readily indicate him to be a truthful speaker and a man to be trusted implicitly. Therefore, because mention was made earlier of the inquiry into the guilt of our brother and fellow bishop Arnulf, it seems to me that we ought to ask Bruno how judgment should be rendered in this case; for he should be the one to moderate the decision of the court, positioned as he is between both parties, owing fidelity to the king and the affection born of kinship to Arnulf. For this reason, he will not be suspected of any kind

nullius doli suspitione tenendus erit, quem fidelitas domini ad iuditium incitabit, et caritas proximi a malivolentia prohibebit.'

58

Responsio Brunonis

Ad haec[143] Bruno episcopus:[144] 'Mentem,' inquit, 'vestram satis plane intelligo. Hic qui reus maiestatis accusatur carnis affinitate mihi coniungitur, utpote avunculi mei Lotharii regis filius. Unde et vestra benignitas mihi fieri iniuriam metuit, si dignum de eo a vobis proferatur iuditium. Sed absit ut amorem consanguinitatis Christi amore preciosiorem habeam. Rem unde agitur sanctitas vestra subtili indagine mecum discutiat, de condemnatione convicto inferenda nihil metuentes, cum aeque iustum sit et reum maiestatis damnari et innocentem laxari.'

of deception. Fidelity to his lord will spur him on to render judgment, while love for his kinsman will prevent him from acting out of malice."[51]

58

Bruno's Response

To this bishop Bruno replied, "I understand full well what you mean. This man who is accused of treason is bound to me by a tie of kinship, inasmuch as he is the son of my maternal uncle, King Lothar. And so, in your sympathy for me, you fear that I would be wronged if a fitting judgment were to be pronounced against him by you. But banish the thought that I should hold love of kin more dear than the love of Christ! Your sanctity must join me in subjecting the matter that is before us to a scrupulous examination. And you should have no fear of convicting him if he is proven guilty, since it is equally just for someone who is guilty of treason to be condemned and for an innocent man to be released."[52]

59

Demonstratio Ratbodi, quod libellum fidelitatis Lothariensium episcopi[145] calumnientur

Ratbodus Noviomensis episcopus dixit: 'Si placet, patres reverendi, libellum fidelitatis, ab Arnulfo quondam regibus de habenda fide porrectum, a vobis nunc discutiendum puto. Videtur enim quod solus in eius dampnatione sufficiat, eo quod fidem iureiurando promissam et manus scripto roboratam sacrilegio periurii penitus violaverit. Sed est quiddam quod remordet, quod scilicet a Lothariensium episcopis, ut fertur, contra illum disputatur. Calumniantur enim contra leges divinas scriptum, lectum, reconditum. Unde et si placet, iam a vobis discutiendus in medium[146] proferatur.' Sinodus dixit, 'Proferatur.'

59

Ratbod Describes How the Bishops of Lotharingia Wrongly Object to Arnulf's Pledge of Fidelity

Ratbod, the bishop of Noyon, now spoke: "If it pleases you, reverend fathers, I think that you should now examine the written pledge of fealty that Arnulf formerly gave to the kings to guarantee his loyalty. For it seems to me that this alone should suffice to condemn him, inasmuch as through the sacrilege of perjury he has completely violated the pledge that he made under oath and confirmed in his own handwriting. There is still something that gives pause, however, namely the fact that the Lotharingian bishops are said to be raising an argument against it. They wrongly claim that it was written, read out, and stored away in contravention of divine laws. And so, if it pleases you, let the document be brought forward so that you may examine it." The synod declared, "Let it be brought forward."[53]

60

Textus libelli fidelitatis Arnulfi

Prolatus est itaque hanc textus seriem habens: 'Ego Arnulfus, gratia dei preveniente Remorum archiepiscopus, promitto regibus Francorum Hugoni et Rotberto me fidem purissimam servaturum, consilium et auxilium eis secundum meum scire et posse in omnibus negotiis prebiturum, inimicis eorum nec consilio nec auxilio ad eorum infidelitatem scienter adiuturum. Haec in conspectu divinae maiestatis et beatorum spirituum et totius aecclesiae assistens promitto, pro bene servatis laturus premia aeternae benedictionis. Si vero, quod nolo et quod absit, ab his deviavero, omnis benedictio mea convertatur in maledictionem, et fiant dies mei pauci, et episcopatum meum accipiat alter. Recedant a me amici mei, sintque perpetuo inimici. Huic ego cirographo a me edito in testimonium benedictionis vel maledictionis meae subscribo, fratresque et filios meos ut subscribant rogo. Ego Arnulfus archiepiscopus subscripsi.'

60

The Text of Arnulf's Pledge of Fidelity

And so they brought forward the document, which read as follows: "I, Arnulf, archbishop of Reims by the grace of God, promise to Hugh and Robert, the kings of the Franks, that I will maintain unadulterated fidelity toward them, that I will provide aid and counsel to them in all their endeavors to the best of my knowledge and ability, and that I will not knowingly provide assistance to their enemies through my aid or counsel, so as to be unfaithful to them. I promise these things as I stand in the sight of the Divine Majesty, the spirits of the blessed, and the whole Church, in the assurance that I will win the rewards of eternal benediction if I keep these promises faithfully. But if I deviate from them (which is not my intention, and may heaven forbid it), then may all of these blessings become a curse upon me. May my days be few, and may someone else receive my bishopric. May my friends abandon me and become my enemies in perpetuity. I append my name to this document that I have drawn up, bearing witness to the blessing and curse that are called down upon me, and I ask my brothers and sons to add their subscriptions as well. I, Archbishop Arnulf, have subscribed."[54]

61

Arnulfus libellum ex parte laudat[147] et ex parte vituperat

Quo recitato, a sinodo investigatur an alicuius reprehensionis aut defensionis vim habere videatur. Tunc venerabilis episcopus Arnulfus, eo quod officium interpretandi ei commissum erat: 'Et pro se,' inquit, 'ex parte defensionem continet, et vires ex parte reprehensoribus accommodat. Causa namque ut scriberetur eius auctor Arnulfus fuit. Qui cum detestandae cupiditatis morbo nimium laboraret, aegit quod reprehendi potest, cum iuratus fidem non servavit. Hoc enim reprehensioni succumbit. Et quod sapientes et boni id effecerunt, quod dolis et astutiae perditissimi hominis contrairet, contra querulos defensioni firmitatem affectat viresque ministrat. Et quicquid illud sit, testimonio tamen roborandum est. Procedat Adalgerus presbiter; adest namque qui rerum seriem proditionis conscius optime novit. Ille, inquam, adsit, et vestrae claritudini inauditum scelus edicat,

61

Arnulf of Orléans Partially Praises and Partially Criticizes the Document

After the document had been read aloud, the synod inquired into whether it contained the power to convict or defend anyone.[55] The venerable bishop Arnulf then spoke, since he had been entrusted with the task of interpreting: "In itself this document contains partly a defense, and it partly lends support to the accusers. Arnulf, the author of this document, was himself responsible for the fact that it was drawn up. Because he was suffering overmuch from the sickness of hateful avarice, he committed an act worthy of censure, in that he did not preserve the fidelity that he swore. For this he is subject to reproach. And the fact that wise and good men saw to it that the document was drawn up in order to oppose the trickery and guile of a most debased man provides a forceful and steadfast defense against those who raise objections. But whatever is the case, it must still be corroborated by testimony. Let the priest Adalger present himself. For there is someone here who, as an accomplice, has an intimate knowledge of the series of events that culminated in the betrayal. Let him come forward, then, and state the facts of this unheard-of crime before this

ut et ubi sit vituperatio habenda cognoscatis, et ubi laus
concedenda videatis.'

62

Admovetur Adalgerus
accusationi[148]

Adalgerus itaque accersitus adest. Super hac re interrogatus et nil moratus respondet: 'Utinam, patres sancti, in
hac vocatione concedatur mihi aliqua remissionis indulgentia. Sed quia ad id deveni, ut si quid quod pro me faciat inve-
niri possit, id contra me stare videatur, verbis brevioribus
quod quaeritis edicam. Dudo, Karoli miles, hortatus est ut
hanc unde hic quaeritis proditionem aggrederer, sic domino
meo placere iuratus. Unde cum ei non crederem, dominum
meum per me interrogavi. Sese id fieri velle respondit. Ut
autem hoc dedecus specie honesti velaretur, Karolo manus
dedi, eiusque factus, proditionem per sacramentum spo-
pondi. Et feci quidem, sed non iniussus. Quod si vobis fal-
sum videatur, paratus sum omnia iuditiorum genera subire.'

illustrious body, so that you may know where abuse is warranted and where praise should be granted."[56]

62

Adalger Is Brought Forward for the Accusers

Adalger was then summoned and came forward. When he was questioned on this matter, he responded without delay: "I wish it were the case, holy fathers, that my appearance before you might win me some remission from punishment. But because I have come to the point where anything that might be found to work in my favor seems instead to impugn me, I will answer your question more concisely. Dudo, one of Charles's vassals, urged me to undertake the betrayal that is the subject of your inquiry, and he swore to me that in doing so I would be obliging my lord. But because I did not trust him, I asked my lord myself, and he told me that this was indeed his will. So that this disgraceful action might be concealed under the guise of honorable conduct, I gave my hands to Charles, and after I had become his man, I swore an oath that I would commit this act of treachery. And I did commit it, but at another's instigation. And if it appears to you that I am not telling the truth, then I am prepared to submit to every type of ordeal."[57]

63

Brevis et dilucida demonstratio criminis a Guidone episcopo

Guido Suessionensis episcopus dixit: 'Ut hic ex ratione huius intelligitur, unius reatus sorte[149] ambo tenentur. Nam cum hic sese effecisse asserat, non est immunis eius dominus, qui facinus perpetrandum suasit, eo quod sceleris causam se ipsum prebuerit. Quoniam ergo utriusque negotium inditiis evidentibus constat, cum alter facinus suaserit, alter effecerit, iuditii censura vestram paternitatem non latet. Est etiam quod iuditio habendo vires prebeat, quod cum ipse episcopus proditionis auctor extiterit, ut suum flagitium melioris zeli fervore tegeret, multae excommunicationis et maledictionis anathemate a corpore et sanguine domini separavit atque ab ecclesia fidelium suspendit Remensium predonum auctores, factores, cooperatores, fautores, et a propriis dominis rerum suarum sub emptionis nomine abalienatores.[150] Sed cum tanti mali episcopus auctor existat, anathemate involutus manifestissime patet. Quod etiam ad eius condempnationem non minimum valet.'

63

Bishop Wido Gives a Clear and Concise Description of the Crime

Wido, the bishop of Soissons, now spoke: "It is clear in this case from the testimony of this man that two people are bound by a single share of guilt. For although Adalger says that he was the one who carried out this wicked deed, nonetheless his lord, who urged him to do it, is not guiltless, because he made himself responsible for the crime. Therefore, since clear evidence shows that both men are involved in this affair—one urging on the deed and the other carrying it out—the judgment to be meted out does not escape you, reverend fathers. And there is something else that adds weight to the verdict that is to be rendered. Although the archbishop himself was the author of this betrayal, in an effort to conceal his wrongdoing behind a facade of pious zeal, he pronounced a terrible anathema of excommunication and malediction against the instigators of the plunderers of Reims, and those who took part, cooperated with, or supported them, as well as those who took property away from the rightful owners under the guise of purchase, cutting them off from the body and blood of the Lord and suspending them from the church of the faithful.[58] But because the archbishop was the one responsible for this great evil, it is quite clear that he is himself bound by this anathema, and this carries no little weight to convict him."

64

Indignatio Gualteri episcopi[151]
in Arnulfum

Gualterus Augustudunensis episcopus dixit: 'An malesanae[152] mentis hic episcopus non est qui pro se defensiones nititur, cum regibus et tot patribus eius iniquitas dilucide pateat, et insuper presbiteri malorum conscii testimonio convincatur? An ipse mali inventor periculum anathematis evadere potuit, cum ipse mali inventor et fautor inventores et factores fautoresque maledictionis telo perfodit? An ipsam divinitatem hec perpendere non animadvertit,[153] cum scriptum sit quod "oculi domini in omni loco contemplantur bonos et malos?" Et certe arbitror, quia "dixit insipiens in corde suo: non est Deus." Animadvertite ergo, patres, quam "corrupti sunt et abominabiles[154] facti sunt in studiis suis" factor et fautor.'

64

Bishop Walter's Indignation
Against Arnulf

Walter, the bishop of Autun, declared: "Can this bishop possibly be in his right mind, striving to defend himself when his wickedness is so obvious to the kings and the many fathers gathered here, and when he is also condemned by the testimony of a priest who was an accomplice to these evil deeds? Was it possible that the very one who contrived this evil could escape the perils of anathema, when he—himself the architect and promoter of this wickedness—transfixed all those who contrived, supported, or carried it out with the shaft of malediction? Is he unaware that God himself weighs these things up, since it is written that 'the eyes of the Lord in every place behold the good and the evil'?[59] I suppose this must be the case, since 'the fool hath said in his heart: there is no God.'[60] Take note, fathers, of how those who promoted this act and those who carried it out 'are corrupt and are become abominable in their ways.'"[61]

65

Odonis episcopi admonitio
de iuditio accelerando

Odo Silvanectensis episcopus dixit: 'Quoniam religionis causa et iussu serenissimorum regum hic collecti sumus, non est differendum habendi iuditii examen. Id enim reges prestolantur. Clerus et plebs idem expectant. Nec est in diversissimis sententiarum rationibus diutius immorandum, cum res sit evidens, et iuditii ratio in promtu sit. De quibus non solum patrum statuta[155] legitis, verum etiam per consequentias rerum equitatis censuram proferre non ignoratis.'

65

Bishop Odo's Admonition to Hasten Their Verdict

Odo, the bishop of Senlis, now spoke: "Because we have assembled here in the interests of our faith and at the behest of our most serene kings, we must not postpone the decision of our verdict. The kings are waiting for it; the clergy and the people expect it. Nor is there any need to allot more time for differences of opinion to be presented, when the facts are so clear, and the grounds for reaching a judgment are so plainly apparent. Not only have you read the statutes of the Fathers concerning these matters, but you are also capable of pronouncing an equitable verdict in accordance with the facts."[62]

66

Arnulfi suasio[156] ad defensores
ut libere disputent

Arnulfus Aurelianensis episcopus dixit: 'Licet, patres venerandi, hec certissime se sic habeant ut de Arnulfo predicantur, plurimisque sententiis patrum iusto iuditio damnari valeat, tamen ne videamur de fratris ruina letantes et in eius damnatione absque iusto ardentes, statuendum communi decreto arbitror ut quicumque in[157] eius defensione aliquid dicere nititur locum defensandi habeat, revolvat volumina, proferat quot vult sententias, atque omnia quae ad defensionem paravit hic coram nil metuens effundat. Atque hoc constituendum reor, ut ultra eis defensandi locus non pateat. Hic tantum nunc cogitata edicant.' Tunc Siguinus episcopus Arnulfi statutum approbat ac decretalibus interdictis[158] violari inhibet. Si quispiam ergo quid dicere habet, ut edicat ammonet.

66

Arnulf of Orléans Urges the Defense to Argue Its Case Freely

Arnulf, the bishop of Orléans, now spoke: "Although what has been said about Arnulf is indisputable, venerable fathers, and although he may be justly condemned by many opinions of the fathers, nevertheless, lest we should seem to take joy in the downfall of one of our brothers and appear overly zealous in our efforts to condemn him, I think that we ought to declare by unanimous consent that whoever desires to say something in his defense should have the opportunity to do so, that he may open up books and cite as many opinions as he wishes, and that he may freely and without fear impart everything that he has prepared in defense of Arnulf. I think that we should take this step so that no further opportunity to defend him will be available to his supporters in the future. Let them state their case here publicly once and for all." Bishop Siguin approved Arnulf's motion and invoked the sanctions of canon law to prevent it from being violated. He then advised that if any person had something to say, he should make a public statement.[63]

67

Defensio scolasticorum pro Arnulfo

Et cum plures ibi assisterent qui in defensione niterentur, maximi tamen defensores fuere abbates Abbo Floriacensis et Ramnulfus Senonensis, atque Iohannes scolasticus Autisiodorensis. Hi enim scientia simul et eloquentia inter suos insignes habebantur. Et indicto silentio, librorum multa volumina aperta sunt, multa quoque ex patrum decretis prolata, nonnulla etiam ad defensionem obiecta. Inter quae quatuor principaliter obiciebant. Aiebant enim inprimis eum suae sedi restituendum; deinde legittimam[159] ei vocationem adhibendam; tum quoque Romano pontifici id innotescendum; et postremo pontificis Romani auctoritate in generali sinodo totum facinus discutiendum. Hoc etiam secundum divinas et humanas leges approbandum asserebant.

67

The Scholars' Defense of Arnulf

Although there were many people in attendance who took Arnulf's side, the most prominent of his defenders were the abbots Abbo of Fleury[64] and Romulf of Sens,[65] and the scholar John of Auxerre.[66] For among the men of their party they were distinguished both for their learning and eloquence. After silence had been called for, many volumes of books were opened, many decrees of the fathers were brought forward, and a number of arguments were also made on behalf the defense, among which were four principal objections: first and foremost, that Arnulf should be restored to his see; second, that he should be given a lawful summons; third, that the pope should be apprised of the proceedings; and finally, that all of his actions should be examined and judged at a general synod under the authority of the bishop of Rome. This, they asserted, was the proper way to proceed according to both divine and human laws.[67]

68

Infirmatio defensionis

Ab altera vero parte responsum est eum sedi pristinae non restituendum, eo quod culpis evidentissimis a probabili accusatore convictus, ad flagicia magis preceps quam ad religionis honorem et dominorum fidem commodus videretur. Nec iam ultra esse vocandum, cum post proditionis nefas per sex continuos menses vocatus fuerit et ad rationem venire contempserit. Romano vero pontifici notificari non posse, eo quod itineris difficultas atque inimicorum minae id plurimum prohiberent.[160] Id vero sceleris iam non esse discutiendum, cum totum constaret, accusator crimen intenderet, ac firmamentum multiplex afferret. Reus vero convictus, nil contra valeret. His episcoporum sententiis multa ratione prolatis, defensores cedunt.

68

A Refutation of the Defense

The other side responded that Arnulf should not be restored to his see because his guilt had been established beyond a doubt by a credible accuser, and because he was more likely to sin again than to prove suitable for high office in the Church or remain faithful to his lord. Nor was there any cause for Arnulf to be called to court on a later occasion; for after his wicked act of betrayal he had been repeatedly summoned over a period of six months, but had declined to come and justify his conduct. There was also no way of notifying the pope, since the difficulty of the journey and threats from hostile parties made this virtually impossible. And there was no need of any further inquiry into his wrongdoing, since the facts were agreed upon and a witness had accused him of the crime and produced a variety of supporting arguments. The defendant had been convicted and there was nothing that he could do for it. In the face of the carefully reasoned arguments advanced by the bishops, Arnulf's defenders yielded.[68]

69

Quibus a defensione cessantibus, episcopi nihil aliud superesse nisi Arnulfum in medium statuendum[161] censebant, ut pro se quae vellet responderet. Vocatus itaque in ordine episcoporum consedit. Cui postquam ab episcopis multa illata fuere quibus conclusus cessavit, et ille ut potuit alia intendit,[162] alia reppulit, victus tamen, argumentorum rationibus succubuit et sese reum ac sacerdotio indignum coram confessus est.

70

Ingressus regum[163] in sinodum

Quod cum regibus suggestum est, ipsi cum primatibus sacro episcoporum conventui sese inferunt, gratias episcopis reddentes eo quod pro se et salute principum diu deliberassent. Petunt[164] quoque gestorum seriem sibi evolvi, et in quo constiterint rationum fine. Tunc etiam omnium gesto-

69

After the defense had abandoned its case, the bishops declared that nothing else remained but for Arnulf to be brought before them so that he might say whatever he wished on his own behalf. He was then called forward and took his seat before the ranks of the bishops.[69] They directed a great many accusations against him that hedged him in and left him unable to respond. He attacked some of them and deflected others as best he could, but in the end he was defeated. He yielded to the logic of their arguments and publicly confessed that he was guilty and unworthy of the priesthood.

70

The Entrance of the Kings into the Synod

When the kings were informed of this, they proceeded forward into the sacred assembly with the magnates. They thanked the bishops for having deliberated so long on their behalf and in the interest of leading men, and they asked them to recount the events of the synod and explain to them the results of their deliberations. The whole sequence of

rum series regibus exposita est. Post auditum narrationis or-
dinem, iam tempus adesse iuditii habendi asseverant. Tunc
episcopi Arnulfum ut regum genibus provolvatur commo-
nent, reatum quoque suum confiteatur atque pro sui vita et
membrorum integritate supplicet. Ille mox dominorum
pedibus prostratus, crimen confessus est, et sacerdotio se
indignum asserens, pro vita et membris suffusus lacrimis
postulabat. Unde et universam sinodum in lacrimas coegit.
Reges multa pietate flexi, vitam et membrorum integrita-
tem indulgent. Sub custodia sui absque ferro et vinculis
habendum decernunt. Et a terra erectus, interrogatur an abdicationem sui canonum auctoritate sollempniter velit cele-
brari.

71

Decretale

Quod cum episcoporum ordinationi totum committeret, mox decretum est ut, quia se indignum sacerdotio confi-
tebatur scelusque non tegebat, sicut gradibus provectus fuit,
ita gradibus deponeretur. Suasus ergo, regibus quae ab eis

events was then related to the kings. After listening to this account, they declared that it was time to render judgment. The bishops then admonished Arnulf to fall at the knees of the kings, confess his guilt, and beseech them for his life and the preservation of his limbs. He immediately prostrated himself at the feet of his lords and confessed his crime. With his eyes full of tears, he declared that he was unworthy of the priesthood, and he entreated them to spare his life and limbs. In so doing, he brought the whole synod to tears. Moved by compassion, the kings granted him his life and the possession of all of his limbs, and they decreed that he would be held in their custody without irons or chains. After he had been made to rise, Arnulf was asked if he was willing for his abdication from office to be ritually solemnized by the authority of the canons.[70]

71

A Decretal

When he declared that he would leave everything for the bishops to decide, they decreed that because he had confessed himself to be unworthy of the priesthood and did not deny his wrongdoing, just as he had been promoted through the priestly orders, so now he would be deposed from them. At their urging he handed over to the kings ev-

acceperat reddidit,[165] sacerdotales vero infulas[166] episcopis sine mora laxavit. Interrogatus etiam an abdicationis et repudii libellum faceret, ad votum episcoporum omnia sese facturum respondit. Et libellum mox scriptum et oblatum, coram regibus in concilio legit atque subscripsit.

72

Textus libelli repudii Arnulfi

Textus autem libelli huiusmodi erat: 'Ego Arnulfus, gratia dei Remorum quondam episcopus, recognoscens fragilitatem meam et pondera peccatorum meorum, testes confessores meos Siguinum archiepiscopum, Daibertum archiepiscopum, Arnulfum episcopum, Godesmannum episcopum, Heriveum episcopum, Ratbodum episcopum, Walterum episcopum, Brunonem episcopum, Milonem episcopum, Adalberonem episcopum, Odonem episcopum, Widonem episcopum, Heribertum episcopum constitui mihi iudices delictorum meorum, et puram ipsis confessionem dedi, quaerens remedium penitendi et salutem animae meae, ut recederem ab officio et ministerio pontificali, quo me recognosco esse indignum, et alienum me reddens pro

erything that he had received from them, and he gave up the episcopal insignia to the bishops without delay.[71] When he was asked whether he would put his abdication and renunciation of office in writing, he replied that he would do everything according to the wishes of the bishops. A document was quickly drawn up and handed over to him. He read it out publicly in the council before the kings and signed his name to it.[72]

72

The Text of Arnulf's Abdication

The text read as follows: "I, Arnulf, formerly bishop of Reims by the grace of God, acknowledging my weakness and the weight of my sins, have established these men as my witnesses and confessors: Archbishop Siguin, Archbishop Daibert, Bishop Arnulf, Bishop Godesmann, Bishop Hervey, Bishop Ratbod, Bishop Walter, Bishop Bruno, Bishop Milo, Bishop Adalbero, Bishop Odo, Bishop Wido, and Bishop Herbert. I have appointed them to be judges over my sins. And seeking the remedy of penance and the salvation of my soul, I have given them a complete confession so that I may withdraw from the duties and responsibilities of the office of bishop, of which I recognize that I am unworthy, making myself a stranger to this see on account of my crimes, which

reatibus meis, in quibus peccasse secreto ipsis confessus sum et de quibus publice arguebar, eo scilicet modo, ut ipsi sint testes et potestatem habeant substituendi et consecrandi alium in loco meo, qui digne preesse et prodesse possit aecclesiae cui actenus indignus prefui. Et ut inde ultra nullam repetitionem aut interpellationem auctoritate canonica facere valeam, manu mea propria subscribens firmavi. Quo ita perlecto, ita subscripsi: Ego Arnulfus, quondam Remorum archiepiscopus, subscripsi.' Necnon et adstantes episcopi ab eo rogati ut subscriberent, subscripserunt atque sic ei responderunt: 'Secundum professionem et subscriptionem tuam, cessa ab officio.' Post hec sacramenti iure hos qui sui fuerant absolvit atque libertatem transeundi in ius alterius victus concessit.

73

Depositio Adalgeri presbiteri
a gradibus

Dum hec multa consideratione gererentur, Adalgerus presbiter, eo quod communione privatus esset, regum pedibus provolutus, multa conquestione quaerebatur, communi-

I privately confessed to these men and of which I was publicly convicted, so that they may stand as witnesses and have the power to replace me and consecrate in my place someone else to be a worthy leader and benefactor of the church of which I have up until now proven an unworthy overseer. And so that I will not be able to make any further claims or appeals in the future with canonical authority, I have confirmed this by signing in my own hand. After reading through this document carefully, I have subscribed as follows: 'I, Arnulf, formerly archbishop of Reims, have subscribed.'" Arnulf also asked the bishops who were standing there with him to sign. They subscribed and then spoke to him as follows: "In accordance with your promise and your subscription, depart from your office." After this he took an oath releasing his former vassals from his service and granting them the freedom to put themselves under someone else's authority now that he had been convicted.[73]

73

The Dismissal of the Priest Adalger from Office

While they were attending to this with careful consideration, the priest Adalger threw himself at the feet of the kings, complaining bitterly that he had been deprived of communion and asking that the sentence of excommunica-

oni petens restitui, parcius sibi inferendam censuram ratus, eo quod iussus domino obtemperavisset. Quem Arnulfus Aurelianensis episcopus adorsus, 'Numquidnam,' inquit, 'iuditii expertem te tua conficta hodie facient? Numquid tu es qui Karolo portas aperuisti et hostiliter cum illo sancta sanctorum ingressus es? Numquid tu es qui adolescentem cum tui similibus perdidisti? Confitere, infandissime!' Quo respondente, 'Negare non possum,' ille mox prosecutus, 'An ideo,' inquit, 'communioni restituendus es, ut domino tuo lugente, tu, nefandissime, rideas?' Tandem decretum est duorum incommodorum[167] utrumlibet ab eo eligi, aut a gradibus deponi, aut perpetuo anathemate teneri. Qui apud se plurima pertractans, tandem maluit gradibus privari quam anathemate perpetuo teneri. Et mox episcoporum iussu indumentis sacerdotalibus vestitur. Quae singula absque ulla miseratione[168] detrahentes, ei singuli dicebant, 'Cessa ab officio tuo.' Laicorum ergo tantum communionem ei reddentes, illum penitentiae subdunt atque sic a sinodo soluti sunt. Si quis autem plenius scire voluerit quid quisque eorum de canonibus et patrum decretis in concilio[169] protulerit, quid quoque ab eis ibi sanccitum sit, quid etiam a regibus et episcopis Romano pontifici directum,[170] quibus quoque causarum rationibus Arnulfi abdicatio roborata,[171] legat librum domni et incomparabilis viri Gerberti, huius Arnulfi in epis-

tion be lifted, arguing that they should show lenience toward him because he had acted in obedience to a command from his lord. Thereupon Arnulf, the bishop of Orléans, accosted him, saying, "Do you really think that your fabrications will make you immune from punishment today? Was it not you who opened the gates of the city to Charles and marched into the holy of holies by his side like an enemy? Was it not you and many like you who corrupted that young man? Admit it, you scoundrel!" When he replied, "I cannot deny this," Arnulf immediately continued: "And for that are you now to be restored to the communion of the Church, so that you may laugh while your lord weeps, you most wicked of men?" In the end they decreed that he had to choose between one of two punishments: either to be stripped of his holy orders, or else to be bound by a perpetual anathema. After giving the matter careful consideration, in the end he chose to be deprived of his orders rather than to be permanently excommunicated. Shortly thereafter, at the order of the bishops, he was dressed in his priestly garments, and as they removed each one of these items from him without pity, they each said to him: "Depart from your office." They subsequently restored him to communion (but only to the communion of the laity) and imposed penance upon him, and with that the synod was dissolved.[74] If anyone would like to obtain a more complete knowledge of the canons and decrees of the fathers that each person put forward at this council, of what was ratified there, of what message the kings and the bishops sent to the Roman pontiff, and of the arguments that were used to strengthen the case for Arnulf's deposition, he should read the treatise written by his lordship the incomparable Gerbert, Arnulf's successor in the

copatu successoris, qui omnia haec digesta continens, mira eloquentiae suavitate Tulliano eloquio comparatur. Obiectionibus namque et responsionibus, conquestionibus atque orationibus, invectivis, coniecturisque et diffinitionibus repletus, luculentissime ac rationabiliter proponit, assumit, atque concludit. Qui non solum sinodalibus causis, sed et status rethoricae cognoscentibus utillimus habetur.

74

Conquestio Odonis apud suos de Miliduni ereptione

Interea[172] Odo rerum suarum augmentum querebat. Unde et apud suos quorum fidem indubitatam sciebat castrum Meledunum in suum ius transfundi parabat, sibi inquiens miserrimum fore quod in Sequana fluvio transmittendis exercitibus nullus sibi transitus pateret. Unde et id animo sibi incidisse, quatinus[173] Milidunum, quod est circumfluente Sequana tutissimum et duplici portu pervium, ad suam partem retorqueret, cum etiam in Ligeri plures sibi portus paterent. Nec de periurii[174] facinore formidandum, cum illud iam ab avo possessum sit, et nunc non regis sed alterius

see of Reims. This work, which contains an account of all of these things, is composed with Ciceronian eloquence and a marvelously pleasant manner of expression. It is filled with objections and responses, laments and speeches, invectives, conjectures, and definitions, and it proposes logical arguments in an elegant form, implements them, and brings them to a conclusion. It is considered very useful not only to those who are involved with cases that come up before synods, but also to anyone familiar with rhetorical issues.

74

Odo's Complaint to His Men Concerning the Capture of Melun

While this was going on, Odo was looking to expand his holdings. To that end, he began to plot with those of his men whose loyalty he knew he could trust to seize control of the castle of Melun. It pained him greatly, he told them, that he did not have access to a crossing over the Seine where he could bring his troops across the river. For this reason he had hit upon the idea of retaking Melun, which was located in an easily defensible position in the middle of the Seine and was accessible by two ports (since he already had a number of ports available to him on the Loire). He had no reason to fear the crime of perjury, since Melun had once

habeatur. Unde et omnibus qui fidem spondebant accelerandum suadebat, ut quacumque ratione valerent ad sui dominium transferrent.

75

Inductio ab legato Odonis in presidem Miliduni

Tunc suorum unus castri presidem petens, firmissimam amicitiam simulat fidemque multam pollicetur. Quod et utrimque sacramento mox firmatum fuit. Presidemque affatus, cuius antehac castrum fuerit quaerit. Ille cuius fuerit non abnuit. Iste quoque, 'Quo,' inquit, 'ordine ad regium ius accessit?' Ille quoque idem prosequitur. Et iste, 'Cur,' inquit, 'Odoni preiuditium fit, cum sepenumero[175] reddi sibi petierit, et se inferior eo nunc potiatur?' 'Quoniam,' inquit, 'id regi sic visum est.' Et iste, 'Putasne,' inquit, 'ipsam divinitatem non offendi, cum mortuo patre pupillus absque re patrimonio frustratur?' Et ille, 'Ita,' inquit. 'Et non solum id, sed

belonged to his grandfather, and at the moment it was held by someone other than the king.[75] He urged all those who owed him fealty to make haste and use any means necessary to bring the castle under his control.

75

The Castellan of Melun Is Led Astray by Odo's Messenger[76]

One of Odo's men then went to the castellan of Melun,[77] feigned steadfast friendship with him, and made a vigorous profession of his loyalty, after which both parties confirmed their agreement with an oath. Odo's man then addressed the castellan and asked him who the castle's previous owner had been. The castellan did not refuse to tell him whose it had been. The messenger asked, "How then, did it come into the king's power?" The castellan also answered this question, whereupon the messenger asked, "Why is Odo being denied that which is rightfully his, when he has asked to have the castle returned to him on many occasions, and it is now held by someone inferior to him?" "Because," the castellan replied, "that was the king's decision." The messenger continued, "Don't you think that God is offended when, after the death of a father, an orphan is deprived of his patrimony without cause?" "Of course," the castellan replied.

et bonorum desperatio fit. Quis enim inter primates Odone potentior? Quis omni honore dignior?' Atque ad haec iste, 'Si,' inquit, 'ad Odonem transverti velles, numquidnam ampliori potentia te non sublimandum arbitrare? Si eius esses, eius sine dubio gratiam, consilium, suppetias haberes. Pro uno castro plurima possideres. Unde et tui nominis gloria eo ulterius iret, quo amplius honoris culmen adipiscereris.' Ille vero, 'Quomodo,' inquit, 'absque peccato et dedecore hec fieri posse confidis?' Et iste inquit, 'Si te cum castro Odoni confers, quicquid sceleris nasci putas meum fiat, meum dicatur. Poenas[176] inde luam et summae divinitati rationem reddam. Consule nobilitati tuae. Fac tuarum rerum augmentum. Instat tempus. Oportunitas id suadet, cum inpotentia regnandi rex sit inglorius, et Odonem prosperior semper sequatur successus.' Ille rerum promissarum cupidus, sacramentum petit. Iste facit, et pro agendo negotio obsides querit. Ille multum honorem sese habiturum arbitrans, obsides dare non distulit. Quos iste receptos domum duxit et Odoni omnia haec retulit. Odoni itaque ut coeptis instet suadet.

"And what is more, this is a source of despair for good men. For who among the magnates is more powerful than Odo? Who is more worthy of every honor?" In response the messenger said, "If you were willing to cross over to Odo's side, don't you think that you would be elevated to a position of greater authority? If you were Odo's man, you can be assured that you would enjoy his favor, his counsel, and his aid. Instead of one castle you would possess many, and the greater the height of the honor that you obtained, the further the glory of your reputation would reach." In response the castellan said, "How can you be sure that all this will happen without my being stained by sin and dishonor?" The messenger answered, "If you give yourself to Odo and turn the castle over to him, then whatever crime you think may result, let it be on my head and charged against me. I will pay the penalty for it, and I will render an account of it to God on high. Now take thought for your own noble status and see to the increase of your fortune. The time to act is now. The circumstances recommend it, for the king's lack of authority has made him contemptible, while Odo is always attended by better fortune." Eager to obtain what had been promised to him, the castellan asked Odo's man to swear an oath. This he did, and in return he asked for hostages to guarantee that the castellan would live up to his promises. Thinking that he would soon gain a position of great importance, the castellan did not delay handing over the hostages. Odo's messenger took possession of them and brought them back with him. He reported everything to Odo and urged him to put his plans into effect.

76

Pervasio Miliduni ab Odone

Interea ab Odone copiae clam parantur, ut castrum ingre-
diatur et optineat. Paratis autem tempore statuto aggressus
appetit et ingreditur. Proditorem simulato furore invadit et
carceri mancipat. Qui non multopost carcere emissus, sacramento coram fidem facit et exinde ad resistendum cum
Odone sese parat. Quae omnia ad regum aures mox delata
feruntur. Reges de castri amissione commoti, in hostes milites parant, proponentes ab obsidione non sese discessuros
donec aut expugnatum recipiant, aut, si res exposcat, cum
hoste comminus vires et arma conferant.

77

Accessus regum ad Milidunum

Paratis itaque copiis, expugnatum accedunt. Et quia castrum circumfluente Sequana ambiebatur, ipsi in litore primo
castra disponunt; in ulteriore accitas[177] piratarum acies ordi-

76

The Capture of Melun by Odo

Meanwhile Odo was secretly readying his forces to infiltrate and seize control of Melun. When his men were ready, he set out at the appointed time, marched to Melun, and entered the castle. He seized the traitor with feigned anger and put him in prison. This man was released a short time later, however, and made a public profession of fidelity to Odo, after which he prepared to defend the castle with him. News of everything that had happened was soon brought to the kings. Dismayed by the loss of their castle, they assembled their fighting men to move against the enemy, resolving to lay siege to Melun until they recaptured it, or to meet their enemies on the field of battle if that were necessary.

77

The Kings' Arrival at Melun

When they had mustered their forces, the kings marched forth to begin the siege. Because the castle was encircled by the Seine, they pitched camp on the near bank of

nant. Et ne quo intercideretur obsidio, classes armatas in
fluvio circumquaque adhibent. Itaque factum fuit ut fluviali
superficie vecti, castrum navali pugna acriter urgerent. Castrenses non impares, inpugnantibus obnituntur; pro viribus
certant; adversariis nullomodo cedunt. Cumque diutius re-
sistentes comminus pugnarent, nec cederent, postico quod
inferius latebat viribus caedentium eruto, piratae admissi
sunt. Et a tergo in muro pugnantibus supervenientes, multa
caede in eis debaccati sunt. Sic quoque factum est ut et reli-
quus exercitus, in litore adhuc persistens, classibus pedester
intromitteretur castrumque repentinus pervaderet.

78

Castrenses capti regi dantur

A quibus castrenses capti et victi, mox regi oblati sunt.
Pro quibus coram rege ab amicis oratione habita, facta regi
fide dimissi sunt, cum non tantum rei maiestatis regiae,

the river, while they deployed the forces of the pirates[78] whom they had summoned on the opposite shore. To ensure that the siege would not be broken at any point, they put warships in the river on every side. In this way the ships were able to keep up a fierce assault upon the castle while borne upon the face of the water. The garrison, who were equal in strength to their besiegers, fought back against them, striving with all of their might and refusing to yield to their enemies. They had been holding out for some time, fighting in hand-to-hand combat and not giving any ground, when the pirates by repeated battering broke down a postern gate that lay concealed at the foot of the walls and gained entrance to the castle. Coming up from behind the men who were fighting on the wall, they wreaked havoc among them with tremendous bloodshed. This allowed the rest of the army, which was still waiting on the shore, to be brought over by ship on foot, whereupon they stormed the castle without warning.

78

The Garrison Is Seized and Turned Over to the King

The garrison was seized and the defeated[79] men were immediately turned over to the king. Some of their friends went to speak to the king on their behalf, however, and they

quantum sui domini fideles dicendi essent. Ad id etiam non perfidiae vitio, sed multa virtute adductos asserebant. His ergo obsidum iure dimissis, et castro domino priori reddito, proditor cuius dolo huiusmodi infortunium accessit mox comprehensus, suspendio secus castri portam defecit. Nec minus eius uxor, inusitato ludibrii genere pedibus suspensa, exuviis circumquaque defluentibus nudata, atroci fine iuxta virum interiit. Cum haec agebantur, Odo cum exercitu haud procul rei eventum opperiebatur, ratus castrum a suis posse contra hostes defendi, insidias[178] piratarum aliquantisper suspectas habens. Dum ergo herens de eventu nutaret, affuere nuntii qui castrum captum suosque comprehensos et inermes factos assererent. Quo audito, exercitum non aequo animo ad sua dimovit. Cui cum a querulis quibusdam intenderetur propter eum virum clarum[179] suspendio interisse, Odo respondisse fertur sese amplius lesum suorum comprehensione quam proditoris suspendio.

were released after taking an oath of fealty, since, it was argued, they were guilty not so much of treason as of faithfulness to their lord. Nor was it the vice of treachery, they said, but their outstanding courage that had spurred them on. When the members of the garrison had given hostages to secure their release, and the castle had been handed over to its former owner, the traitor whose schemes had brought about this misfortune was soon caught and hanged in front of the gates of the fortress. Moreover, in a novel form of indignity, his wife was hung up by her feet, with her clothing hanging down all around her exposing her nakedness, and there beside her husband she suffered a cruel death. Meanwhile, Odo was waiting nearby with his army to see what happened. He thought that his men could probably hold the castle against his enemies, but he had been worried about the treachery of the pirates for some time. As he was hesitating, wavering about the outcome in his mind, messengers arrived to tell him that the castle had been taken and his men captured and disarmed. Crestfallen at the news, he led his army home. When certain discontented people subsequently accused him of being responsible for the hanging of such an eminent man, he reportedly replied that the capture of his men grieved him more than did the hanging of a traitor.

79

Rixa Odonis et Fulconis
de Brittannia

Nec multopost bella civilia reparata sunt. Etenim Fulco, qui regum partibus favebat, exercitum in Odonem parabat, quaesiturus ab eo Brittanniae partem quam non multo ante ei[180] abstulerat. Collegit itaque IIII, qui[181] non comminus confligerent, eo quod eorum vires Odonis potentiae non sufficerent, sed eius terram incendiis et rapinis afficerent. Et tandiu id faciendum arbitrabatur, donec Odo aut tedio victus redderet, aut pro ea aliam non inparem conferret.[182] Preceps itaque fertur, terramque predis[183] combustionibusque affecit.[184] Et cum apud Blesum[185] loca suburbana succenderet, incendiis aura flante circumquaque erumpentibus, in coenobium monachorum sancti confessoris Laudomari ignis plurimus evolavit. Quod mox combustum, dirutum fuit; cibi quoque consumpti. Unde nec monachorum migratio defuit. His exemptis, in loca alia exercitum retorquet et vastat. Post cuius digressum Odo in eius terram versa vice exercitum induxit, sic in ea efferatus ut nec tugurium vel gallum relinqueret, hostem provocans et ut dimicaturus veniat invitans. Ille autem copias non sufficere sibi cognoscens, provo-

79

The Dispute Between Odo and Fulk Over Brittany

Not long after this, civil war flared up again. It began when Fulk,[80] who was a supporter of the king, assembled an army against Odo in order to retake the part of Brittany that had been seized from him a short time earlier.[81] He mustered four thousand men, not intending to meet his adversary in open battle, since his forces were inferior to Odo's, but instead to visit burning and plundering upon his lands. He planned to keep this up until Odo gave in out of exhaustion and restored his lands to him, or else gave him something of equal value in return. Fulk advanced rapidly, pillaging and burning Odo's territory. When he set fire to the outskirts of Blois, the wind scattered the flames in all directions, and a wall of fire engulfed the monastery of Saint-Lomer, rapidly burning it to the ground. All of the monks' provisions were consumed in the flames, and they left to go elsewhere. On the heels of this destruction, Fulk led his army into a different area and devastated it. After his departure, Odo in turn led his army into Fulk's territory, where he meted out such savagery that he did not leave so much as a single cottage or a rooster behind him, challenging and inciting his adversary to come forth and do battle against

canti cessit atque ad sua rediit. Atque haec fere per biennium.

80

Oratio legatorum Odonis apud regem de Miliduni pervasione[186]

O do interea, castro amisso frustratus, etiam in hoc sese
cautissimum habebat. Arbitrabatur etenim duplici calamitate se posse torqueri, cum de castri amissione plurimum
doleret, et a rege irato non mediocriter valeret urgeri. Unde
et regi legatos direxit, per quos sese optime ratiocinari posse
de obiectis quibuscumque suggereret, sese in nullo regiam
maiestatem lesisse ostensurum. Si de Miliduno agatur, contra regem nil mali molitum, cum non regi sed suo commili-
toni illud abstulisset. Regi nihil derogatum fuisse, cum ipse
regis aeque sit ut ille cui abstulit. Nihilque interesse quantum ad regiam dignitatem quicumque teneat. Sese etiam
iustis causis id effecisse, cum illud a suis precessoribus olim
possessum approbari possit. Unde etiam videri posse a se

him. Fulk, however, realizing that he did not have sufficient forces, yielded in the face of these provocations and returned home. This lasted for almost two years.

80

The Speech of Odo's Envoys to the King Concerning the Capture of Melun

Although he was frustrated by the loss of Melun, Odo proceeded very cautiously in this matter. He realized that he risked a double calamity: not only was he vexed by the loss of the castle, but the king's anger could make life very difficult for him. For this reason, he sent envoys to the king to inform him that he could be vindicated in the face of any allegations that had been made against him, and to prove that he had not committed treason against him in any way. With regard to Melun, he had intended no harm to the king, since he had not taken it from him, but from one of his vassals, a man equal in status to himself.[82] And in the end, Hugh had suffered no loss, because Odo was just as much a vassal of the king as the man from whom he had taken it. As far as the crown was concerned, it made no difference who held the castle. Moreover, his actions had been justified because he could prove that Melun had previously been held by his ancestors. So from this perspective it could be seen as more

dignius teneri debere quam ab alio quocumque. Tandem si quid piaculi factum est, in sese poenam dedecoris redundasse, tantumque scelus pari ignominia abstersum. Unde et facilius sibi indulgendum atque in tanta iniuria amplius parcendum. Rex orationis vim advertens, legatis satisfacit benivolentiamque petenti mandat. Haec legati Odoni referunt. Odo itaque regem adiit. Coram quo oratione utiliter usus, eius gratia potitus est, tanta affabilitate insignis ut amicitiam pristinam renovarent, et in nullo suspectus regi haberetur.

81

Bellum inter Odonem et Fulconem de Brittannia

Hac tempestate itidem civilia bella reparata sunt. Nam Fulco, Brittanniae parte frustratus, insidias adhuc parare contendebat. Collectoque exercitu, in Brittanniam preceps fertur Namtasque appetit. Cuius custodes alios auro corru-

fitting that he should hold Melun rather than someone else, whoever he might be. Finally, if there had been any wrong-doing on his part, he had already been punished by the shame that he had endured. As great as the crime was that had been committed, it had been wiped away by a disgrace of equal magnitude. Considering what he had already suf-fered, the king should be all the more ready to forgive him and offer him pardon. Recognizing the power of these argu-ments, the king granted the envoys what they sought and sent them back with a message of goodwill for Odo. When they returned with the news, Odo went before the king, and after effectively pleading his case, he was restored to his favor. Odo demonstrated such an amiable demeanor that the good relations that had formerly existed between them were restored, and the king did not harbor any suspicions against him.

81

Fulk and Odo Go to War Over Brittany

At this time civil war broke out again because Fulk, who had been dispossessed of part of Brittany, was still scheming to get it back. After raising an army, he advanced swiftly into Brittany and marched on Nantes. By bribing some of the

992

pit, alios quibusdam pollicitationibus illexit. Eis quoque usque ad effectum suasit quo sibi satisfacerent, ut scilicet urbis introitum panderent. Qui suasi, sacramento tempus constituunt, nec multopost et in urbem admittunt. Ingressusque pervadit et a civibus iure sacramenti obsides accepit. Arcem solam expugnare non valuit, eo quod milites magnanimos haberet. Unde et cessit, sese recedere deliberans, ut copiis amplioribus congressurus rediret arcemque expugnaret.

82

Conanus in exterioribus Brittaniae partibus qui locus Bruerech dicitur de rebus bellicis apud suos pertractabat, cum ad eius aures haec delata sunt. Magisque coepto negotio insistens, exercitum congregat[187] bellumque fieri parat. Et quoniam obsidioni instandum tempus suadebat, collectum exercitum urbi inducit eique ad[188] unum latus obsidionem per terram ordinat. Ad alterum vero per Ligerim classes piratarum adhibet.[189] Undique ergo obsidione disposita, a piratis per fluvium, a Brittannis per terram urbani[190] vehementer urgentur. Nec minus qui in arce remanserant a superioribus iaculorum diversa genera precipitabant. Parique inpugnatione superiorum atque inferiorum qui medii erant vexabantur. Nam qui in arce et in obsidione certabant

city's guards with gold and enticing others with promises of various sorts, he persuaded them to comply with his wishes and open the gates of the city to him. Those whom he had won over swore an oath and fixed a time for his arrival, and not long thereafter they actually admitted him into the city. Upon entering, he seized control of the city and took hostages from the townsmen under oath. The only part of the city he could not take was the citadel, which was by garrisoned by stout-hearted soldiers. And so he abandoned the attempt, planning to leave temporarily and come back later with reinforcements to capture it.

82

Conan[83] was in outer Brittany at a place called Broerec, holding a council of war with his men, when the news reached him. Applying himself all the more urgently to the task at hand, he mustered an army and prepared for war. Because the time was right to commence a siege, he led the army that he had just assembled to Nantes, investing one side of the city by land and deploying a pirate fleet on the Loire against the other side. The city was now completely surrounded, with the townsmen under violent assault from the pirates on the river and from the Bretons on land. In addition, the men who remained in the citadel were hurling various sorts of projectiles at them from above, leaving them caught in the middle, subject to attacks from above and below. The men inside the citadel and those taking part in the

Conani partes tuebantur; urbani vero pro Fulconis victoria operam dabant. Nec minus Fulco copias parabat et exercitum tam de suis quam conducticiis congregabat. Comperto[191] vero Conanum urbi obsidionem adhibuisse, mox legionem[192] Brittanniae infert.

83

Dolus Fulconi paratus

Erat campus non valde procul, longitudine sui et latitudine vastus, filicetum in se maximum habens. Hic Conanus locum gerendi belli constituens, insidiarum dolos infodit. Nam fossas quam plures ibi inmergens, virgis et viminibus stipulisque earum hiatus desuper operuit, intus surculis defixis qui superiora sustinerent[193] et soliditatem superficiei

siege were supporters of Conan, while the townsmen were fighting on behalf of Fulk. Fulk himself, meanwhile, was readying his forces and assembling an army composed of both his own men and hired soldiers. When he heard that Conan had laid siege to Nantes, he immediately led his army into Brittany.

83

The Trap Prepared for Fulk

Not far from the city there was a huge field the whole length and breadth of which was uncultivated and overgrown with ferns.[84] Conan decided that this was the place where the battle would be fought, and he set about digging up the ground to prepare traps for his enemies. He dug as many ditches as he could there, and covered them with branches, twigs, and grass. Inside he planted stakes to support this material, giving the appearance that the ground above was solid. To ensure that this artificial surface remained completely hidden, he gathered up ferns and scat-

simularent. Et ut simulata superficies penitus lateret, filicem collectam desuper respersit insidiasque dissimulavit.

84

Fraus[194] Conani contra hostes

Post insidias[195] ipse acies ordinans, sic fraude usus est ut diceret se ibi mansurum, nec ulterius hostes quaesiturum. Si hostes urgerent, ibi tantum vitam defensurum. Nec ob metum id facturum, at ut hostes, si sese querant et impetant, contra ius id faciant. Sic enim eorum ruina facilius provenire possit, cum sua temeritate quietos et innoxios aggrediantur. Ibi itaque acies ordinavit, insidias in prospectu habens. Herebat ergo, hostesque excepturus opperiebatur. Fulco Conanum herentem videns, nec ab eo loco exiturum,[196] cum insidias nesciret, suos multo hortatu suadebat quatinus vehementi[197] conamine impetum facerent, hostesque aggredi non dubitarent. De victoria[198] non diffiderent, cum virium spes optima non desit, si divinitas aversa non sit. Dato ita-

tered them on top, covering up the snares that lay hidden
below.

84

Conan's Ruse Against His Enemies

After drawing his men up in rank behind the line of pit-
falls, he declared by way of a ruse that he was going to hold
his ground and advance no further against the enemy. If his
foes pursued him there, he would only be defending his own
life. He was not doing this out of fear, he claimed, but to ensure that if his enemies came to attack him, they would be
doing so unjustly. For in that case they would be all the more
likely to meet with disaster, since they would be recklessly
attacking peaceful men who had done them no harm. And
so he deployed his battle lines, keeping the snares that he
had set in front of him, and waiting to catch his enemies.
Fulk knew nothing of these traps, and when he saw Conan
biding his time, with no intention of moving from that spot,
he repeatedly exhorted his men to charge forward and attack their foes resolutely. They need not have any doubt that
they would prevail, he said, for they could trust in their superior strength as long as God was not against them. With

que signo, irruunt. Arbitrati quoque solidum iter, fossis in-
dubitate propinquant.

85

Precipitatio hostium a Conano

Cumque Brittannos metu herentes arbitrarentur, telis
obnitentes ad fossas irruunt. Precipitatique cum equis in-
merguntur, ac caeca ruina confusi, ad $\overline{\text{XX}}$ inmersi atque
compressi sunt. At posterior exercitus, priori precipitato,[199]
terga dedit. Unde et Fulco vitae tantum consulens, profugio
eripi conabatur.

that, he gave the signal and his men rushed forward. Because they assumed that there was solid ground in front of them, they advanced toward the ditches without hesitation.

85

The Downfall of Conan's Enemies

Thinking that the Bretons were staying put out of cowardice, they charged headlong toward the ditches with their lances at the ready, whereupon the ground beneath them gave way, plunging them to the bottom of the pit along with their horses. In the blind chaos of their fall twenty thousand of them were trapped and crushed to death. When the men in the rear saw the disaster that had befallen the front ranks, they turned and fled. Thereupon Fulk, thinking only of his own safety, tried to escape and save himself.

86

Interfectio Conani

Q uem cum fuga exagitaret,[200] Conanus interim in dume-
tum cum tribus sese recepit, armisque depositis, corporis
fervorem ad auram[201] mitigabat. Quem quidam adversariorum intuitus, facto impetu illum adorsus, gladio transfixit,
Fulconisque victoriam extulit. Fulco, animo resumpto,
Namtas repetit atque ingreditur, qui in arce erant acriter
vexans. Qui principe destituti, pene exanimes inpugnanti
cedunt fidemque postulati faciunt.

87

Repudium reginae Susannae
a rege Rotberto

H is ita sese habentibus, Rotbertus rex, cum in XVIIII
aetatis anno iuventutis flore vernaret, Susannam uxorem,
genere Italicam, eo quod anus esset, facto divortio repudia-

86

The Death of Conan

As Fulk was being driven headlong in flight, Conan retired into a thicket with three of his men, stripped off his armor, and began to cool himself off in the breeze. One of his enemies caught sight of him, however, and charged forward to attack, running him through with his sword and proclaiming Fulk the victor. Thereupon Fulk recovered his courage and returned to Nantes, entering the city and mounting a fierce assault upon the men who remained in the citadel. Bereft of their leader and half dead from exhaustion, they surrendered to their attacker and swore fealty to him when it was demanded of them.

87

King Robert's Repudiation of Queen Susanna

Meanwhile King Robert, who had reached the age of nineteen and was in the bloom of youth, divorced and repudiated his wife Susanna, an Italian by birth, on the

vit. Quae repudiata, cum ea quae ex dote acceperat repetere vellet, nec ei rex adquiesceret, aliorsum animum transvertit. A qua etiam die, sua quaerens, regi insidias moliebatur. Nam Monasteriolum castrum, quod in dote acceperat, ad suum ius refundere cupiens, cum id efficere non posset, secus eum aliud nomine . . . extruxit, rege interim occupato circa Odonis et Fulconis facinora. Ex cuius munitione arbitrabatur posse omnem navium convectationem prohiberi, cum sibi advenientes sese prius offerrent, unde[202] et eis transitum ulterius inhibere valeret.

88

Reprehensio repudii

Huius repudii scelus a[203] nonnullis qui intelligentiae purioris fuere satis laceratum eo tempore fuit, clam tamen, nec patenti refragatione culpatum.

grounds that she was an old woman.[85] When, after the repudiation, she subsequently tried to recover what she had been given by way of a dower, and the king refused to return it to her, she turned her thoughts to other methods. From that day forward she began to plot secretly against the king to get back what belonged to her. She wanted to seize control of the castle of Montreuil, which she had been given as part of her dower, but when she was unable to do so, she built another castle next to it by the name of . . .[86] while the king was busy dealing with the mischief caused by Fulk and Odo. She thought that this fortress would enable her to put a stop to maritime trade, because any ships that arrived would have to come to her first, and she would be able to prevent them from going any further.[87]

88

Condemnation of the Divorce

At the time many people of sounder judgment condemned this sinful act of repudiation, but only in private; the criticism did not rise to the level of open opposition.

89

Sinodus Chelae habita

Huius temporis diebus cum a papa Romano Benedicto abdicatio Arnulfi et promotio Gerberti plurimis epistolarum scriptis calumniarentur, episcopi quoque rei huiusmodi auctores simulque et alii cooperatores diversis reprehensionibus redarguerentur, placuit episcopis Galliae in unum convenire et super hac reprehensione consulere. Quibus Chelae collectis, sinodus habita est. Cui rex Rotbertus presedit, considentibus metropolitanis Gerberto Remensi, cui tota sinodalium causarum ratio discutienda commissa fuit, Siguino quoque Senonensi, Erchembaldo Turonico, Daiberto Bituricensi, aliisque horum comprovintialibus nonnullis. In qua postquam ex patrum decretis rationes de statu sanctae aecclesiae promulgarunt, inter nonnulla utilia constitui et roborari placuit ut ab ea die idem sentirent, idem vellent, idem cooperarentur, secundum id quod scriptum est: 'Erat eis cor unum et anima una.' Decerni et illud voluere, ut si in qualibet aecclesia quaecumque tirannis emergeret quae telo anathematis ferienda[204] videretur, id inprimis ab omnibus consulendum et sic communi decreto agitandum. Et qui anathemate relaxandi forent, decreto communi similiter relaxandos, iuxta quod scriptum est:

89

The Synod of Chelles

992/994

Because at this time Pope Benedict[88] had written a number of letters unjustly condemning the deposition of Arnulf and the elevation of Gerbert, and subjecting both the bishops responsible for it and those who had cooperated with them to various criticisms, the bishops of Gaul decided to meet and discuss what they should do about his reprimand. They assembled at Chelles[89] and a synod was held, presided over by King Robert and attended by Archbishops Gerbert of Reims (who was entrusted with administering all of the issues to be dealt with by the synod), Siguin of Sens, Erchembald of Tours, and Daibert of Bourges, as well as a number of their suffragans. After they had issued decisions concerning the status of the Holy Church in accordance with the decrees of the fathers, among a number of other useful provisions they resolved and confirmed that from that day forward they should be united in thought, will, and purpose, according to the scripture that says "they had but one heart and one soul."[90] They also decreed that if in any church an oppressive regime should arise that warranted destruction through the weapons of anathema, then they should all deliberate on the matter and resolve it through a communal decision. In a similar fashion, those who were to be released from the bonds of anathema should be released by virtue of a communal decree, according to what is writ-

'Consilium a sapiente perquire.' Placuit quoque sanciri,[205] si quid a papa Romano contra patrum decreta suggereretur, cassum et irritum fieri, iuxta quod Apostolus ait: 'Hereticum hominem et ab ecclesia dissentientem penitus devita.' Nec minus abdicationem Arnulfi et promotionem Gerberti, prout ab eis ordinatae et peractae essent, perpetuo placuit sanciri, iuxta quod in canonibus scriptum habetur: 'Sinodo provinciali statutum, a nullo temere labefactandum.'

90

Impetus Odonis et Fulconis inter se

Hac tempestate bella civilia reparata sunt. Cum enim tirannorum insidiis Odonis et Fulconis de Brittanniae principatu rixa resurgeret, illis dissidentibus reliqui etiam regnorum principes moti dissensere. Rex Fulconis partes tutabat. Odo suorum necnon et piratarum qui rege deserto ad se transierant Aquitanorumque copiis fretus incedebat. Unde Fulco in Odonem preceps, eius terram depopulatur, et post

ten: "Seek counsel from a wise man."[91] In addition, the council ordained that if the pope propounded anything that was contrary to the decrees of the fathers, it would be considered null and void, in accordance with the saying of the Apostle: "Completely avoid the man who is a heretic and dissents from the Church."[92] They also ratified in perpetuity the deposition of Arnulf and the elevation of Gerbert, just as these things had been decided and carried out by them, according to the text of the canon: "Let no one presume to undermine what has been established by a provincial synod."[93]

90

The Feud Between Fulk and Odo

At that time civil war broke out anew. For when the dispute over Brittany flared up again thanks to the machinations of the tyrants Odo and Fulk, their quarreling provoked the other magnates of the realm to take up arms against one another. The king took Fulk's side. Odo went into battle supported by forces composed of his own men, the pirates who had deserted the king and gone over to him, and the Aquitainians.[94] Fulk moved quickly against Odo, ravaging

994–996

in ea non procul ab urbe Turonica oppidum[206] exstruit atque munit. Copias ponit; militibus implet. Et quia ad hoc
diruendum Odonem adventurum sperabat, regem petiit
auxilia imploraturus. Cui cum rex auxilium polliceretur, ob-
stinatiore animo ferebatur. Itaque copias contra hostem
congressurus parat, exercitum colligit, bellumque Odoni in-
dicit. Odo pudore tactus, a Gallis Belgis[207] subsidia petit; si
adsint, gratiam sese recompensaturum spondet. Illi liberaliter annuunt fidemque faciunt. Nec minus Flandrenses[208] ac-
cersit, ab eisque tutelam petiit, vicem pollicens si quod petit
non abnuant. Illi quoque animo liberali quesita accommo-
dant. Piratis etiam legatos dirigens, copias sibi non negari
deposcit. Tempus et locus omnibus constituitur quo collecti
sese conferant. Odo interim suos placat, colligit, et incitat.
Ratusque Belgas et piratas tempestivos, cum suorum paucis
tanta celeritate in Fulconem fertur, ut in certamine plus $\overline{IIII}$
pugnatorum non haberet. Castro tamen obsidionem adhi-
bet armiferosque disponit. Castrenses multo conatu adur-
get.

his lands and later constructing on them a walled stronghold not far from the city of Tours.[95] He established a garrison there as well, and filled the stronghold with soldiers. And because he expected that Odo would soon be coming to try to destroy it, he went to the king to ask for help. When the king promised to assist him, Fulk became even more headstrong. He readied his forces for battle with the enemy, assembled his army, and declared war on Odo. Moved by this affront, Odo sought help from the Belgic Gauls. They agreed gladly and pledged fealty to him. He also called upon the men of Flanders, asking them for protection and promising the same in return if they did not refuse him. They, too, generously acceded to his requests.[96] He sent envoys to the pirates as well, beseeching them not to deny him troops. A time and a place were set for all of these forces to assemble. In the meantime he appeased, assembled, and encouraged his men. Calculating that the pirates and the men of Belgica would be arriving soon, he took a few of his troops and advanced against Fulk, moving with such haste that he had no more than four thousand men at his disposal. In spite of this, he laid siege to the castle, deploying his fighting men all around it and mounting a major assault upon the garrison.

91

Fulconis supplicatio apud[209] Odonem[210] per legatos

Fulco regem morantem non auxiliaturum et Odonis exercitum intolerabilem ratus, remissiori mox animo habitus est. Itaque per legatos Odonis amicitiam expetit. Pro Conani interitu C pondo[211] argenti sese impensurum mandat. Loco militis interfecti filium suum pro eo militaturum offert. Castrum extructum in eius honore sese eversurum atque a suis evacuaturum. Sese quoque ei sponte militaturum ire, si id regi iniuriosum non foret. Quod quia absque regis iniuria fieri non poterat, eius filio manus per sacramentum daret. Itaque fieret ut ipse cum nato[212] militaret, cum filium suum Odoni pro Conano daret et sese Odonis filio militaturos committeret. Daturum se etiam fidem sacramento contra omnium causam, preter regis et horum quibus speciali consanguinitate carius addictus est, utpote nati, fratris, ac nepotum. His Odo perceptis, suorum usus consilio, haec sese excepturum optime mandat, si Namtas Brittanniae ur-

91

Fulk Sends Envoys to
Ask for Terms

Fulk, realizing that the king was delaying and would not
be coming to his aid, and recognizing that he himself could
not resist Odo's army, soon adopted a more pliant demeanor.
He sent envoys to ask for Odo's friendship, offering to pay
one hundred pounds of silver as compensation for the death
of Conan, and volunteering his own son[97] to serve in place of
Odo's slain vassal. He promised to tear down the castle that
he had built on Odo's fief and remove all of his men. He
would even be willing to serve as Odo's vassal if that were
not contrary to the king's interests. But because there was
no way that he could do this without injury to the king, he
would instead take an oath and give his hands to Odo's son.[98]
In this way he and his son would be doing military service,
since he would be giving his own son to Odo in place of Conan, while at the same time he would be committing them
to serve Odo's son.[99] He would also swear an oath of fealty
to Odo that superseded all other claims upon him, except
for those of the king and those to whom he was bound by
particularly close ties of kinship, such as his son, brother,
and nephews.[100] After hearing what they had to say, Odo
took counsel with his men and sent word that he would be
glad to agree to these terms if Fulk restored Nantes to him
(the city in Brittany that he had treacherously seized) and

bem dolo captam reddat et a suis evacuet. Iniuriosum enim
id videri, si ablata prius non repetat, et non redditis cum
hoste pacem faciat.

92

Abruptio[213] supplicationis
ab Fulcone

Haec dum exagitarentur, et Odo exercitum suum pau-
latim augeri arbitraretur, priusquam copias congrediendi
haberet, rex cum $\overline{\text{XII}}$ affuit, cum Fulconem $\overline{\text{VI}}$ suorum sti-
parent. Quibus mixtis, exercitus armatorum densatus est.
Unde et Fulco insolentior factus, quae ante supplex obtule-
rat spernit. Ut bellum fiat fervidus instat. Et ut vada Ligeris
qui eis interfluebat pertranseant hostemque impetant, hortatur atque suadet. Odo suos ut spoponderant non venisse
advertens, eo quod exercitibus colligendis huius temporis

removed his men from it. For it would be seen as an insult to him if he did not first demand back what had been taken from him, and if he made peace with his enemy without recovering it.

92

Fulk Breaks off His Request for Terms

During the negotiations Odo expected that his army would be gradually growing larger, but before he could assemble a force sufficient to go into battle, the king arrived with twelve thousand men, adding to the six thousand Fulk already had. Their forces were combined together to form a dense throng of fighting men. Fulk grew more brazen as a result, and rejected the terms that he had obtained earlier through humble entreaties. He now eagerly pressed for war, urging and exhorting his men to cross the ford over the Loire that separated them from their foes and attack the enemy. Meanwhile, Odo was in a highly agitated state, having realized that his allies had not come as promised because

brevitas non sufficeret, animo nimis turbato ferebatur. Atta-
men cum IIII refragratus,[214] vada Ligeris prohibebat.

93

Rex vadi incessu prohibitus, ad Ambatiam castrum retorquet exercitum, quod non procul in eodem litore flumi-
nis inter rupes eminebat, ut ibi transiens et post obliquatus
hostibus a tergo inprovisus adsistat eosque adurgeat. Odo
regis exercitum non sustinens, legatos ei dirigit, hostem
suum non regem sese impetiisse mandans, nec contra regem
quicquam molitum, at contra inimicum. Si rex iubeat, se
mox ulterius iturum et sibi de omnibus satisfacturum. Rex
rationis consequentiam advertens, tantum virum absque
causa a se laesum suspectum habebat. Unde et ne penitus a
se deficeret, ab eo obsides sub pace sequestra accepit, de
omnibus quae ei intenderet post rationem ab eo auditurus.
Unde et exercitum reducens, Parisium devenit. Odo quoque
nihil amittens, indempnis Meldim cum suis devenit.

there had not been enough time for them to assemble their troops. Nonetheless he held out with his four thousand men and defended the crossing over the Loire.

93

Because the king was prevented from entering the ford, he led his army back to the nearby castle of Amboise, which was perched high in the hills on the same side of the river.[101] He intended to cross the river there and then change directions so that he could come up from behind his enemies unexpectedly and press the attack. Odo could not withstand the king's army, and he sent messengers to declare that it was his own enemy and not the king whom he had attacked. His quarrel had only been with his foe, not with the king. If the king commanded it, he would come over to him at once and make satisfaction to him on all counts. The king pondered his next step, mistrustful of this eminent man whom he had injured without cause. To ensure, therefore, that Odo would not abandon him completely, he took hostages from him under terms of truce and agreed to let him answer to the charges that he had directed against him at a later date. With that, he took his army away and went back to Paris. Odo, meanwhile, having lost nothing, returned to Meaux with his men, unscathed.

94

Obitus Odonis

Inde etiam post dies non multos castrum quod Dunum dicitur sua dispositurus petiit. Unde cum de suis quos sub pace sequestra regi delegaverat plurima consultatione deliberaret, humorum superfluitate pro temporis immutatione vexatus, in egritudinem quae a phisicis synantica dicitur decidit. Quae cum intra gulae interiora sedem habeat, ex fleumatis reumatismo progressa, tamen aliquando ad maxillas et genas, aliquando ad toracem et pulmones tumorem cum dolore gravi immittit. Quibus tumentibus atque ferventibus, excepta initii die post diatritum patientem perimit. In hanc igitur Odo lapsus, infestis gulae doloribus circumquaque pulsabatur. Arteriarum quoque fervor sermonis intercisionem operabatur. Nec petiit huiusmodi dolor capitis superiora, at precordia pertemptans, pulmonem et epar peracuto dolore stimulabat. Fuit itaque militum luctus, famulorum clamor, feminarum frequens exclamatio, eo quod dominum inconsultum amittebant, et natis dominandi spes nulla relinqueretur, cum reges patri adhuc animo irato perstarent, et Fulco insolentiae spiritu pacem multifariam turbaret. Et tamen in brevi victurus, regibus legatos celeres mi-

94

The Death of Odo

A few days later Odo set out for the castle of Châteaudun to attend to some of his affairs. While he was engaged in careful deliberations concerning the men whom he had turned over to the king to secure a truce, he began to suffer from an excess of humors brought on by the change of seasons, and he was taken ill with the sickness that physicians call synanche. It begins in the inner part of the throat, arising from rheumatic phlegm, before spreading to the jaw and the cheeks, and eventually inducing swelling and severe pain in the chest and lungs. These parts of the body become feverish and inflamed, and on the third day (not counting the day of onset) it kills the patient. After lapsing into this illness, Odo was struck on all sides by terrible pains in his throat, and the inflammation in his breathing passages caused him to have difficulty speaking. The top of his head remained relatively unaffected, but his diaphragm, lungs, and liver were afflicted with acute pain. There was mourning among his fighting men, wailing from his servants, and repeated cries from the women. For they were all losing their lord unexpectedly, and no hope remained that his sons would rule in his place, since the kings were still irate at their father, and Fulk, in his spirit of brazen arrogance, continued to threaten the peace in various ways. Even so, recognizing that he had only a short time to live, Odo sent swift messen-

sit, qui pro se supplices suasorie rogarent et pro iniuriis illatis iustissimam[215] recompensationem sponderent. Rex veteranus malorum correctionem ab legatis excipere volens, a filio indignante inhibitus est. Unde et legatorum allegationem penitus sprevit atque illos immunes redire coegit. Quibus in itinere moram agentibus, antequam redissent, die quarta natae synanticae facta, Odo monachus factus defecit atque sic vitae finem habuit; ad sanctum Martinum delatus et in loco quod Maius Monasterium dicitur cum multo suorum obsequio sepultus.

95

Iohannes papa Leonem abbatem in Gallias mittit ut Arnulfi abdicationem discutiat[216]

Per idem tempus cum a Germanorum episcopis domno Iohanni papae per epistolas saepenumero suggestum foret ut Gerberti Remorum metropolitani promotionem abdicaret et Arnulfi abdicationem preter ius factam indignaretur, a papa in Germaniam tunc directus est Leo monachus et abbas, qui vicibus papae potitus cum episcopis Germaniae

gers to the kings to solicit them persuasively as suppliants on his behalf, promising to provide just compensation for the injuries that they had suffered. The old king wanted to accept the envoys' offer and let Odo atone for his misdeeds, but he was prevented from doing so by his son's resentfulness. And so he flatly rejected the offer brought by the envoys and ordered them to leave without any reward. The envoys were held up during the journey home, and before they could make it back, Odo, who had since taken the vows of a monk, succumbed and died on the fourth day after the onset of synanche.[102] He was carried to Saint-Martin and buried at the place called Marmoutier amidst a great throng of his followers. 996

95

Pope John Sends Abbot Leo to Gaul to Investigate the Deposition of Arnulf

All this time the bishops of Germany had been sending a steady stream of letters to Pope John, advising him to invalidate the elevation of Gerbert to the see of Reims and express his outrage at the illegal deposition of Arnulf. In response the pope sent the monk and abbot Leo[103] to Germany as his representative, with instructions to conduct an inves- 995

403

atque Galliarum huius negotii et indaginem faceret et iuditium diligens inde proferret.[217] Qui humanissime ab episcopis[218] exceptus, de habenda sinodo super hoc negotio cum
eis tractabat. A quibus Gallorum regibus, Hugoni videlicet
eiusque filio Rotberto, legati directi sunt qui papae manda-
tum necnon et episcoporum voluntatem super hoc aperiant,
eisque ut cum suis episcopis conveniant rationabiliter sua-
deant,[219] locum etiam tempusque quo et quando convenien-
dum esset a regibus discerent, eorumque animum ex hoc
sibi referrent.

96

Quod regibus indicatum[220] sit episcopos Germaniae in sinodum convenire

Legati igitur directi sunt. Legatio quoque prolata, quam[221]
etiam reges serenissima mente excipientes, papae et episcoporum mandatis in nullo tunc refragati sunt; sese consilium
super hoc quaesituros respondentes atque aequitatem de
omnibus facturos. Legatis itaque abductis, per quosdam re-

tigation into this affair together with the bishops of Germany and Gaul and to render judgment after careful consideration. Leo received a very hospitable reception from the German bishops and discussed with them the need to hold a synod to deal with this matter. Envoys were sent to Hugh and his son Robert, the kings of the Gauls, to inform them of the pope's directive and the will of the bishops in this matter, to persuade them through reason to attend the council with their bishops, and also to learn from the kings a time and place when and where it would be convenient for them to meet, and based upon this to report back to them about their intentions.

96

The Kings Are Informed That the Bishops of Germany Are Convening a Synod

And so the envoys were dispatched. Their message was delivered, and the kings received it calmly, raising no objections at that time to the demands of the pope and the bishops. In response they said that they would deliberate on the matter and do what was fair for all parties concerned. After the envoys had been led away, certain people informed the kings that this was all part of a scheme devised by Bishop

gibus indicatum est Adalberonem Laudunensem episcopum haec dolo ordinasse; omnino etiam apud Odonem illud pridem pertractasse. Eorum utrumque in voto habuisse ut Ottonem regem Galliis inducerent et reges ingenio et viribus foras expungerent. Episcopos quoque Germaniae ideo convenire ut dolum quaesitum expleant. Reges itaque, fraude percepta, episcopis iam ad locum designatum[222] convenientibus per legatos indicavere sese illuc non ituros, eo quod suorum precipuos penes se non haberent, sine quorum consilio nihil agendum vel omittendum videbatur. Indignum etiam sibi videri si correctioni episcoporum Germaniae suos subdat,[223] cum isti non minus nobiles, non minus potentes, aeque etiam aut amplius sapientes sint. Ipsi ergo si indigent, in Gallias properent, unde volunt edicant. Alioquin redeant et sua ut libet curent. Horum ergo res in contrarium relapsa est. Adalbero enim, qui horum ministrum sese prebuerat, cum delationis[224] nescius reges moneret ut occurrentibus obveniret,[225] rex veteranus, fraudium non ignarus,[226] Ludovicum Karoli filium ab eo reposcit, quem in captione Lauduni captum ei custodiendum commiserat. Repoposcit etiam eiusdem urbis arcem, quam similiter commiserat.

Adalbero of Laon, who in fact had worked out the whole thing with Odo some time ago. Both of these men wanted to bring Otto into Gaul as king and to depose Hugh and Robert by stratagem and force of arms; and it was to put this plot that they had devised into effect that the bishops of Germany had assembled. Having now been apprised of this trickery, the kings sent messengers to tell the bishops (who had already assembled at the designated location) that they would not be coming there because they did not have their most important men with them and they could not make any decisions about what to do or what not to do without their advice. It also seemed dishonorable for them to submit their own bishops to a German synod for punishment, since these men were no less noble and no less powerful than their German counterparts, and just as wise, if not more so. If the bishops found it necessary to do so, they should come quickly to Gaul and deliver a pronouncement on whatever subject they wished. Otherwise they should go home and attend to their own affairs as they saw fit. In the end their plans suffered a complete reversal. For when Adalbero, who had offered himself up as an accomplice to the conspirators and was unaware that he had been betrayed, advised the kings to go meet with the bishops, the old king, who was well acquainted with the bishop's treachery, demanded in return that he hand over to him Louis, the son of Charles, who had been seized during the capture of Laon and entrusted to Adalbero for safekeeping. He also demanded back the citadel of the same city, which he had similarly placed under his control.

97

Adalbero totius fraudis causa deprehenditur[227]

Quo credita reddere reniso, regii stipatores animo indignante subinferunt: 'Cum tu, o episcope, in perniciem regum et principum apud Ottonem regem et Odonem tirannum plurima quaesieris, quomodo hic ante dominos tuos reges tam magnifica confingere non vereris? Quid Ludovicum et arcem reddere metuis, si fidem regibus te servasse non dubitas? Quid ergo est credita nolle reddere, nisi contra reges infausta moliri? Evidentissime fidem abrupisti, cum apud Odonem[228] de regum interitu tractasti, eorumque honorem subruere temptasti. Unde et periurii reatu detineris. Legationem[229] etiam tamquam ab eis missam Ottoni regi pertulisti, ac apud eum dolose ordinasti ut ipse cum paucis[230] adveniret et militum multitudinem non longe[231] expeditam haberet. Regibus quoque nostris adversario cum paucis occurrere suasisti, atque nihil mali ex hoc proventurum spopondisti. Hanc etiam collocutionem utrimque utillimam fieri dicebas, cum hos et illum de communibus et privatis familiariter collocuturos simulabas. Verum aliter[232] tibi visum

97

Adalbero Is Revealed to Be Responsible for the Whole Plot

When Adalbero balked at returning what had been entrusted to him, the king's retinue responded angrily: "How is it, O bishop, that you are not afraid to tell such extravagant lies here in the presence of your lords the kings, when you have worked so diligently with King Otto and the tyrant Odo to destroy them and the leading men? If you are certain that you have always preserved your oath of fealty to the kings, then why do you fear to hand over Louis and the citadel of Laon? What other reason could you have for refusing to give back what has been entrusted to you, except that you are plotting some mischief against the kings? It is quite clear that you violated your oath of fealty when you discussed the destruction of the kings with Odo and attempted to undermine their sovereignty, thus implicating yourself in the crime of perjury. In addition to this, you brought a message to King Otto, pretending that it had been sent by Hugh and Robert, and treacherously arranged with him to have him come to meet them with a small retinue, all the while keeping a large band of soldiers at the ready nearby. You then persuaded our kings to go meet their enemy with only a few men to accompany them, promising them that no ill would befall them as a result. You assured them that the discussions would be beneficial to both sides, claiming that the

erat, cum hoc ideo pretendebas, ut ab Ottone rege dominos tuos reges comprehendi faceres, regnumque Francorum in ius illius transfunderes,[233] ut tu videlicet Remorum metropolitanus, Odo vero Francorum dux haberetur. Idque tunc nobis omnino patuit, sed ad tempus suppressum fuit. Et o summae divinitatis miserationem inestimabilem, quantis miseriis erepti, quanto ludibrio subtracti sumus! Instat tempus quo paratae insidiae effectum promittunt. Episcopi etenim sub specie religionis acsi de promotione et abdicatione Gerberti atque Arnulfi episcoporum quaesituri, premissis legatis adveniunt. Otto quoque rex Metti adest; a quo non longe exercitus collectus predicatur. Si ergo imus, aut pugnabimus aut capiemur. Si vero non imus, periurii arguemur. Sed ire reges non expedit, eo quod militum copia sufficiens eis non sit. Periurii vero reatus in te redundabit, cum tu solus regibus nesciis iuratus sis.'

parties involved would speak on amiable terms over private matters and issues of common interest. But in truth you had something quite different in mind. You arranged the meeting in order to deliver your lords the kings into the hands of King Otto and place the kingdom of the Franks under his authority. In return for this, you were to become archbishop of Reims, and Odo was to be made duke of the Franks. This was all known to us at the time, but we chose to keep it quiet temporarily. O unfathomable mercy of God on high! From what misfortunes have we been rescued! From what mockery have we been spared! The time is now at hand when these plots of yours are supposed to be bearing fruit. The bishops have sent out messengers and are assembling under the guise of piety, ostensibly for the purpose of holding an inquiry into the deposition of Arnulf and the elevation of Gerbert. King Otto is now at Metz, and it is said that his army has gathered nearby. Thus, if we go to meet him, we must either fight or be captured. If, on the other hand, we refuse to go, then we shall be accused of breaking our oath. And yet it would be foolish for the kings to go, because they do not have a sufficient number of fighting men at their disposal. Nonetheless, the guilt of perjury will be upon your head, because you swore the oath by yourself, without informing them."

98

Ad haec episcopus erubescens obmutuit. Quem cum unus suorum his exterritum vidit, contra haec responsurus surrexit, et sic oblocutorem adorsus est:[234] 'Horum omnium obiector mihi loquatur. Adsum qui pro criminato rationem reddo. Unus tantum haec proferat; caput quoque suum meo obiciat; arma quoque armis comparet; necnon et vires viribus conferat.' Hunc pro domino suo insanientem et fervidum Landricus comes sic alloquitur: 'O optime miles, harum, ut video, fraudium penitus es ignarus. Quae licet te ignorante, tamen ut predicantur quaesitae sunt. Unde et tempera animum, mitiga fervorem. Belli necessitatem non tibi imponas. Non te impellas unde ingressus redire non poteris. Sed nunc meo usus consilio, paululum hinc secede, dominumque tuum de his an vera sint interroga. Si te ad pugnam hortatur, congredere. Si dicit cessandum, furori parce.' Secessit ergo, dominumque vocatum an sic[235] res habeatur interrogat. Episcopus, utpote a conscio convictus, rem ita esse quaerenti confessus est. Unde et pugnam inhibuit. Sedato itaque tanto fervore militis, res penitus inno-

98

In response the bishop blushed and said nothing. One of his men, however, when he saw how frightened his lord had become, stood up to offer a response, accosting the man who had made the charges: "Let the person responsible for all of these allegations address himself to me. I am here to respond on behalf of the accused. Only one man need uphold these charges. Let him risk his life against mine. Let him make trial of arms with me and match his strength against mine." Count Landry[104] replied to the man who was raving so furiously on behalf of his lord: "Brave warrior, as far as I can tell you are ignorant of these deceptions. But whether you are aware of it or not, they have indeed been practiced, just as we have heard. So calm down and temper your anger. Do not impose upon yourself the obligation to fight, nor commit yourself to a course of action from which there is no return. Take my advice: step aside for a little while and go ask your lord if these things are true or not. If he urges you to fight, then do so. But if he tells you to stand down, then cease your madness."[105] And so the warrior went off to the side, and calling over his lord, he asked him whether the situation was as it had been represented to him. When questioned, the bishop, whose guilt had now been established by someone with knowledge of the affair, admitted the truth to him and prohibited him from fighting. Thus, when the warrior's fury abated, Adalbero's guilt became obvious to everyone. He was apprehended on the order of the

tuit. Detentus ergo regum iussu, utpote desertor custodibus datur. Cuius milites mox regibus sacramento alligati sunt.

99

Synodus quae Mosomi pro Arnulfo[236] habita est

Dum haec agerentur,[237] et[238] Galliarum episcopi ab regibus prohibiti essent ut ad sinodum statutam non venissent, episcopi tamen Germaniae, ne doli arguerentur si non accederent, statuto tempore Mosomum conveniunt, domni papae legatum secum habentes. Collecti ergo in basilica sanctae dei genitricis Mariae, ordinatim more ecclesiastico consedere, scilicet Sugerus Mimagardvurdensis, Leodulfus Treverensis, Nocherus Leodicensis, et Haimo Virdunensis. Horum medius abbas Leo resedit, vicesque domni papae obtinuit. Contra quos etiam Gerbertus Remorum metropolitanus, qui solus ex Galliarum episcopis, regibus etiam interdicentibus, advenerat, pro se responsurus ex adverso resedit. Consederunt quoque diversorum locorum abbates ac clerici nonnulli, laici etiam Godefridus comes cum duobus filiis suis, atque Ragenerus Remensium vicedominus.

kings and taken into custody as a traitor, and his men were subsequently bound to the kings under oath.

99

The Synod Held at Mouzon on Behalf of Arnulf

Although the bishops of Gaul had been prohibited by their kings from attending the upcoming synod, the German bishops, in an effort to avoid raising suspicions by not coming, assembled at Mouzon at the appointed time in the presence of the papal legate.[106] They gathered in the church of Mary, the Holy Mother of God, and took their seats in order of rank, in accordance with ecclesiastical custom. They were Swidger of Münster, Liudolf of Trier, Notker of Liège, and Haimo of Verdun. Abbot Leo, who was serving as the papal vicar, was seated in their midst, and across from them sat Archbishop Gerbert of Reims, who alone out of the bishops of Gaul had come, in spite of the royal prohibition, in order to plead his case. Many abbots from different places also took their seat there, in addition to a number of clerics and also the laymen Count Godfrey,[107] with his two sons, and Rainier, the *vidame*[108] of Reims.[109]

100

Praelocutio Haimonis Virdunensis episcopi de causa sinodi

Quibus circumquaque silentibus, episcopus Virdunensis, eo quod linguam Gallicam norat, causam sinodi prolaturus surrexit: 'Quoniam,' inquiens, 'ad aures domni papae sepissime perlatum est Remorum metropolim pervasam et preter ius et aequum proprio pastore frustratam, non semel et bis litteris suggessit quatinus nobis in unum collectis, tantum facinus iusta lance utrimque pensaremus, et sua auctoritate per nos correctum ad normam reduceremus. Sed quoniam impediente rerum diversitate id facere distulimus, nunc post tot ammonitiones domnum hunc abbatem Leonem et monachum mittere voluit, qui vices suas teneat et rem memoratam nobis oboedientibus discuciat. Per quem etiam scriptum suae voluntatis allegavit, ut si quid oblivio derogaret, scripto commendatum haberetur. Quod et inpresentiarum audire utile est.' Et statim protulit scriptum atque in aures considentium recitavit, quod quia brevitati studemus et nobis minus fuit accommodum, nostris scriptis inserere vitavimus.

100

The Address of Bishop Haimo of Verdun Establishing the Reason for the Synod

When everyone around him was silent, the bishop of Verdun arose to declare the reason for the synod, since he knew the Gallic language. "The pope has been informed many times now that the metropolitan see of Reims has been usurped and deprived of its rightful bishop in contravention of both law and justice, and for this reason he has written to us on several occasions to ask us to come together to conduct a fair and impartial investigation into this most serious crime, so that after we have corrected it by virtue of his authority, we can reestablish proper order. But since we have been forced to put it off for a variety of different reasons, now, after so many reminders, he has chosen to send this man, the monk and abbot Leo, to serve as his vicar and to examine the aforementioned matter with our compliance. And he has sent with him a document attesting to his wishes, so that if we forget anything, we will have it in writing to remind us. I think it will be useful for us to listen to it now." He then produced the document and read it aloud before the synod.[110] But because I am striving to be concise and I did not find it to be very relevant,[111] I have refrained from including it in my work.[112]

IOI

Oratio Gerberti pro se in concilio[239] recitata

Post cuius recitationem Gerbertus surrexit atque orationem pro se scriptam in concilio mox recitavit. Satisque apud illos luculenter peroravit. Sed hanc addere hic placuit, quod plena rationibus plurimam lectori utilitatem comparat. Cuius textus huiusmodi est:

(102)

Exordium

'Semper quidem, reverentissimi patres, hanc diem pre oculis habui, spe ac voto ad eam intendi, ex quo a fratribus meis admonitus, onus hoc sacerdotii non sine periculo capitis mei subii. Tanti erat apud me pereuntis populi salus, tanti vestra auctoritas, qua me tutum fore existimabam. Recordabar preteritorum beneficiorum dulcis atque affabilis beni-

101

Gerbert's Speech on His Own Behalf Before the Council

After it had been read out, Gerbert stood up and delivered a speech that he had set down on his own behalf, speaking before the council with admirable clarity.[113] I have decided to include this speech here, because it is full of arguments, and the reader will derive great profit from it. It reads as follows:[114]

[102]

Exordium

"Most reverend fathers, I have always anticipated this day, and I have looked forward to it with hope and longing ever since I undertook the burden of episcopal office at the behest of my brothers, in spite of the danger to my own life. So important to me was the salvation of a perishing people, and so much faith did I put in your authority, in which I thought that I would find safety. I recalled the past kindnesses of your sweet and generous good nature, which I en-

volentiae vestrae, qua sepenumero cum multa laude prestan-
tium usus fueram. Cum ecce, subitus rumor vos offensos
insinuat, vitioque dare laborat quod magna paratum virtute
inter alios constabat. Horrui, fateor, et quos ante formida-
bam gladios pre indignatione vestra posthabui. Nunc quia
propitia divinitas coram contulit quibus salutem meam semper commisi, pauca super innocentiam meam referam et
quonam consilio urbi Remorum prelatus sim edisseram. Ego
quippe post obitum divi Ottonis augusti, cum statuissem
non discedere a clientela patris mei beati Adalberonis, ab
eodem ignorans ad sacerdotium preelectus sum atque in
eius discessu ad deum coram illustribus viris futurus aecclesiae pastor designatus. Sed simoniaca heresis in Petri solidi-
tate me stantem inveniens reppulit, Arnulfum pretulit. Cui
tamen plus quam oportuerit fidum obsequium prebui, donec eum per multos et per me apostatare palam intelligens,
dato repudii libello, cum omnibus suis apostaticis dereliqui,
non spe nec pactione capessendi eius honoris, ut mei emuli
dicunt, sed monstruosis operibus diaboli[240] territus in effi-
gie hominis latitantis. Non, inquam, ideo illum dereliqui,
sed ne illud propheticum incurrerem: "Impio prebes auxilium, et iis qui oderunt me amititia iungeris, et idcirco iram
quidem domini merebaris." Deinde sanctionibus aecclesias-

joyed on so many occasions with the praise of my benefactors. But behold: suddenly a rumor began to circulate that you were displeased with me, a rumor that imputed to me as a fault what others agreed had been achieved through the exercise of great courage. I admit that I shuddered with fear, for the swords that I had trembled at earlier meant little to me when compared with your anger. But now, because merciful God has seen fit to bring me before you, to whom I have always entrusted my safety, I intend to say a few words about my innocence and explain to you the reason for which I was elevated to the see of Reims. Upon the death of the divine Emperor Otto, after I had made the decision to remain in the service of my blessed father Adalbero, unbeknownst to me he chose me in advance as his successor, and before an assembly of the most eminent men I was designated as the pastor of this church in the event of his death. But the heresy of simony sought me out, driving me from where I stood on the solid foundation of Peter and promoting Arnulf instead of me. In spite of this, I offered him my loyal service (more indeed than was deserved), until I learned for myself and from many other people that he had openly apostatized. Then, after presenting him with a written repudiation,[115] I abandoned him and all of his fellow apostates, not, as my rivals claim, because I hoped to succeed to his office[116] or because I had made a bargain to do so, but because I was terrified by the monstrous deeds of the devil lurking in the guise of a man. It was not, I repeat, for that reason that I abandoned him, but so that I would not incur the prophet's rebuke: 'Thou helpest the ungodly, and thou art joined in friendship with those that hate me, and therefore thou didst deserve indeed the wrath of the Lord.'[117]

ticis per longa temporum spatia peractis, legeque perhemp-
toria consumata, cum nichil aliud restaret nisi ut iudiciaria
principis potestate coherceretur, et tanquam seditiosus ac
rebellis a principali cathedra removeretur lege Africani concilii, iterum a fratribus meis et regni primatibus conventus
et commonitus sum ut excluso apostata, curam discissi et
dilaniati susciperem populi. Quod quidem et diu distuli et
postea non satis sponte adquievi, quoniam quae tormento-
rum genera me comitarentur omnimodis intellexi. Haec est
viarum mearum simplicitas, haec innocentiae puritas, et coram deo et vobis sacerdotibus in his omnibus munda consci-
entia.'

(103)

Particio

'Sed ecce, ex adverso occurrit calumpniator; vocum novi-
tatibus, ut maior fiat invidia, delectatus obloquitur: "Dominum tuum tradidisti, carceri mancipasti, sponsam eius ra-
puisti, sedem pervasisti!"'

It was only after a long period of time, when all the sanctions of the church had been exhausted, and the peremptory law[118] had run its course, when nothing else remained but for him to be turned over to the secular arm of the law for punishment and to be removed from the archbishop's chair as a rebel and a traitor in accordance with a law of the African Council, that I was once again called upon by my brothers and the chief men of the realm to undertake the care of an abused and divided people, now that this apostate had been debarred from office. I hesitated for a long time, and in the end I submitted only grudgingly, because I was all too aware of what sort of torments awaited me. Observe the simplicity of my ways and the purity of my innocence. Before God and you, the bishops, my conscience is clear in all that I did."[119]

[103]

Partition

"But behold, a slanderer comes forward who delights in employing novel words so that he may arouse greater ill will, and he reproaches me thusly: 'You betrayed your lord; you delivered him over to a prison cell; you ravished his bride; you usurped his see!'"[120]

(104)

Confirmatio et reprehensio alternatim digeste

'Itane ego dominum, cuius numquam servus fuerim, cui etiam nullum sacramenti genus umquam prestiterim? Etsi enim ad tempus famulatus sum, fecit hoc imperium patris mei Adalberonis, qui me in Remensi aecclesia commorari precepit quoadusque pontificis in ea sacrati mores actusque dinoscerem. Quod dum opperior, hostium preda factus sum, et quae vestra munificentia magnorumque ducum largitas clara et precipua contulerat, violenta predonum manus abstulit, meque pene nudum gladiis suis ereptum doluit. Denique postquam illum apostatam dereliqui, vias et itinera eius non observavi, nec quolibet modo ei communicavi. Quomodo ergo eum tradidi, qui ubi tunc temporis fuerit nescivi? Sed neque eum carceri mancipavi, qui nunc nuper sub presentia fidelium testium seniorem meum conveni ut propter me nec ad momentum ulla detineretur custodia. Si enim auctoritas vestra pro me staret, in tantum Arnulfus vilesceret ut michi minimum valeret obesse. Quod si contraria mihi, quod absit, sententia vestra decerneret, quid mea interesset utrum Arnulfus an alius Remorum constitueretur

[104]

Confirmation and Refutation
Set Forth Alternately

"And yet was he really my lord if I was never his servant and never swore any kind of oath to him? Even if I did serve him for a time, I did so under orders from my father Adalbero, who instructed me to remain in the church of Reims until I learned more about the character and deeds of the man who had just been consecrated bishop. But while I was waiting, I became the prey of my enemies, and what your generosity and the celebrated and outstanding liberality of the great dukes had bestowed upon me was stolen by a violent band of robbers who, after leaving me almost naked, rued the fact that I had managed to escape from their swords. Finally, when I left the service of that apostate, I stopped paying attention to the roads that he traveled and the journeys that he took, and I ceased all communications with him. How then could I have betrayed him, when I did not even know where he was at the time? Nor did I consign him to a prison, since I recently addressed my lord in the presence of faithful witnesses and asked that Arnulf not be held in custody even for a moment on my account. If you put your authority behind me, then Arnulf will become so discredited that he will be powerless to oppose me. But if, God forbid, you decide against me, then what difference does it make to me whether Arnulf or some other person is

episcopus? Iam de sponsa rapta sedeque pervasa quod dicitur ridiculosum est. Dico enim primum numquam illius
fuisse sponsam, quam pro legitima donatione spiritualis do-
tis collatis ante beneficiis expoliavit, proscidit, ac dilaniavit.
Necdum sacerdotali anulo insignitus erat, et iam omnia quae
denominatae sponsae fuisse videbantur satellites Symonis
vastaverant. Dico etiam si concederetur quolibet modo illius sponsa fuisse, utique esse desiit postquam pollutam et
violatam et, ut ita dicam, adulteratam suis predonibus pro-
stravit. Num igitur eam, aut quam non habuit aut quam suo
scelere perdidit, illius sponsam rapui? Sedem autem populo-
rum multitudine refertam advena et peregrinus, nullis fretus
opibus, pervadere qui potui? Sed forte apostolica sedes nobis opponitur, tamquam ea inconsulta summum hoc negotium discussum sit, vel ignorantia, vel contumatia. Certe
nichil actum vel agendum fuit quod apostolicae sedi relatum
non fuerit, eiusque per decem et VIII menses expectata
sententia. Sed dum ab hominibus consilium non capitur, ad
filii dei supereminens eloquium recurritur: "Si oculus tuus
scandalizat te," et reliqua. Et fratrem peccantem coram tes-
tibus coramque ecclesia commonitum, et non obaudientem,
decernit habendum tanquam ethnicum[241] et publicanum.
Conventus ergo Arnulfus, et commonitus litteris et legatis
episcoporum Galliae ut a cepto furore desisteret, et si vale-

established as bishop? As for what has been said about me ravishing his bride and usurping his see, this is absurd. In the first place, I tell you, she could never have been his bride, since in exchange for the lawful gift of a spiritual dowry he despoiled her of the gifts that had previously been bestowed upon her, rending her and tearing her to pieces. He had not even been honored with the ring of office yet, and already those minions of Simon[121] had plundered everything that belonged to his intended spouse. But even if we somehow grant that she was his bride at one time, she certainly ceased to be so after he befouled, polluted, and, so to speak, defiled her, before prostituting her to his band of brigands. Is it really possible, then, that I ravished his bride, when either he never had a bride in the first place, or else he forfeited her through his own wickedness? Could I, a foreigner and a stranger with no resources upon which to rely, really have usurped control over such a populous see? Now perhaps the apostolic see is invoked against us, on the grounds that a matter of such consequence was decided without consulting them, either through negligence or insolence. But in fact nothing was done (nor should it have been done) without their being informed of it, and we waited for their decision for eighteen months.[122] But when no advice is forthcoming from men, it is natural to look to the supreme eloquence of the Son of God: 'If your eye offends you,' and so forth.[123] And it also decrees that a sinning brother who has been warned in the presence of witnesses and the Church, and who still refuses to obey, is to be treated as a heathen and a publican.[124] Now Arnulf was summoned and warned, both in writing and by the envoys of the bishops of Gaul, to cease his madness and defend himself against the charge of trea-

ret quoquo modo se a proditionis scelere purgaret, dum mo-
nita salubria contempnit, habitus est tamquam ethnicus[242]
et publicanus. Nec tamen idcirco diiudicatus ut ethnicus[243]
ob reverentiam sedis apostolicae sacerdotiique sacri privile-
gia. Sed a se ipso in se ipsum dampnationis sententia lata,
hoc solum eum in omni vita sua preclare egisse diiudicatum
est. Quia nimirum, si eum se ipso dampnante episcopi absol-
verent, poenam sceleris eius incurrerent. "Si," inquit magnus
Leo papa, "omnes sacerdotes et mundus assentiat dampnan-
dis, dampnatio consentientes involvit, non prevaricationem
consensus absolvit. Hoc enim deus omnium indicavit, qui
peccantem mundum generali diluvio interemit." Et papa
Gelasius: "Error qui semel est cum suo auctore dampnatus,
in participe quolibet pravae communionis effecto, execrati-
onem sui gestat et poenam." Excluso itaque illo a Remensi
aecclesia, mihi reluctanti multumque ea quae passus sum et
adhuc patior formidanti, a fratribus meis Galliarum episcopis hoc honus sacerdotii sub divini nominis obtestatione
impositum est. Quod si forte a sacris legibus quippiam
deviatum est, non id malitia, sed temporis importavit necessitas. Alioquin tempore hostili omne ius omneque licitum
cavere, quid est aliud quam patriam perdere et necem in-
ferre? Silent equidem leges inter arma, quibus ille feralis
bestia Odo[244] ita abusus est, ut reverentissimos sacerdotes

son if there was any way that he could, but when he spurned these salutary admonitions, he was regarded as a heathen and a publican. In spite of this, he was not adjudged a heathen out of deference to the Holy See and the privileges of his sacred office. And yet when he passed the sentence of excommunication against himself, it was deemed to have been the only occasion in his entire life on which he had acted nobly. Now if the bishops had absolved him of his guilt after he had convicted himself, they assuredly would have incurred the penalty for his crime. For 'if,' says Pope Leo the Great, 'the entire priesthood and the whole world are in agreement with those who ought to be condemned, then the condemnation affects all of them as well. The fact that they are in agreement does not wipe away the transgression. The God of all made this clear when he destroyed the sinning world in a universal flood.'[125] And Pope Gelasius says that 'when an error has been condemned along with its author, the malediction and the punishment that it carries with it apply to anyone who is a member of the community of wrongdoers.'[126] And so, after he had been expelled from the Church of Reims, the burden of this office was imposed upon me under a sacred oath by my brothers, the bishops of Gaul, in spite of my reluctance and my apprehension of the sufferings I have experienced and still do experience to this day. Now if by chance there was any deviation from the laws of the Church, this was not done with malicious intent, but because the situation at the time demanded it. Otherwise what would a scrupulous obedience to every point of law and procedure during a time of war lead to, except death and the destruction of the fatherland? For laws fall silent when surrounded by arms,[127] arms which that savage beast Odo so

429

dei quasi vilia mancipia caperet, nec ab ipsis sacrosanctis altaribus temperaret, commeatus publicos intercluderet.'

(105)

Epilogus

'Redeo ad me, reverentissimi patres, cui specialiter ob salutem pereuntis populi totiusque rei publicae curam mors furibunda cum omnibus suis incubuit copiis. Hinc dira aegestas horreas et apothecas armata manu sibi vindicat; illinc foris gladius et intus pavor dies ac noctes reddiderunt insomnes.[245] Sola vestra auctoritas ut tantorum malorum levamen fieret expectata est, quae tantum vim habere creditur ut non solum Remensi, sed etiam omni ecclesiae Gallorum desolatae et pene ad nichilum redactae subsidio esse valeat; quod divinitate propitia expectamus et ut fiat omnes in commune oramus.'

misused at the time[128] that he imprisoned the most reverend priests of God as if they were lowly serfs, declined to spare even the sacred altars, and put a stop to all public traffic."[129]

[105]

Epilogue

"But let me return to my own case, most reverend fathers. While I have been devoting myself to the salvation of a perishing people and to the concerns of the whole realm, frenzied death has fallen upon me with all of its forces. On one side dire poverty claims my granaries and storehouses for itself with an armed band; on the other, 'the sword without and the terror within'[130] have rendered my days and nights sleepless. My only hope for the alleviation of these woes is your authority, which is believed to possess such power that it can help not only the church of Reims, but also the whole Gaulish church, which is now forsaken and reduced almost to nothing. God willing, this is what we are waiting for, and we all pray with one accord that it may come to pass."[131]

106

Quam perlectam, legato papae mox legendum porrexit. Tunc episcopi omnes cum Godefrido comite, qui eis intererat, simul surgentes seorsumque[246] seducti, quid agendum inde esset deliberabant. Et post paululum ipsum Gerbertum invitant. Cui cum[247] post aliquot sermones a domno papa corpus et sanguinem domini ac sacerdotale officium sub presentia legati prohibere vellent, ille mox ex canonibus et decretis confidenter astruxit nulli hoc imponendum, nisi aut ex crimine convicto, aut post vocationem venire ad concilium vel rationem contempnenti. Huic penae non sese esse obnoxium, cum ipse etiam prohibitus accesserit, et cum nullo adhuc crimine convictus sit. Simulque hoc ex Africano et Toletano conciliis asserebat. Sed ne domno papae omnino reniti videretur, a missarum celebratione sese cessaturum usque in alteram sinodum spopondit. Et statim his dictis sessum reversi sunt.

106

When he had finished reading out his speech, he handed it over to the papal legate for him to read. Then all of the bishops and Count Godfrey, who was there with them, stood up together and went off by themselves to discuss what they were going to do. A short time later they called Gerbert back in. After a few preliminary remarks, they went before the papal legate and declared that on behalf of the pope it was their will that Gerbert be debarred from the body and blood of Our Lord and from the office of archbishop. Gerbert responded immediately and with assurance, citing canons and decrees to show that no such punishment could be imposed upon anyone unless he had been convicted of a crime or else refused a summons to appear before a council and defend himself. He himself was not liable to this punishment, because he had come before the synod despite the fact that he had been prohibited from doing so, and because he had not yet been convicted of any crime. He cited the councils of Africa and Toledo to the same effect. To avoid giving the appearance that he was completely flouting the pope's authority, however, he pledged to refrain from saying mass until the next synod was held. When he had finished speaking, they all returned to their seats.[132]

107

Quibus considentibus, Virdunensis episcopus iterum surgens, eo quod sinodi interpres habebatur ad alios qui episcoporum consilio non interfuere, sic concionatus ait: 'Quoniam,' inquiens, 'hoc unde hic agitur diffiniri nunc non potest, eo quod controversiae pars altera deficit, placet his domnis episcopis ut vobis demonstretur presentis rationis causam in aliud tempus transferendam, ut ibi qui intendat et qui refellat ante iudicem consistant, ut singulorum partibus discussis, recti iudicii proferatur censura.' Ab omnibus conceditur et laudatur. Destinatur ergo locus Remis apud coenobium monachorum sancti Remigii; tempus quoque die VIII post natale sancti Iohannis baptistae. Quibus constitutis et dictis, sinodus soluta est.

108

Tempore statuto Silvanecti sinodus episcoporum collecta est, ubi etiam inter Gerbertum et Arnulfum presentaliter ratio discussa est sub presentia Leonis abbatis et monachi legati, aliorumque quam plurium.

107

When they had taken their seats, the bishop of Verdun, who had been assigned the task of explaining the proceedings of the synod to those who had not participated in the bishops' deliberations, stood up again and spoke as follows: "Since the matter at issue here cannot be resolved because one of the parties to the dispute is absent, the bishops have instructed me to tell you that the case under consideration should be postponed to a future date, so that both the accuser and the defendant may come before a judge, and a just verdict may be rendered after both sides have been heard." This proposal met with agreement and praise from everyone, and it was decided that a synod would be held at the monastery of Saint-Rémi at Reims eight days after the nativity of Saint John the Baptist.[133] When these decisions had been made and the speeches were concluded, the synod was dissolved.

108[134]

At the appointed time a synod of bishops assembled at Senlis,[135] where an inquiry was held into the dispute between Gerbert and Arnulf, with both parties in attendance, and in the presence of the monk and abbot Leo (the papal legate) and many others.

July 1, 995

435

Berta Odonis uxor suarum rerum defensorem atque advocatum Rotbertum regem accepit.

Richardus pyratarum dux apoplexia minore periit, Hilduinus quoque vinolentia.

Sinodus quinque episcoporum in Monte sanctae Mariae habita est.[248]

Alia item sinodus apud Engleheim indicta est sanctae Agathes festivitate habenda, quae et suo tempore habita est.

Berta, Rotberto nubere volens, Gerbertum consulit ac ab eo confutatur.

Gerbertus Romam ratiotinaturus vadit, ac ibi ratione papae data, cum nullus accusasset,[249] alia sinodus indicitur.

109

Hugo rex papulis toto corpore confectus, in oppido Hugonis Iudeis extinctus est.

Rotbertus rex patri succedens, suorum consilio Bertam duxit uxorem, ea usus ratione, quod melius sit parvum aggredi malum, ut maximum[250] evitetur.

Bertha,[136] the wife of Odo,[137] took King Robert as the guard- ian and advocate of her property.

996

Richard, the duke of the pirates, died of minor apoplexy, and Hilduin[138] of intoxication.

Nov. 21, 996

A synod of five bishops was held at Mont-Notre-Dame.

Another synod was scheduled to be held at Ingelheim on the feast of Saint Agatha, and it took place at the appointed time.

Feb. 5, 996

Bertha, wishing to marry King Robert, consulted Gerbert, who rejected the idea.[139]

Gerbert went to Rome to argue on his own behalf. After he had presented his case to the pope[140] and no one had appeared to argue against him, another synod was scheduled.

May 996

109

King Hugh was afflicted with pustules all over his body and died at his stronghold at Les Juifs.

October 996

After succeeding to his father's throne, King Robert took the advice of his counselors and married Bertha, reasoning that it was worth committing a minor wrong in order to avoid a great evil.

Rotbertus rex, ducta Berta uxore, in Fulconem, qui Odonis adversarius fuerat, fertur et ab eo urbem Turonicam et alia quae pervaserat <per> vim[251] recipit.

Rotbertus rex in Aquitania ob nepotem suum Wilelmum obsidione Hildebertum[252] premit.

Gerbertus iterum Romam adit, ibique cum moram faceret, Arnulfus a Rotberto rege dimittitur.

Gerbertus, cum Rotberti regis perfidiam dinosceret, Ottonem regem frequentat, et patefacta sui ingenii peritia, episcopatum Ravennatem ab eo accipit.

Gregorius papa tandiu permittit Arnulfo officium sacerdotale, donec in tempore racionabiliter aut legibus adquirat, aut legibus amittat.

After his marriage to Bertha, King Robert moved against 997
Fulk, Odo's old enemy, and used force to take back the city
of Tours and whatever else he had seized.

In Aquitaine King Robert laid siege to Hildebert[141] in order
to help his nephew William.[142]

Gerbert went to Rome again, and while he was there, Arnulf
was released by King Robert.

When Gerbert learned of King Robert's treachery, he went 997
to the court of King Otto, and when the depth of his intel- 998
lectual attainments became clear, he received the bishopric
of Ravenna from him.[143]

Pope Gregory permitted Arnulf to retain the office of arch- 997
bishop until such time as a decision had been reached in accordance with the law to grant or deny him the office.

Note on the Text

Richer's *Historia* survives only in the author's autograph manuscript: Bamberg, Staatsbibliothek MS Hist. 5. The folio that contained Richer's account of Gerbert's speech at the synod of Mouzon has gone missing or perhaps was never inserted into the manuscript. All of Richer's editors have reconstructed this section (chapters 4.102–5) from Gerbert's *Acta* of the synod, which are found in an eleventh-century manuscript from Saint-Mesmin-de-Micy and in the *Ecclesiastical History* of the Magdeburg Centuriators. Frutolf of Michelsberg (d. 1103) and Johannes Trithemius (1462–1516) both made use of a revised version of the *Historia* that once existed at Bamberg and which contained only the first two books. Many of their variant readings, which almost certainly represent revisions that Richer made to the text found in Bamberg MS Hist. 5, are included below.

Georg Heinrich Pertz produced the first edition of Richer's *Historia* for the *Monumenta Germaniae Historica* in 1839. Georg Waitz revised Pertz's edition for the *MGH* in 1877, and Robert Latouche published a two-volume edition and translation of the *Historia* with some emendations to Waitz's text in 1930 and 1937. Hartmut Hoffmann produced a comprehensive new edition of the *Historia* for the *MGH* in 2000; his is now the authoritative text. The text printed

here is based on Hoffmann's edition, kindly made available by the *MGH,* with some minor changes. While Hoffmann prints Richer's punctuation from Bamberg MS Hist. 5, the text here has been punctuated to accord with modern conventions.

Notes to the Text

ABBREVIATIONS

Frutolf = Frutolf of Michelsberg, *Chronicon,* ed. G. Waitz, *MGH SS* 6. Hanover: Hahn, 1844, pp. 33–223.

Hoffmann = Hartmut Hoffmann, ed., *Richeri Historiarum Libri IIII, MGH SS* 38. Hanover: Hahn, 2000.

L = *Acta concilii Mosomensis,* Leiden, Bibliotheek der Rijksuniversiteit, Voss. lat. Q 54, ff. 82r–84r.

Latouche = Robert Latouche, ed. and trans., *Richer: Histoire de France (885–995).* Les classiques de l'histoire de France au moyen âge. 2 vols. Paris: H. Champion, 1930 and 1937.

MS = Bamberg, Staatsbibliothek MS Hist. 5.

Pertz = G.H. Pertz, ed., *Richeri historiarum libri IIII.* Hanover: Hahn, 1839, pp. 561–657.

Poinsignon = A.-M. Poinsignon, *Richeri Historiarum quatuor libri—Histoire de Richer en quatres livres.* Reims: P. Regnier, 1855.

Trithemius = Johannes Trithemius, *Annales Hirsaugienses.* Saint-Gall, 1690.

Waitz = Georg Waitz, ed., *Richeri historiarum libri IIII, MGH SRG* 51. Hanover: Hahn, 1877.

Book 3

1   eo *omitted by Waitz*

2   *correction for* aderat, *which has not been expunged*

3   caedit *MS*

4   petiit *Pertz*

5   pemeria *MS*

6   fecit *Pertz*

7   aliquanto *added by a later hand*

8   secunda *Pertz*

9   egrediantur *corrected from* exeant

10   l cum boni quique capitis quocumque tegmine contenti sint. Hi ergo a religiosis dissidentes non sunt? Cum enim vestium dignitate delectantur, vilium procul dubio abiectionem unde ex parte religio recognoscitur penitus abhorrent *expunged after* induere

11   splen *expunged after* colore

12   De calciamentorum superfluitate *Pertz*

13   operibus *Pertz*

14   erunt *Waitz*

15   haec *Pertz*

16   studuiis *MS*

17   Romam *corrected from* in <Galliam>

18   quo *Pertz*

19   *faint marginal chapter title* Quod Atto Romae moratus decessit; *perhaps erased by Richer*

20   indicitur *Pertz*

21   de arte sua *Pertz*

22   servavit *Pertz*

23   in orizonte *in margin, expunged*

24   *After* reconderet *appear the words* Sed hoc ad circulos intellectibiles. Quanto etiam studio errantium quoque siderum circulos aperuerit, dicere non pigebit. Qui *All are expunged except* errantium quoque siderum circulos

25   *After* vero *appear the words* cuius nihil ante Galliae scriptum habebant, quantus labor expensus sit, sermo impar dicere non sufficit. *All are expunged except* labor expensus

444

26   C. *MS*

27   id negotium perpenderant, et ob hoc *expunged after* qui

28   eorum doctissimo *expunged after* Otrico

29   Non enim ignoro quemcumque bonum calumniis malivolorum
        assidue insectari *expunged after* sit

30   *sic MS*

31   Quod continentius sit rationale quam mortale *Hoffmann*

32   *sic Latouche* : in regem per Germanos et Belgas *Pertz* : a Germanis
        et Belgis *Waitz*

33   Tractant atque ordinant Galli Celtae. Quod. *expunged after* negotii

34   centuriati *expunged before* itaque

35   allici *corrected from* adici

36   cum principibus *expunged after* videndum

37   coepisset *MS*

38   favonium *corrected from* Gallos

39   viri clarissimi *Pertz*

40   Nec pretermittendus videtur congressus duorum, quorum alter
        Germanus, alter Gallus fuit *expunged before* cum

41   vel tirones *written above* milites, *which is not expunged*

42   furentem repellant et a tanta ignominia purgati *corrected from*
        canem latrantem repellant, et a tanta ignominia non solum sese,
        sed et totam gentem suam emundent, ac per infinita tempora.

43   *the name* IVO *is expunged*

44   vita *corrected from* armis

45   digressus *Waitz*

46   fuga *Pertz*

47   vel decretum *written above* deliberatum, *which is not expunged*

48   primatibus *corrected from* principibus

49   ergo *expunged after* Vos

50   quos et ingenium cogitandi et ratio dicendi reddidit clariores.
        Quos non dubito de pernitie bonorum dolere, quibus ingenti
        virtutue propositum sit improbis displicere. Et *expunged after*
        idoneos

51   etiam *expunged after* vos

52   a mente *corrected from* ab animo

53   Ad haec primates . . . quantis periculis *corrected from* Hac conques-

tione principes suscepta, non solum novimus inquiunt, vir illustris quanto periculo

54 gloriosissime *expunged after* est
55 Quod ut facilius fiat *expunged after* adipisceris
56 sessio *Pertz*
57 aegit *MS*
58 portaturum *Pertz*
59 Conrando *MS*
60 Vale *Pertz*
61 *corrected from* senatus consultum
62 Ludovici *corrected from* Rotberti
63 per omnia *expunged after* sese
64 supplicicem *MS*
65 efficatiter *MS*
66 habitum *written above* vestes, *which is not expunged*
67 operatum *Pertz*
68 descendentes *expunged above* vibratis
69 Belgica atque *expunged after* tempestate
70 hostis *expunged after* Otto
71 paucosque multitudini cedere *expunged after* posse
72 Gallis *corrected from* hostibus
73 millena *corrected from* mille
74 *sic Pertz* : *De* repetito *Waitz*
75 abducta *above* eiecta, *which is not expunged*
76 exstructa *above* educta, *which is not expunged*
77 Stamtimque *MS*
78 *correction for* in captis
79 personat *above* concrepitat, *which is not crossed out*
80 *corrected from* purpurea

Book 4

1 cultu *Pertz*
2 suarum urbium *expunged after* palatiis
3 com<morandum> *above* immorandum, *which is not expunged*
4 amicorum *corrected from* cognatorum

5   semperque dum in vita fuero potissimum vigebit *expunged after* valet

6   Aequum namque, ut pravus iusto supplitio damnetur. Utile vero, ut *expunged after* videtur

7   Eorum *corrected from* Eius

8   copiorus *MS*

9   curassent *corrected from* curarent

10   divae *Pertz*

11   suspitionem *corrected, perhaps from* suspectum

12   Purgato *expunged before* Ergo

13   vel immobili *above* obstinato, *which is not expunged*

14   Divae *Pertz*

15   orbi *corrected from* ab hac vita

16   imperatoribus . . . precipitatis *corrected from* imperatores . . . precipitatos

17   deus propitius esto *in the margin*

18   ab omnibus *expunged after* rex

19   fecit *corrected from* dedit

20   creari *corrected from* ordinari

21   citerioris *corrected from* interioris

22   alterum *Pertz*

23   bellico tumultu *corrected from* in bello Hispanico

24   *sic MS*

25   amici *corrected from* o amici mei

26   aliquam misericordiam ostendere *expunged after* affinitas

27   Mox omnes commoti *corrected from* Qua omnes commoti conquestione

28   et celare possent, et *expunged after* qui

29   eiusdem urbis *corrected from* Laudunensis

30   bona *expunged after* eis

31   Ergo inter vinearum sepes latuerunt, donec *expunged after* advenit

32   misitque *corrected from* missi

33   advenisse *corrected from* adesse

34   Karolum *Hoffmann*

35   non sine tumultu *expunged after* devexa

36   a muro *expunged after* vigiles

37	lapidibusque *corrected from* proditores lapidibus
38	personabant *corrected from* personantesque
39	cum esset *expunged after* unus
40	observatoribus *corrected from* osservatoribus
41	Deputavit ergo vigiles quingentenos *corrected from* Deputati ergo sunt vigiles quingenteni
42	ligna *corrected from* millenae trabes
43	incombendum *corrected from* incumbendum
44	sui *expunged after* eminentia
45	regem *apparently corrected from* reges *or vice versa*
46	mitiori *corrected from* mitiore
47	adhibuerunt *corrected from* suspenderunt
48	tracta *corrected from* tractus
49	eminet *corrected from* eminebat
50	quadam *corrected from* aliquan : die *added above the line*
51	aggravatis *corrected from* gravatis
52	annueret *above* sponderet, *which is not expunged*
53	absumpta videbat *corrected from* absumptae erant
54	et *corrected from* rex
55	hanc etiam *expunged*
56	adveniens *corrected from* advenit : adventans *Pertz*
57	plurimam *MS*
58	archiepiscopatum *Pertz*
59	quosdam *corrected from* Burch.
60	Hugonis *Latouche*
61	Divae *Pertz*
62	aliquos *corrected from* eos
63	suffecti *corrected from* facti
64	est *above* videtur, *which is not expunged*
65	Conferamus *corrected from* Conferantur
66	manachorum *MS*
67	Divae *Pertz*
68	eodem *Pertz*
69	cibum *expunged after* videri
70	tanta *above* multa, *which is not expunged*
71	patruum *expunged after* Karolum

72	solus *expunged after* is
73	adventaret *corrected from* adesset : adveniret *Pertz*
74	irruenti *corrected from* ruenti
75	secreti fidem *corrected from* secretum hoc numquam proditurum
76	ergastulo *above* custodiae, *which is not expunged*
77	v̄c *MS* : viros consulares *Pertz*
78	Karolus *above* exercitus, *which is not expunged*
79	intromitendus *MS*
80	commites *MS*
81	unanimiter *corrected from* unamimiter
82	enuntiaretur *above* predicaretur, *which is not expunged*
83	Arnulfus *above* episcopus, *which is not expunged*
84	regis *above* regum, *which is not expunged*
85	*sic MS*
86	*corrected from* V̄Ī itaque militum collegit, in tirannum ire disponens
87	terra *MS*
88	Exercitum tripertito ordinat *Hoffmann*
89	impetus *corrected from* tumultus
90	agere *above* fecisse, *which is not expunged*
91	iura *corrected from* ius
92	diffiderent *corrected from* diffidant
93	tempestiva *corrected from* intempestiva
94	et *expunged after* repentini
95	machinatio *Pertz*
96	ab se digressi sunt *above* abscesserunt, *which is not expunged*
97	effunderet *over* aperiret, *which is not expunged*
98	atque *corrected from* et
99	promis<sam> *expunged after* largitatem
100	his *above* eis, *which is not expunged*
101	omnia *expunged before* quae
102	explicans *corrected from* explicat
103	Nam *expunged before* Super
104	cunctos *corrected from* cunctis
105	plebem *above* populum, *which is not expunged*
106	accelerari *probably corrected from* accelerare

107   adhuc *corrected from* ad hunc
108   super *Pertz*
109   cloro *MS*
110   de omnibus sibi obiciendis *expunged after* quo
111   sententia *corrected from* sentia
112   st̄ *MS* : sunt *Hoffmann*
113   *omitted by Pertz*
114   Choi *corrected from* Coi
115   semotim *Pertz* : secrete *Waitz*
116   *corrected from* tertio
117   tortus *above* vexatus, *which is not expunged*
118   amicorum *corrected from* scolasticorum
119   edicto *corrected from* decreto
120   omnes *expunged after* episcopi
121   convictum *corrected from* captum : et convictum *expunged above*
           dampnarent
122   Remensis quidem metropolitani comprovinciales *corrected from* Ex
           provincia quidem Remensi
123   Lugdunensis metropolitani comprovinciales *corrected from* Ex
           provincia Lugdunensi
124   diversorum *corrected from* diversarum
125   prelatura *perhaps corrected from* prelaturae : prelaturae *Pertz*
126   habendarum rationum *corrected from* habendae rationis
127   Elocutio *Pertz*
128   vivaciter *corrected from* contra aemulum
129   criminatur *corrected from* dicitur
130   quantotius *corrected from* quam cito
131   capite *Pertz*
132   Ratiocinatio *corrected from* Oratio : Sermocinatio *Pertz*
133   pro *Pertz*
134   Daibertus *corrected from* episcopus
135   sententiam *corrected from* severitatem
136   cuius *corrected from* qua
137   istud *corrected from* id
138   magnanimitatem *MS*
139   et *omitted by Hoffmann*

140 constituatur *Pertz* : proferatur *Waitz*

141 affinitatis *corrected from* consanguinitatis

142 Ergo *corrected from* At

143 Ad haec *corrected from* Et

144 respondit *expunged after* episcopus

145 Lothariensium episcopi *Latouche* : episcopi Lothariensium per-
peram *Pertz*

146 medium *corrected from* medio

147 probat *Pertz*

148 accusationi *Pertz* : accusationis causa *Waitz*

149 forte *Pertz*

150 Cuius anathematis *expunged before* Sed

151 episcopi *omitted by Pertz*

152 malesanae *corrected from* malaesanae

153 animadvertit *perhaps corrected to* animadvertis *or* animadverti *Hoffmann*

154 abominabiles *corrected from* abhominabiles

155 statuta *corrected from* decreta

156 persuasio *Pertz*

157 in *corrected from* pro

158 inter interdictis *MS*

159 *sic MS*

160 Discutiendum vero multa ratione *expunged before* Id

161 statuendum *corrected from* producendum

162 alia intendit *corrected from* plurima intenderet

163 Regum ingressus *Pertz*

164 ergo *expunged after* Petunt

165 episcopi *expunged before* sacerdotales

166 ante *expunged after* infulas

167 alterum *expunged after* incommodorum

168 miseratione *corrected from* misericordia

169 concilio *corrected from* consilio

170 sit *expunged after* directum

171 sit *expunged after* roborata

172 Interea *corrected from* Nec multopost

173 quatinus *corrected from* quod

174 periurii *corrected from* peccati

175 sepenumero *corrected from* sine dubio

176 Poenas *corrected from* Penas

177 accitas *Pertz* : accita *MS*

178 tantum *expunged after* insidias

179 v̄c *MS* : virum consularem *Pertz*

180 ei *corrected from* sibi

181 quae *Hoffmann*

182 conferret *corrected from* redderet

183 predis *above* manubiis, *which is not expunged*

184 affecit *above* percutit, *which is not expunged*

185 castrum *expunged after* Blesum

186 pervasione *corrected from* captione

187 congregat *above* parat, *which is not expunged*

188 ad *above* per, *which is not expunged*

189 adhibet *above* adhibuit, *which is not expunged*

190 urbani *corrected from* urbs

191 Audito *Pertz*

192 Comperto vero Conanum urbi obsidionem adhibuisse mox legionem Britanniae infert *corrected from* Et collectum Britanniae infert

193 continerent *Pertz*

194 Dolus *Pertz*

195 insidias *corrected from* quas

196 advertens *expunged after* exiturum

197 vehementi *corrected from* multo

198 victoria *corrected from* viribus

199 priori precipitato *above* fronte precipitata, *which is not expunged*

200 et per *expunged after* exagitaret

201 mitiorem *expunged after* auram

202 sibi advenientes sese prius offerrent unde *corrected from* prius advenientibus sese offerret

203 an *MS*

204 ferienda *above* iugulanda, *which is not expunged*

205 ut *expunged* ; sanciri *corrected from* sancciri

206 oppidum *above* castrum, *which is not expunged*

207 a Gallis Belgis *corrected from* Gallos Belgas
208 Flandrenses *corrected from* Frandrenses
209 *omitted by Pertz*
210 Odoni $\overline{Pertz}$
211 $\overline{\text{o.p.}}$ or $\overline{\text{c.p.}}$ *MS*
212 nato *corrected from* natis
213 Abiectio *Pertz*
214 *sic MS*
215 iustissimam *above* aequissimam, *which is not expunged*
216 dissolvat *Pertz*
217 diligens inde proferret *corrected from* diligentissime promulgaret
218 Germaniae *expunged after* episcopis
219 Qui postquam impetrarent, et *expunged before* locum
220 nuntiatum *Pertz*
221 quam *corrected from* Quod
222 designatum *corrected from* quem reges designaverant
223 subdat *perhaps a mistake for* subdant
224 delationis *corrected from* proditionis
225 *sic MS* ; *perhaps an error for* obvenirent
226 non ignarus *corrected from* gnarus
227 reprehenditur *Pertz*
228 Ottonem *Pertz*
229 namque *expunged after* Legationem
230 ad locum quod Mosomum appellatur *expunged after* paucis
231 Non longe *corrected to* iuxta Mettim *and then restored*
232 id *expunged after* aliter
233 transfunderes *corrected from* transfundi faceres
234 adorsus est *corrected from* locutus est
235 sese *expunged after* sic
236 Synodus quae Mosomi pro Arnulfo *corrected from* Concilium quod
       pro Arnulfo Mosomi
237 Dum haec agerentur *corrected from* Interea cum
238 <et> *Hoffmann* : *Pertz retains* cum
239 in concilio *corrected from* et a se lecta
240 diaboli *omitted in L*
241 hetnicum *L*

242   hetnicus *L*

243   hetnicus *L*

244   O. *L*

245   illinc foris gladius et intus pavor dies ac noctes reddiderunt insom-
        nes *omitted in L*

246   *orsumque MS*

247   inter *expunged*

248   Heinrihcus quoque dux obiit *expunged after* est.

249   accusaret *Pertz*

250   penitus *expunged after* maximum

251   vi *Poinsignon*

252   Hildebertum *corrected from* illum

Notes to the Translation

ABBREVIATIONS

Acta concilii Mosomensis = Ernst-Dieter Hehl ed., *Die Konzilien Deutschlands und Reichsitaliens 916–1001,* vol. 2, *MGH Concilia* 6.2. Hanover: Hahn, 2007, pp. 495–507.

Acta concilii Remensis = Ernst-Dieter Hehl, ed., *Die Konzilien Deutschlands und Reichsitaliens 916–1001,* vol. 2, *MGH Concilia* 6.2. Hanover: Hahn, 2007, pp. 380–450.

Barth = Rüdiger E. Barth, *Der Herzog in Lotharingien im 10. Jahrhundert.* Sigmaringen: Thorbecke, 1990.

Bubnov = N. Bubnov, ed., *Gerberti Opera Mathemtica.* Berlin: R. Friedländer, 1899.

Flodoard, *Annales* = Philippe Lauer, ed., *Les Annales de Flodoard,* Collection de texts pour servir à l'étude et à l'enseignement de l'histoire. Paris: Alphonse Picard, 1905.

Flodoard, *HRE* = Martina Stratmann, ed., *Flodoardus Remensis: Historia Remensis Ecclesiae, MGH SS* 36. Hanover: Hahn, 1998.

Gerbert, *ep.* = Pierre Riché and J. P. Callu, eds., *Gerbert d'Aurillac: Correspondance,* Les classiques de l'histoire de France au moyen âge. 2 vols. Paris: Les Belles Lettres, 1993.

Hoffmann, "Die *Historien*" = Hartmut Hoffmann, "Die *Historien* Richers von Saint-Remi." *Deutsches Archiv für Erforschung des Mittelalters* 54 (1998): 445–532.

Hoffmann, *Historiae* = Hartmut Hoffmann, ed., *Richer von Saint-Remi: Historiae, MGH SS* 38. Hanover: Hahn, 2000.

JK = Philipp Jaffé, ed., *Regesta pontificum Romanorum ab condita ecclesia ad annum post Christum natum MCXCVIII,* 2nd ed. by F. Kaltenbrunner, P. Ewald, and S. Loewenfeld. 2 vols. Graz: Akademische Druck, 1956 [Leipzig, 1885–1888].

Latouche = Robert Latouche, ed. and trans., *Richer: Histoire de France (885–995).* Les classiques de l'histoire de France au moyen âge. 2 vols. Paris: H. Champion, 1930 and 1937.

Lauer, *Louis IV* = Philippe Lauer, *Le règne de Louis IV d'Outre-Mer.* Geneva: Slatkine, 1977 [Paris: É. Bouillon, 1900].

Lauer, *Robert Ier et Raoul de Bourgogne* = Philippe Lauer, *Robert Ier et Raoul de Bourgogne, rois de France (923–936).* Geneva: Slatkine, 1976 [Paris: H. Champion, 1910].

Lot, *Hugues Capet* = Ferdinand Lot, *Études sur le règne de Hugues Capet et la fin du Xe siècle.* Geneva: Slatkine, 1975 [Paris: É. Bouillon, 1903].

Lot, *Les derniers Carolingiens* = Ferdinand Lot, *Les derniers Carolingiens, Lothaire, Louis V, Charles de Lorraine (954–991).* Geneva: Slatkine, 1975 [Paris: É. Bouillon, 1891].

MGH = *Monumenta Germaniae Historica.* Hanover, etc. 1826ff.

PL = Jacques-Paul Migne, ed., *Patrologiae cursus completus, series latina.* 221 vols. Paris: 1841–1864.

SRG = *Scriptores rerum germanicarum in usum scholarum separatim editi*

SS = *Scriptores* (in folio)

Book 3

1   In 953 Otto deposed Duke Conrad the Red and turned the duchy of Lotharingia over to his brother Bruno, who had been appointed archbishop of Cologne a short time earlier.

2   Flodoard, *Annales, s.a.* 954, p. 138.

3   Lothar was crowned on November 12, 954.

4   Flodoard, *Annales s.a.* 954, p. 139.

5   Flodoard, *Annales s.a.* 955, pp. 140–41.

6   Flodoard, *Annales s.a.* 955, p. 141.

7   Flodoard, *Annales s.a.* 956, p. 143. Hugh the Great died on June 16/17, 956.

8   Duke Boleslav I of Bohemia (ca. 935–972). Richer is alluding to Otto's campaign against the Hungarians in the summer of 955, which culminated in his decisive victory at Lechfeld on August 10. Flodoard, *Annales s.a.* 955, p. 141, reports that Boleslav fought *with* Otto against the Hungarians, not against him.

9   Flodoard, *Annales s.a.* 955, pp. 141–42.

10   Count Reginar III of Hainaut (d. after 958), grandson of Reginar Longneck and nephew of Gislebert of Lotharingia.

11   Flodoard, *Annales s.a.* 956, pp. 142–43. Flodoard says nothing about the role of Richer's father in the capture of Mons.

12   Flodoard, *Annales s.a.* 956, p. 143.

13   Flodoard, *Annales s.a.* 959, p. 147, *s.a.* 960, p. 148.

14   Flodoard, *Annales s.a.* 959, p. 147.

15   Flodoard, *Annales, s.a.* 960, p. 148. According to Flodoard the traitor's father was a certain Count Odelric.

16   Hugh Capet, duke of the Franks and later king (987–996).

17   Otto, duke of Burgundy (956–965).

18   Flodoard, *Annales s.a.* 960, p. 149.

19   Flodoard, *Annales s.a.* 961, p. 150. Artald actually died on November 1, 961. See Hoffmann, *Historiae,* p. 178, ch. 14 n. 2.

20   Flodoard, *Annales s.a.* 962, p. 151.

21   In the manuscript Richer omits the location of the synod, which is not found in Flodoard and was presumably unknown to him.

22   Archbishop Archembald of Sens (958–967).

23   Flodoard, *Annales s.a.* 962, p. 151.

24   Octavian was actually the given name of Pope John XII (955–964), who succeeded Agapitus II.

25   Flodoard, *Annales s.a.* 962, p. 153.

26   Flodoard, *Annales s.a.* 962, p. 153.

27   Flodoard, *Annales s.a.* 962, pp. 153–54.

28   Flodoard, *Annales s.a.* 962, p. 154.

29   Flodoard, *Annales s.a.* 963, p. 164.

30   Flodoard, *Annales s.a.* 964, p. 155.

31   Odo, the future count of Blois and Chartres.

32   Flodoard, *Annales s.a.* 964, p. 155, *s.a.* 965, p. 156.

33   Arnulf's son Baldwin III actually predeceased his father. Flodoard
        says nothing about Lothar granting Flanders to Arnulf's son (or
        grandson).

34   Flodoard, *Annales s.a.* 965, p. 166. At this point in his history Richer
        ceases using Flodoard's *Annals* as a source; in the next chapter
        he skips from the year 965 to 969.

35   That is, Archbishop Odelric, who died in 969. There is a gap in the
        manuscript between this and the preceding chapter.

36   See Song of Sol. 3:9–10.

37   Cf. Heb. 9:4. The relics of the saints located within the chest are
        compared to the manna and the rod of Aaron, which were kept
        inside a golden vessel within the Ark of the Covenant.

38   Not a mechanical clock, but a device that measured the passing of
        time by the flow of water or sand.

39   Pope John XIII (965–972).

40   The papal privilege for the monastery of Saint-Rémi is dated to
        April 23, 972.

41   The full text of the papal privilege was presumably on a folio that
        has since fallen out of the manuscript.

42   The date of this synod of abbots is unknown. Hoffmann, *Histo-
        riae,* p. 187, ch. 32 n. 1 suggests that it was held between 972 and
        974.

43   Rodulf appears to be employing the dialectical topic of *notatio,*
        whereby an argument about the meaning of a word is derived
        from an analysis of its constituent parts (see Cicero, *Top. 35–36*).

44   The monastery of Saint-Gerald at Aurillac.

45   Count Borrell of Barcelona (947–992).

46   Bishop Hatto of Vich (d. 971/972).

47   Richer (see below, chs. 45, 49–54) uses the word *mathesis* ("mathe-
        matical arts") to denote the arts of the quadrivium: arithmetic,
        geometry, music, and astronomy.

48   Pope John XIII.

49   Logic here includes both dialectic and rhetoric, and possibly grammar as well.

50   The best candidate for the "G" of the manuscript is the archdeacon Gerannus, but this identification is uncertain. See Hoffmann, *Historiae,* p. 193, ch. 45 n. 2.

51   Marius Victorinus's translation of Porphyry's *Isagoge* is no longer extant and was almost certainly not available at Reims. Richer is probably referring to Boethius's translation of the *Isagoge,* the first edition of which contained many quotations from Victorinus's translation.

52   *On Differential Topics, On the Categorical Syllogism, On Hypothetical Syllogisms,* and *On Division* were all treatises by Boethius. *On Definition* was written by Marius Victorinus but attributed to Boethius in the Middle Ages.

53   Technically *modi locutionum* are tropes, a class of figure in which a word is used to refer to something other than its natural signification, but Richer is probably using the term generally to refer to both tropes and figures of speech.

54   The Roman poet Lucan (AD 39–65) was the author of an unfinished epic poem in ten books, the *Bellum Civile* (or *Pharsalia*), which dealt with the civil war between Julius Caesar and Pompey.

55   Cicero, *Inv.* 1.6.8.

56   The three musical genera were the diatonic, chromatic, and enharmonic.

57   I.e., by demonstrating the ratios that made up these intervals on the monochord.

58   Richer may be describing the use of a horizon stand, which made up part of the framework supporting the celestial globe. In addition to containing the cardinal directions and degree markings, it may also have enumerated the stars that make up the major constellations and the rising and setting times of the signs of the zodiac.

59   The instrument described here is a form of compound sighting tube, or "dioptra," of the sort mentioned by the first-century

BC astronomer Geminus ("Introduction to the Phenomena," 5.11, 12.4). Richer does not mention a fixed stand to which the device is attached, but if it was used to trace the daily rotation of the celestial circles around the earth, then it must have been attached to one.

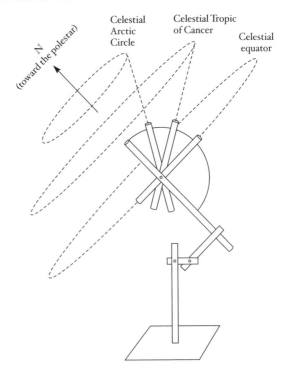

Celestial Arctic Circle

Celestial Tropic of Cancer

Celestial equator

N (toward the polestar)

60 Or possibly a hemisphere, such as the one Gerbert describes in a letter to Constantine of Fleury (ep. 3 in Appendix 5, Riché and Callu, vol. 2, pp. 680–87).

61 Richer is referring here to the prograde and retrograde motion of the planets.

62 The *colures* are a pair of longitudinal celestial circles, one passing through the solstices and the other the equinoxes.

63   The five parallels are, from north to south, the Arctic Circle, the Tropic of Cancer, the equator, the Tropic of Capricorn, and the Antarctic Circle.

64   The division of the parts of the hemisphere described here produces a value of 54° of latitude for the Arctic Circle (as well as the Antarctic Circle). Although the modern celestial Arctic Circle is fixed at 66° north latitude, ancient astronomers understood that the location of the Arctic Circle would shift according to the latitude of the observer. The division of the hemisphere into thirty intervals, with the Arctic and Antarctic Circles located six intervals from the poles, derives ultimately from Eratosthenes and is found in Macrobius's *Commentary on the Dream of Scipio* (2.6.2–6).

65   The "oblique band" is the zodiac, at the center of which is the ecliptic.

66   The apogee of a planet is the point in its orbit when it is furthest from the earth; its altitude is its elevation above the horizon. Richer, however, may have been using the astronomical terminology of Martianus Capella, who employed *absis* to mean the point where a planet reached its highest elevation above the earth and *altitudo* to mean apogee.

67   That is, it was not an armillary sphere.

68   These are Hindu-Arabic numerals.

69   Constantine (d. 1021/1022), a friend and correspondent of Gerbert, served as a monk at Fleury before moving to the monastery of Saint-Mesmin at Micy, where he was eventually made abbot. The book on the abacus that Richer mentions here may be the treatise *De divisione numerorum,* which is found, along with an introductory letter addressed to Constantine, in Bubnov, pp. 6–22.

70   Otric was the master of the cathedral school at Magdeburg.

71   In the Aristotelian division of the sciences, which was subsequently adopted by Boethius and Cassiodorus, mathematics, physics, and theology were the three branches of theoretical knowledge.

72   Richer is referring here to Otto II (973–983), whose accession to the throne is not announced until chapter 67 below.

73   Adso, abbot of Montier-en-Der (d. 992).

74   Cf. Boethius, *De institutione arithmetica* 1.1.

75   Richer must mean the fourth-century Neoplatonist scholar Marius Victorinus, rather than the first-century BC architect and engineer Vitruvius.

76   Richer is relying here on an ontological hierarchy outlined by Boethius in his commentary on Porphyry's *Isagoge*. That which is intellectible (*intellectibilis*) is divine, unchanging, and understood by the mind alone; the intelligible (*intelligibilis*) is perceived by the mind but participates in the corporeal world; the natural (*naturalis*) has bodily existence and is perceived via the senses.

77   The Latin could be also be rendered as "I am not wrong in placing mathematics beneath physics," and this is clearly what Otric thinks Gerbert has done. But for Gerbert to claim here that he is subordinating mathematics to physics directly contradicts his assertion in the next chapter that they are coequal species of the same genus. The confusion between Otric and Gerbert may be a result of the terms that Gerbert attaches to physics, mathematics, and theology. By referring to "natural physics" and "intelligible mathematics," Gerbert may be claiming a kind of ontological superiority for mathematics (or at least that may be how Otric understands him). Yet even if Gerbert is claiming that mathematics is somehow superior to physics by virtue of its greater distance from the physical world and its closer proximity to the world of the divine, that does not mean that mathematics stands in a relationship to physics as genus to species.

78   Richer writes "coeval" *(coeaevus),* perhaps harking back to Boethius's use of *aequaevus* in his commentary on Aristotle's *Peri Hermeneias* (1.1): *Quod autem prius negationem, postea proposuit affirmationem, nihil interest, cum omnes species aequaevae sibimet sint, et uni generi aequaliter supponantur.* See Hoffmann, *Historiae,* p. 201, ch. 59 n. 1, and p. 202, ch. 61 n. b.

79   Based on his reading of Boethius, Richer understood physiology and physics to be synonymous terms, like philosophy and philology, the latter of which is to be construed broadly here as encompassing all of the liberal arts.

80 As Waitz (p. 108) notes in his edition of the text, this title applies much better to the contents of the following chapter.

81 In the manuscript (fol. 35v), the words *eodem tempore* occur immediately after 3.54, and chapters 55–65 are added on two inserted folios. Hence it is not clear whether the synod of Saint-Macre took place before or after the disputation at Ravenna. See Hoffmann, *Historiae,* p. 205 n. 1, who concludes that the synod took place some time between 977 and 983.

82 The church of Saint-Macre at Fismes.

83 The bottom lines of the folio (35v) have been cut away and can no longer be read.

84 Cf. Hegesippus, *Bellum Iudaicum* 2.13.1.

85 Cf. Hegesippus, *Bellum Iudaicum* 1.1.

86 Both here and at 3.74 below Richer treats centurions as scouts or advance troops.

87 Sallust, *Cat.* 20.17.

88 Sallust, *Cat.* 20.10.

89 Sallust, *Cat.* 20.7.

90 Lothar's mother, Gerberga, was a sister of Otto I, which made Lothar and Otto II cousins.

91 That is, Lothar could no longer rely on the duke because he had gone behind Hugh's back in forging an alliance with Otto.

92 Alternatively: "It is not without the fruits of the expedient and the useful that advice is sought from wise men."

93 Hugh Capet's mother, Hadwig, was a sister of Otto I, which made Hugh, like Lothar, a cousin of Otto II.

94 Count Burchard of Vendôme (d. 1005).

95 These "indispensable men" may have included Adalbero of Reims and Gerbert.

96 Adelaide was the sister of King Conrad of Burgundy and the mother of Otto II of Germany by her second husband, Otto I. Emma was her daughter by her first marriage, to King Lothar of Italy (d. 950).

97 Literally, "the inseparable accidents of his whole body." Cf. Boethius, *In Isagogen Porphyrii Commenta* 4.8, 5.17, 5.23.

98 Cf. Livy 1.58.2.

99 Richer's chronology here is highly problematic. In his version of

463

events, the feuding between Hugh and Lothar is supposed to have broken out after Hugh's trip to Rome in 981. There followed a reconciliation between the two men, after which Hugh undertook to arrange the coronation of Lothar's son Louis (3.91). In fact, the coronation of Louis as Lothar's successor took place in 979, two years before Hugh's journey to Rome. See Hoffmann, *Historiae,* p. 219, ch. 89 n. 1.

100   June 8, 979.

101   Adelaide (d. 1026) was the sister of Geoffrey Grisegonelle, count of Anjou (960–987).

102   If Richer is correct on this detail, Raymond of Gothia was most likely Count Raymond IV of Toulouse (d. 978), who is very thinly attested in the sources. Adelaide had been previously married to Stephen, the count or viscount of Gévaudan.

103   Geoffrey Grisegonelle.

104   That is, the throne of Aquitaine.

105   Sallust, *Iug.* 14.7.

106   William I, count of Arles and marquis of Provence (d. 993).

107   Otto II was defeated by the Saracens at the Battle of Capo delle Colonne in Calabria in July of 982.

108   Otto died on December 7, 983.

109   Otto III, king of Germany (983–1002) and Holy Roman Emperor (996–1002).

110   Duke Henry "the Quarrelsome" of Bavaria (955–976, 985–995), cousin of Otto II. Hezilo was a nickname for Henry.

111   Sallust, *Iug.* 14.3.

112   Breisach, on the right bank of the Rhine.

113   Hegesippus, *Bellum Iudaicum* 4.15.2

114   Hegesippus, *Bellum Iudaicum* 4.15.1.

115   Count Odo I of Blois and Chartres (d. 996).

116   Count Heribert the Younger of Troyes (d. 994/995).

117   Heribert the Old (d. 980/984).

118   Cf. Hegesippus, *Bellum Iudaicum* 4.1.1.

119   Cf. Hegesippus, *Bellum Iudaicum* 4.1.2.

120   Duke Thierry I of Upper Lotharingia (d. 1027/1033).

121   Count Godfrey of Verdun (d. after 997).

122   Count Siegfried of Luxemburg (d. 998).

123   Count Gozelo of Bastogne (d. before 993/996).

124   Among those not named by Richer was Count Godfrey's son Frederick. All of these men were part of the same Lotharingian noble family and were relatives of Archbishop Adalbero of Reims. Duke Thierry was Adalbero's cousin, Godfrey of Verdun was his brother, and Siegfried of Luxemburg was his uncle. Bardo and Gozelo were Adalbero's nephews, and brothers of Adalbero of Laon.

125   That is, a shield wall employed to protect soldiers from incoming projectiles.

126   Hegesippus, *Bellum Iudaicum* 4.1.3.

127   The prisoners were held by Odo and Heribert.

128   Lothar died on March 2, 986, a year after the capture of Verdun.

129   Cf. Hegesippus, *Bellum Iudaicum* 1.45.10.

130   Cf. Hegesippus, *Bellum Iudaicum* 1.45.12.

131   All of the information that Richer supplies here is incorrect. Otto I died in 973 and Otto II in 983, so that Lothar did not outlive either of them by exactly ten years. Louis IV died in 954, meaning that Lothar died in the thirty-second year after he had succeeded to his father's throne. And Lothar was born in late 941, making him forty-four when he died, ruling out the possibility that he had been crowned forty-eight years earlier!

132   Cf. Hegesippus, *Bellum Iudaicum* 1.46.2.

133   Most likely Lothar's son and heir, Louis.

134   Thirty Roman miles or twenty-seven and a half English miles.

135   Cf. Hegesippus, *Bellum Iudaicum* 1.46.2.

BOOK 4

1   King Louis V (986–987).

2   Hegesippus, *Bellum Iudaicum* 1.46.2.

3   Sallust, *Jug.* 14.1.

4   Sallust, *Jug.* 14.1.

5   This Rainier is probably the *vidame* of Reims mentioned at 4.99.

See Lot, *Les Dernier Carolingiens,* p. 192, and Hoffmann, *Historiae,* p. 234, ch. 4 n. 2.

6   Lothar was buried at the monastery of Saint-Rémi at Reims. See 3.110.

7   *Inter intellectibilia translato* echoes Gerbert's use of the phrase *inter intelligibilia disposito* to describe the death of Archbishop Adalbero. See ep. 153, p. 374.

8   Charles's speech draws heavily on Adherbal's speech to the Roman senate at Sallust, *Iug.* 14.8–24.

9   Otto II, who appointed Charles duke of Lower Lotharingia in 977.

10   I.e., to assist him in mounting a horse.

11   Isa. 5:20.

12   Hegesippus, *Bellum Iudaicum* 1.35.1.

13   Ibn Abi Amir (Al-Mansur), who ruled the Umayyad caliphate of Córdoba in the name of the caliph Hisham II from 981 until his death in 1002, adopted a hostile stance toward the Christian kingdoms of Spain. In July of 985 his army sacked and burned Barcelona.

14   At Orléans.

15   Hegesippus, *Bellum Iudaicum* 1.42.3.

16   It is not clear in this case whether Richer is referring to crossbowmen or to men operating a ballista, a siege weapon that resembled a large-scale crossbow.

17   Livy 25.24.6.

18   Cf. Gerbert, ep. 121, pp. 288–91.

19   I.e., fever.

20   Arnulf, archbishop of Reims (989–991/998–1021), was an illegitimate son of King Lothar.

21   A chirograph was an official document drawn up in duplicate and then divided in half so that both parties to an act could retain a copy.

22   Among this group were certain Lotharingian bishops. See 4.59.

23   Ws. 1:5.

24   Pope John XV (985–996).

25   Counts Gislebert of Roucy and Wido of Soissons, both cousins of Arnulf. See Lot, *Les derniers Carolingiens,* p. 255.

26 A shortened form of Adalger, the name Richer uses to refer to him
      at 4.61, 4.62, and 4.73.

27 Hegesippus, *Bellum Iudaicum* 5.22.1.

28 Adelaide, daughter of Duke William III of Aquitaine.

29 Cicero, *Inv.* 1.1.1.

30 According to Isidore of Seville (*Etym.* 4.4.1), Hippocrates was the
      founder of the rational school of medicine (*logica*), as distinct
      from the methodist and empiricist sects.

31 The *Aphorisms* of Hippocrates, a common medical text in the Mid-
      dle Ages.

32 Abbot Arbod of Saint-Rémi (d. 1007).

33 The identity of the abbot of Orbais is not known.

34 Chapter thirty-one of the Benedictine Rule.

35 Around midnight.

36 The monastery of Saint-Basle-de-Verzy, some 15 kilometers south
      of Reims. The synod of Saint-Basle took place on June 17 and 18,
      991. Richer's account of its proceedings is based on the *Acta*
      written by Gerbert.

37 Bishop Wido II of Soissons, not the Wido mentioned above.

38 *Acta concilii Remensis,* ch. 1, pp. 394–95.

39 *Acta concilii Remensis,* ch. 1, p. 395.

40 The thirty-first chapter of the fourth council of Toledo (633) al-
      lowed ecclesiastical courts to hear cases of treason if remission
      of punishment *(supplicii indulgentia)* was promised to the defen-
      dant. The relevant chapter is cited in *Acta concilii Remensis,* ch. 3,
      p. 396.

41 *Acta concilii Remensis,* chs. 2–3, pp. 395–96.

42 *Acta concilii Remensis,* ch. 4, p. 397.

43 Arnulf was the son of King Lothar and thus the nephew of Charles
      of Lorraine.

44 *Acta concilii Remensis,* ch. 4, p. 397.

45 Bruno had offered himself as a hostage to guarantee Arnulf's fidel-
      ity to the king.

46 Bruno's mother, Alberada, was a half-sister of Lothar, which made
      him a cousin to Arnulf. Bruno was also the brother of Counts
      Gislebert of Roucy and Wido of Soissons (see 4.34 above).

47   This statement implies that Arnulf was among the friends and kinsmen who recommended that Charles investigate the possibility of capturing Laon. See 4.14–15 above.

48   Count Manasses of Rethel.

49   Count Roger III of Porcien.

50   *Acta concilii Remensis,* ch. 5, pp. 397–98.

51   *Acta concilii Remensis,* ch. 6, p. 398.

52   *Acta concilii Remensis,* ch. 6, pp. 398–99.

53   *Acta concilii Remensis,* ch. 7, p. 399.

54   *Acta concilii Remensis,* ch. 7–8, p. 399.

55   It is not clear exactly what power of defense Arnulf's *libellus* contained. One explanation is that only a man of a certain moral fiber would have drawn up such a document. Alternatively, it might show the confidence placed by "wise and good men" in Arnulf. A third possibility is that the document does not defend Arnulf. Instead, the "powers of defense" mentioned by Richer refer to the unimpeachable quality of the document itself, which convicts Arnulf precisely because it was drawn up by wise and good men and must therefore be taken as appropriate evidence against him. It is possible that Richer misunderstood his source here. In Gerbert's *Acta* (ch. 9, p. 400), Arnulf mentions that the *libellus* contains "subtle powers of defense," but he is interrupted by the arrival of the priest Adalger before he can explain what he means.

56   *Acta concilii Remensis,* ch. 9, p. 400.

57   *Acta concilii Remensis,* ch. 11, pp. 400–401. In Gerbert's *Acta,* Adalger refers specifically to the ordeals of fire, boiling water, and hot iron.

58   *Acta concilii Remensis,* ch. 12, p. 402.

59   Prov. 15:3.

60   Ps. 13:1.

61   Ibid. Cf. *Acta concilii Remensis,* ch. 13, p. 403.

62   In the *Acta* of the synod, Odo speaks before Walter and the content of his speech is different. He relates the contents of the letter addressed by Arnulf to those who had sacked Reims, the letter mentioned by Wido of Soissons at ch. 63 above. See *Acta concilii Remensis,* ch. 12, pp. 401–2.

63   *Acta concilii Remensis,* ch. 17, p. 407.

64   Abbo (ca. 940–1004) was abbot of Fleury (Saint-Benoît-sur-Loire)
     from 988 until his death in 1004.

65   Romulf was the abbot of either Saint-Rémi of Sens or Saint-Pierre-
     le-Vif of Sens.

66   John was the master of the cathedral school of Auxerre and later
     bishop (996–998).

67   *Acta concilii Remensis,* ch. 19, p. 408; ch. 23, p. 416.

68   *Acta concilii Remensis,* ch. 23, pp. 416–17.

69   *Acta concilii Remensis,* ch. 30, p. 431.

70   *Acta concilii Remensis,* ch. 50, p. 446; ch. 53, p. 448.

71   Arnulf gave the king the ring and staff of office with which he had
     been invested, and he gave the bishops the pallium that he
     had received from the pope. See *Acta concilii Remensis,* ch. 53,
     p. 448.

72   *Acta concilii Remensis,* ch. 53, p. 448.

73   *Acta concilii Remensis,* ch. 54, p. 449.

74   *Acta concilii Remensis,* ch. 55, p. 450.

75   Melun was held by Burchard of Vendôme, a vassal of the king. It
     had previously belonged to Odo's maternal grandfather, Herib-
     ert II of Vermandois. Heribert's daughter Liutgard had married
     Theobald le Tricheur, and Odo was their son.

76   In classical rhetoric *inductio* was a form of argument in which the
     speaker attempted to win his interlocutor's assent to a series of
     uncontroversial propositions, with the ultimate goal of getting
     him to agree to a more doubtful proposition that was in some
     way analogous to the earlier ones. See Cicero, *Inv.* 1.31.51.

77   We learn from other sources that the castellan's name was Walter.
     See G. Waitz, ed., *Historia Francorum Senonensis, MGH SS* 9 (Han-
     over: Hahn, 1851), p. 369.

78   The Normans, under the leadership of Duke Richard I.

79   It is possible that Richer meant to write *vincti* ("bound") instead of
     victi ("defeated") here. See Waitz, *Historia Francorum Senonensis,*
     p. 165.

80   Fulk Nerra, count of Anjou (987–1040).

81   In 990, Conan, the count of Rennes and an ally of Odo I of Blois
     and Chartres, seized Nantes and laid claim to the title of duke

of Brittany. It was in revenge for this that Fulk ravaged Odo's lands that same year. Confusingly, Richer recounts Fulk's expedition against Blois after the recapture of Melun by the king and his allies, which took place in the summer of 991.

82 Count Burchard of Vendôme.

83 Count Conan I of Rennes (d. 992).

84 The plain of Conquereuil, where the battle between Fulk and Conan was fought.

85 Susanna, whose given name was Rozala, was the daughter of King Berengar II of Italy. She married Robert after the death of her first husband, Count Arnulf II of Flanders, in 988.

86 There is a blank space in the manuscript (fol. 52v) where the name of the stronghold should be.

87 Montreuil was located near the mouth of the Canche River. Although it is not clear from Richer's account, presumably Queen Susanna constructed the new fortress downstream from Montreuil to prevent ships coming in by sea from sailing upriver.

88 Richer is in error here. It was not Pope Benedict VII (974–983) but John XV (985–996) who criticized the deposition of Arnulf.

89 The exact date of the synod is unknown. It took place at some point between 992 and 944. See Hoffmann, *Historiae*, p. 291, ch. 89 n. 1.

90 Acts 4:32.

91 Tob. 4:19.

92 A loose rendition of Titus 3:10: "A man that is a heretic, after the first and second admonition, avoid."

93 The canon that Richer cites here is apocryphal and, according to Hoffmann, "Die *Historien*," pp. 488–89, probably invented by Richer.

94 William IV Iron Arm, count of Poitou and duke of Aquitaine (963–993), was married to Odo's sister, Emma of Blois. Hence Odo could count on his support.

95 The castle of Langeais.

96 Count Baldwin IV of Flanders (989–1035) was the son of Queen Susanna. His hostility to King Robert after the king's repudiation of his mother and his subsequent refusal to return Mon-

treuil to her led him to join with Odo in opposing Fulk, an ally of the king.

97   At the time of the siege of Langeais Fulk did not have a son. Evidently a future child is meant.

98   Either Odo's eldest son, Robert, or his second son, Theobald, the future count of Blois.

99   Because Odo was an adversary of the Capetian kings, Fulk could not pledge fealty to him without harming their interests and undermining his own oath of fidelity to them. Pledging fealty to Odo's son seems to have been a solution devised to get around this problem.

100   At the time Fulk had a half-brother, Maurice, and at least one nephew, Count Geoffrey-Berengar of Rennes, the son of his sister, Ermengard-Gerberga.

101   Amboise was actually on the left bank of the Loire, opposite the army of the king, who was approaching Langeais from the northeast.

102   Odo died on March 12, 996.

103   Leo was abbot of the monastery of Saint-Boniface-and-Alexis at Rome.

104   Count Landry of Nevers (d. 1028).

105   Ps. 77:50.

106   The abbey of Mouzon was located on the Meuse River, just inside German imperial territory but within the ecclesiastical province of Reims. The synod took place on June 2, 995.

107   Count Godfrey of Verdun, brother of the deceased Adalbero of Reims.

108   The *vidame* (*vicedominus*) was a high-ranking official who exercised certain judicial, military, and administrative functions on behalf of a bishop, who was prevented from doing so by the nature of his office. The *vidame* served a role analogous to that of the advocate of a monastery or church.

109   *Acta concilii Mosomensis,* pp. 502–3.

110   *Acta concilii Mosomensis,* p. 503.

111   Or "because I found it difficult to obtain."

112   Richer chose not to include the pope's letter either because it pre-

sented arguments hostile to Gerbert or because he did not have access to it (see n. 111 above). The letter is also missing in Gerbert's *Acta* of the synod.

113   *Acta concilii Mosomensis,* p. 503.

114   Although Richer evidently meant to include Gerbert's speech from the synod of Mouzon in his history, either he never got around to it or the folios on which it was written have fallen out of the manuscript. Chapters 102–5 are taken from Gerbert's *Acta* of the proceedings.

115   Gerbert, ep. 178, pp. 442–47.

116   Gerbert, ep. 197, pp. 524–25.

117   2 Chron. 19:2.

118   Cf. Gerbert, ep. 217, p. 622. The "peremptory law" refers to the authority of a Church council to issue a summons which, if ignored, could result in the delinquent party being declared in contempt.

119   *Acta concilii Mosomensis,* pp. 503–4.

120   *Acta concilii Mosomensis,* p. 504.

121   Arnulf, who is compared with Simon Magus (see Acts 8:9–24).

122   Probably the eighteen-month period between December of 989 and the synod of Saint-Basle in June of 991. Cf. Gerbert, ep. 217, p. 588.

123   Matt. 5:29.

124   Cf. Matt. 18:15–17.

125   The quotation is not by Pope Leo the Great but from a letter written by the Roman clergy to a priest named John in the time of Pope Vigilius. Gerbert presumably found the quotations in the writings of Hincmar, where it appears several times. See Hoffmann, *Historiae,* p. 304 n. 9.

126   Gelasius, ep. 26, ch. 4, in Andreas Thiel, ed., *Epistolae Romanorum pontificum genuinae* (Braunsberg: Edward Peter, 1867–1868), vol. 1, p. 399; JK 664, vol. 1, p. 88. Both this and the citation from Leo are found together in Hincmar, *Opusculum XV capitulorum,* ch. 36, *PL* vol. 126 col. 433.

127   Cicero, *Mil.* 4.11.

128   That is, during the late spring and early summer of 991, when Odo

captured Melun and then defended it from the king. See Lot, *Hugues Capet,* p. 93 n. 4 and p. 159 n. 1

129   *Acta concilii Mosomensis,* pp. 504–6.

130   Deut. 32:25.

131   *Acta concilii Mosomensis,* pp. 506–7.

132   *Acta concilii Mosomensis,* p. 507.

133   June 24.

134   Richer's history ends on folio 55v. The rest of the folio is blank, as is folio 56r. Folio 56v contains two letters written to Gerbert in another hand. Folio 57r contains a set of brief annalistic notices that were evidently intended as material for a future continuation.

135   Possibly a mistake, since Richer previously said that the synod was scheduled to be held at the monastery of Saint-Rémi at Reims.

136   Bertha (d. after 1007) was the daughter of King Conrad the Peaceful of Burgundy.

137   Count Odo I of Blois and Chartres.

138   Perhaps Count Hilduin I of Arcis-sur-Aube. See Hoffmann, *Historiae,* p. 307 n. 5.

139   Bertha and Robert were both great-grandchildren of Henry I of Germany and hence second cousins, which placed their marriage within the prohibited degrees of consanguinity. Equally problematic from the standpoint of the Church was the fact that Robert was godfather to one of Bertha's children from her first marriage.

140   Pope Gregory V (996–999).

141   Count Hildebert (Aldebert) I of Périgord and La Marche.

142   William V, count of Poitou and duke of Aquitaine (990–1030).

143   The papal bull announcing Gerbert's appointment to the see of Ravenna is dated April 28, 998.

Bibliography

EDITIONS

Hoffmann, Hartmut. *Richeri historiarum libri IIII, Monumenta Germaniae Historica SS* 38. Hanover: Hahn, 2000.

Pertz, G. H. *Richeri historiarum libri IIII,* in *Monumenta Germaniae Historica SS* 3, pp. 561–657. Hanover: Hahn, 1839.

Waitz, Georg. *Richeri historiarum libri IIII, Monumenta Germaniae Historica SRG* 51. Hanover: Hahn, 1877.

TRANSLATIONS

Guadet, Jerome. *Richer, Histoire de son temps.* 2 vols. Paris: Jules Renouard, 1845–1846.

Latouche, Robert. *Richer: Histoire de France (885–995).* Les classiques de l'histoire de France au moyen âge. 2 vols. Paris: H. Champion, 1930 and 1937.

Poinsignon, A.-M. *Richeri Historiarum quatuor libri—Histoire de Richer en quatres livres.* Reims: P. Regnier, 1855.

Von der Osten-Sacken, Karl. *Richers vier Bücher Geschichte.* Berlin: Besser, 1854.

SELECTED STUDIES

Giese, Wolfgang. *"Genus" und "Virtus": Studien zum Geschichtswerk des Richer von St. Remi.* Augsburg: W. Blasaditsch, 1969.

Glenn, Jason. *Politics and History in the Tenth Century: The Work and World of Richer of Reims.* Cambridge, Cambridge University Press, 2004.

475

Hoffmann, Hartmut. "Die *Historien* Richers von Saint-Remi." *Deutsches Archiv für Erforschung des Mittelalters* 54 (1998): 445–532.

Kortüm, Hans-Henning. *Richer von Saint-Remi: Studien zu einem Geschichtsschreiber des 10. Jahrhunderts.* Stuttgart: Franz Steiner, 1985.

Lauer, Philippe. *Le règne de Louis IV d'Outre-Mer.* Geneva: Slatkine, 1977 [Paris: É. Bouillon, 1900].

——. *Robert Ier et Raoul de Bourgogne, rois de France (923–936).* Geneva: Slatkine, 1976 [Paris: H. Champion, 1910].

Lot, Ferdinand. *Les derniers Carolingiens, Lothaire, Louis V, Charles de Lorraine (954–991).* Geneva: Slatkine, 1975 [Paris: É. Bouillon, 1891].

——. *Études sur le règne de Hugues Capet et la fin du Xe siècle.* Geneva: Slatkine, 1975 [Paris: É. Bouillon, 1903].

MacKinney, L. C. "Tenth-Century Medicine as Seen in the *Historia* of Richer of Rheims." *Bulletin of the Institute of the History of Medicine* 2 (1934): 347–75.

Riché, Pierre. *Gerbert d'Aurillac, le pape de l'an mil.* Paris: Fayard, 1987.

Index